Divine
Simplicity

Divine Simplicity

CHRIST THE CRISIS OF METAPHYSICS

Paul R. Hinlicky

BakerAcademic
a division of Baker Publishing Group
Grand Rapids, Michigan

© 2016 by Paul R. Hinlicky

Published by Baker Academic
a division of Baker Publishing Group
P.O. Box 6287, Grand Rapids, MI 49516-6287
www.bakeracademic.com

Printed in the United States of America

Library of Congress Cataloging-in-Publication Data
Names: Hinlicky, Paul R., author.
Title: Divine simplicity : Christ the crisis of metaphysics / Paul R. Hinlicky.
Description: Grand Rapids : Baker Academic, 2016. | Includes bibliographical references and index.
Identifiers: LCCN 2015051494 | ISBN 9780801048999 (cloth)
Subjects: LCSH: God (Christianity)—Simplicity—History of doctrines.
Classification: LCC BT148 .H56 2016 | DDC 231/.4—dc23
LC record available at http://lccn.loc.gov/2015051494

16   17   18   19   20   21   22   7   6   5   4   3   2   1

green press INITIATIVE

In thanksgiving for sixteen years (1999–2015)
in the *studia humanitatis*
with the students, faculty, staff,
administration, and board
of Roanoke College of Salem, Virginia

Contents

Preface

I first conceived of this book during a decade-long intensive study of Islamic thought following the horrific events of September 11, 2001. My initial hunch was that the Aristotelian version of the doctrine of simplicity, "thought thinking itself," taken up by St. Thomas Aquinas owed much—perhaps too much—to the Muslim philosopher Avicenna, who had Neoplatonized Aristotle with a notion of deity as "thought thinking and willing itself." This amplification, also known to Augustine, provided dynamism to the notion of the simple deity expressed by emanation to form the great chain of being in the cosmic system. The Christian revision that Thomas accomplished demarcated the Creator's act of being as pure actuality in strong ontological distinction from the creature's imperfect actualization, and in this way supposedly blocked emanation and replaced it with repetition by way of analogy. I was further thinking that, liberated from Thomas's Christian revision, strong simplicity, by virtue of the "power of the negative," progressively outstripped attempts to tame it for Christian purposes until it reappeared in pristine beauty in Spinoza's doctrine of an eternal world viewed in the alternate modes of *natura naturans* and *natura naturata*. To a degree, these hunches are still at work in the book laid before you now, but no longer are they the matter of central importance as I had originally conceived.

What intervened and now runs like a red thread through this book is the discovery, via St. Augustine's difficulty with it, of Paul the apostle's ruminations on the oneness of God in his First Letter to the Corinthians. Paul begins with the word of the cross that delivers Christ as the paradoxical power and wisdom of God in 1 Corinthians 1:24; centers the letter in the prototrinitarian confession of 8:6; and culminates it in the doxological "theopanism" of 15:28. This too is a doctrine of divine simplicity, but in an eschatological rather than protological key and so in an ontologically weaker sense than the tradition that originates with the pre-Socratics, passes through Plato and Aristotle, and achieves its sublime expression among the ancients in Plotinus.

All this is here acknowledged as a brief preface and by way of expressing thanks to Baker Academic and my editor there, R. David Nelson, for their patience as the extended process of investigation produced a book somewhat different than originally proposed. I am also indebted to a veritable stable of theological stallions who in the interim have lent me their aid, reading and commenting on all or parts of this book, beginning with the aforementioned R. David Nelson. So I would also like to acknowledge with gratitude Rob Saler, David Bruner, the late—and sainted—Stephen Webb, Piotr Małysz, Derek Nelson, Jacob Goodson, Dennis Bielfeldt, and Hans Zorn for their interest, comment, and criticism as the draft evolved.

I think it was Stanley Hauerwas whom I once heard say that his "method" in theology was to read a lot of books, think hard, and then write his own book. Whether or not Stanley deserves credit for that bon mot, I have made it my own. As it seems to me, it is more important to converse than to monologue, to intervene in a conversation with a timely truth than to silence conversation by pretending to deliver a timeless one. I mention this here by way of justifying a definite selectivity in the authors and treatments of the topic engaged in this book. This selectivity is, among other things, a way of recommending said literature to the reader for fuller understanding. Yet the principle of selection is that these are the works that I have thus far found significant and so worth discussing in public, not to end debate but ecumenically to advance it. Usually, then, as I am giving an account of an author, unless and until explicitly noted otherwise, I should be understood as appropriating that author's line of thought into my own argument, striving to recognize truth even in positions that I will ultimately find inadequate. The proof of this dialogical "method" is in the pudding, then, whether the book succeeds according to its idiosyncratic way in advancing the argument about what it means for Christians to affirm of the Three of the gospel narrative that they are the one true God. Naturally, success is for the reader to judge.

I intend gender inclusivity, but not gender eliminationism, with respect to our common humanity by the strategy in English of alternating the nonspecific third-person personal pronouns between "he" and "she" and "him" and "her." With respect to the divine, I defer to the primary language of faith in the Scriptures and the ecclesiastical terminology based on it that is useful for articulating the strong trinitarian personalism presupposed in this book. My intention throughout is hardly to idolize the masculine gender but rather to signal a specialized usage in theology for the God who is the Father of the Son in the Holy Spirit by capitalizing "Him" or "His" when the third-person singular pronoun is used in reference to the trinitarian persons. The divine nature, being nothing but a conceptual abstraction from the Three who are the Beloved Community, could be referred to in the neuter gender, as an "It." But such an alienating innovation makes too much of a pseudoproblem that in material fact is under suspicion in the pages that follow.

In a work that delves deeply into the Western theological tradition, the use of ecclesiastical Latin (and some Greek and German) is unavoidable. Recognizing that some readers may need assistance in this connection, I have added a glossary of foreign language words and phrases.

This book is dedicated to my academic home for the longest and happiest period of my seesaw career in scholarship: Roanoke College of Salem, Virginia. It is one of the increasingly rare institutions of higher learning that sustains commitment to the liberal arts; that acknowledges and honors its relationship to the Christian tradition while welcoming people of all faiths and no faith; and that supports scholarship as well as excellence in teaching. Excellence in scholarship cannot be readily quantified in a cost-benefit analysis according to the economy of the quid pro quo; nor can it accommodate the creeping commoditization of all things that will be, if it is not already, the ruin of the humanities if not also of our humanity. Excellence in scholarship is and will ever be a sacrificial act of resistance whose reward is in heaven. But here on earth I happily sing my thanks to "dear old Roanoke."

Paul R. Hinlicky
Epiphany 2015

Introduction

"Hear, O Israel: The LORD our God, the LORD is one" (Deut. 6:4 NIV). Paul the apostle agrees with this axiom of Israel's faith—sort of. "We know," he writes to the Corinthians, "that 'no idol in the world really exists,' and that 'there is no God but one'" (1 Cor. 8:4). It appears that he is quoting from a letter that the Corinthians had written to him, themselves quoting from the Scriptures of Israel. But Paul adds to this affirmation from Israel of the oneness of God that he shares with the Corinthians: "Indeed, even though there may be so-called gods in heaven or on earth—as in fact there are many gods and many lords—yet for us there is one God, the Father, from whom are all things and for whom we exist, and one Lord, Jesus Christ, through whom are all things and through whom we exist" (1 Cor. 8:5–6). God is one, for Paul, but not *simply* so.

Rather, God is one complexly in several different senses. First, there are many contenders in heaven and on earth for the title of deity, the one true God (whatever that may be); second, it is "for us"—believers in Paul's gospel—that idols have no real existence in the sense of a true or valid claim upon them; third, even so, for this liberation to have come about for Paul and the Corinthians, it seems that for God there are internal differentiations constituting corresponding external relations. In this passage Paul attributes primacy to one "God, the Father" as the source of all things and hence as the goal of the believers' lives. At the same time, he assigns the instrumental agency of this primary source and goal to the one Lord Jesus Christ, by whom both the creation and the believers' lives as new creation of the one God have come about.[1] Since 1 Corinthians in many respects is the canonical paradigm of the gospel's encounter with the world of many gods and lords, we will return to its theology of the oneness of the God of the gospel throughout this book.

For the moment, the introductory point is merely to indicate how the received doctrine[2] of divine simplicity is ambiguous. Some account of divine unity, indeed some ontological account, certainly is required if Christian theology is to affirm with understanding the Shema of Israel, as it must, that God is one; yet what account accords with and does not rather subvert robust Christian trinitarianism as the articulation of the saving God of the gospel has never been self-evident and is even less so today with the collapse of Christendom and its erstwhile theological certitudes.

1. N. T. Wright, "Monotheism, Christology and Ethics: 1 Corinthians 8," in *The Climax of the Covenant: Christ and the Law in Pauline Theology* (Minneapolis: Fortress, 1992), 120–36.

2. In this book I will turn in chap. 2 to its classical statement by St. Thomas Aquinas (*Summa Theologiae* Ia.3.7 and *Summa contra Gentiles* I.18), who drew on St. Augustine's trinitarian ruminations (also in *De civitate Dei* 11.10) as mediated by Anselm (*Proslogion* 18 and *Monologion* 16–17), but I could as well have turned to its codification and elaboration in Reformed orthodoxy; see Richard A. Muller, "Simplicity, Spirituality, Immutability and Related Attributes," in *Post-Reformation Reformed Dogmatics: The Rise and Development of Reformed Orthodoxy, ca. 1520 to ca. 1725*, vol. 3, *The Divine Essence and Attributes*, 2nd ed. (Grand Rapids: Baker Academic, 2003), 271–324, where a central problem, even "possible contradiction," in the doctrine is identified: "On the one hand," Muller notes, "the attributes are identical to the divine essence and 'differ only in our apprehension . . .' differ[ing] not among themselves nor from the divine essence," while, on the other hand, the attributes are "'actually and operatively in God,'" which "seems to posit distinctions between the attributes" (203). In the conclusion of the present book I will take up the alternative to my own case, resourced from both Thomistic and Reformed orthodoxy, which has been recently argued by James E. Dolezal, *God without Parts: Divine Simplicity and the Metaphysics of God's Absoluteness* (Eugene, OR: Pickwick, 2011). A similar case is made by Steven J. Duby, "Divine Simplicity, Divine Freedom, and the Contingency of Creation: Dogmatic Responses to Some Analytic Questions," *Journal of Reformed Theology* 6 (2012): 115–42, which heavily trades upon the absolute-relative distinction in predicating God in Reformed orthodoxy that I will trace back to Augustine in chap. 3 and criticize as an optical illusion that forces a modalist interpretation of the Trinity: the quaternity of immutable but unknowable essence taken absolutely but the Three of the Gospel narrative taken relatively. In the end, Duby owns up to the choice involved in reconciling immutability and freedom in God: "Any enigma remaining here [with respect to the freedom of creation by an immutable and fully actual divine being] is preferable to the problems with denying the real identity of God and God's perfections and to the problems attending the inclusion of accidents in God" (137). That statement of preference is in fact a costly theological choice that is determined on grounds other than analysis of ideas. The utter innocence of trinitarian patrology, as we will see, with which Duby argues against the thesis that the divine "will is really distinct from the divine essence," since this distinction must "posit another increate or uncaused along with God," is as striking as the necessitarian implication of his affirmation that "God's employment of an instrument [i.e., will] that is really distinct from himself [i.e., immutable essence] undermines the immediacy and instantaneity of the production of creation and the immediacy of God's relation to creation" (137).

The fundamental discovery driving Christian trinitarianism is the theological need both to distinguish correctly and to relate properly the Jesus who at the depths of His solidarity with us cried abandonment to His Abba Father, who had sent Him in the power of the Spirit to drink that cup of divine wrath.[3] For that is how the one Lord Jesus Christ mediates His Father's reconciliation with us when by the same Spirit we die to sinful idolatries under the wrath of the God of love and mercifully are raised to live for the living and true God (1 Thess. 1:9). The key to making this proper distinction and relation, however, lies in the One whom Paul momentarily neglected to mention in the cited passage from 1 Corinthians 8:4–6 (though he had devoted the preceding chapters 2–4 to Him): the Spirit of this Father and Son, who sustained the Son in His decision to take responsibility for us idolaters before God and as such presented anew the incarnate, crucified, dead, and buried Son, shrouded in the sin of the world, to that same Father for recognition and vindication as the Father's own love for the creation lost to sin's tyranny. The Spirit's resurrection of the crucified Jesus, vindicating His faith in the Father's self-surpassing love for the sinful world, and the Spirit's communication of this reconciliation to newborn faith properly relate not only the Father and the Son to each other but also correspondingly to the world being reconciled in Christ the Son by the Spirit's proclamation of news that is truly good. This complex event of trinitarian advent is the dawning of the Beloved Community of God in contest with many so-called gods in heaven and on earth.

In adopting and articulating this social model of the Trinity in my systematic theology,[4] I frequently indicated ambivalence regarding the traditional doctrine of divine simplicity without actually devoting a separate treatment to it. The reason for that neglect is that the traditional doctrine presupposes what today can no longer be taken for granted—namely, the cultural plausibility of an axiomatic Creator/creature distinction[5] that in fact comes from revelation with the corresponding assumption of the viability of a revelation-friendly natural theology: the rational ascent to the unconditioned protological Source of the visible world of multiplicity, complexity, and dynamism. Surely, the ontology of the Creator/creature distinction and the epistemological way of

3. Paul R. Hinlicky, *Divine Complexity: The Rise of Creedal Christianity* (Minneapolis: Fortress, 2009).

4. Paul R. Hinlicky, *Beloved Community: Critical Dogmatics after Christendom* (Grand Rapids: Eerdmans, 2015). Passages on the following pages, in varying degrees of relevance to the present book, may be consulted: 110, 115–16, 126, 216, 252, 339–40, 507n25, 590, 637–38, 697, 702, 705–6, 766, 796, 823, 871, 873n16.

5. Brent Adkins and I exposed the problem of theology on the contemporary "plane of immanence" in *Rethinking Philosophy and Theology with Deleuze: A New Cartography* (London: Bloomsbury Academic, 2013).

natural theology are in principle separable, and the case to be made in this book depends on executing this separation. But in historical fact, the synthesis of these two in the conclusion that Thomas Aquinas drew from each of his five demonstrations of God's existence, "and this is what everyone means by God," has been uncritically assumed in Christendom. On this basis of divine simplicity, to which Occam and Scotus hold as devotedly as Thomas, the medieval schools could contend with one another on the basis of the cultural plausibility regarding a First and Necessary Being. Today, however, this is no longer the case (even though nostalgia for that lost world in which "God is in heaven and man is on the earth" is palpable in the more aggressive recent attempts to retrieve the metaphysics of divine simplicity).

But in my systematic theology it was labor enough to require that Christian theology own up to post-Christendom and hence also to the loss of the cultural plausibility of the hypothesis of a perfect being precisely on the terrain of so-called natural theology and the concomitant realization that the strong Creator/creature distinction is a predicate of trinitarian revelation, specifically, the founding kerygma of the resurrection of the Crucified One.[6] Since the Creator/creature distinction, articulated christologically in terms of the so-called two-natures doctrine, is an inalienable aspect of Christian doctrine—just as is the oneness of God—my intention, of course, was to come to such essential distinctions by another route than building on a foundation of natural theology.

In the previous theological generation a similar set of issues and concerns was articulated as an argument about whether God is capable of suffering. The need to affirm the Christian God's solidarity with His suffering creation was palpable after the ethical catastrophes of twentieth-century Euro-America in Hitler, Hiroshima, and Stalin. God cannot be aloof from this carnage. God in Christ must be hanging right there on the gallows, suffering with us. "Only a suffering God can help," as Bonhoeffer famously wrote from his prison cell. God is the great "fellow sufferer," as Whitehead supposed. But several difficulties have emerged from the protracted debate about this supposed radicalization of the theology of the cross and the consequent weakening of the doctrine of two natures. The first is a basic problem of coherency. What distinguishes God the sufferer as God in our understanding, who thus seems rather more like us creatures in all things, excepting (perhaps) sin? The suspicion of critics that the twentieth century's suffering God secretes atheism in this one-sided christological reduction is, truth be told, not far from wrong.

6. See the section "God Was Not Always Creator," in T. F. Torrance, *The Trinitarian Faith: The Evangelical Theology of the Ancient Catholic Church* (Edinburgh: T&T Clark, 1993), 84–89.

But Christianly speaking, what help, really, is a great big fellow sufferer? He is and can be little more than Plato's token of ethical resistance in the figure of Socrates, whose piety leads him to the critique of the gods, whose divinity is responsible only for the good. Of course, that is something, but it is not the God of exodus and Easter—the God who rescued Hebrew slaves and exalted the crucified "king of the Jews" and appointed Him judge and coming king of a renewed creation.

Moreover, there comes with this (today increasingly maudlin) kerygma of the suffering God a twofold danger of misrepresenting the wrath of the God of love against what is against love and therewith of proffering a sentimental consolation for us intellectuals who read and write books like this, while our world merrily continues on its juggernaut way to further catastrophes of sin unrecognized and unrepented. Here the insight from the history of doctrine is that the ancient church rejected patripassianism not to deny God's solidarity in Christ with the world's just and unjust sufferings but rather to specify it christologically (as per the third, fourth, and fifth ecumenical councils) within the antecedently established trinitarian framework (of the first and second councils).

Theologically, that christological specification entailed rejection of modalism, which effaces the real differentiation, for God as for us, between God the Father, our source and goal, and the Lord, Jesus Christ, the Father's Son and saving agent in the mediation of the same God's reconciliation. Modalism effaces the real distinction of persons here and thus the very possibility of the exodus-Easter new harmonization of the Father and Son for us and our salvation following their diastasis at Golgotha. But, as the Spirit insists, God kills *in order to* make alive, and God suffers with us *in order to* overcome suffering. Unless we can find the way in the Spirit to genuine reconciliation of those who are different, and so also to genuine healing that ends unjust suffering and puts just suffering into a newly redemptive light, we fall short of the Christian gospel theologically. In that light, the real problem is not divine suffering, which an adequate trinitarianism can account for christologically, but rather the ambiguous doctrine of simplicity that can front for modalism—and in the West especially has done so. In this precise respect, the previous generation was barking up the wrong tree with its pleas to recognize a generic divine pathos.

In any case, today our order of knowledge lies on Gilles Deleuze's plane of immanence, and our language is plausible here only on the supposition of univocity—at a minimum semantically, and perhaps also ontologically. Today the resort to analogy to ascend to a protological First Being seems nothing but a mystification of what is in fact a religious construction. Our present "natural theology" is thus far more comfortable with "figures" appearing on the plane of immanence that pretend to anchor immanence in transcendence, thus funding a new polytheism of many so-called gods and lords. On the plane of immanence, however, immanence is transcendent only to immanence; there are no necessary beings, first causes, unconditioned conditions, or transcendental subjects that do not, on analysis, reduce to appearances: religious figures—"idols" in Paul's language, "icons" perhaps less polemically—suspect of being illusions, though undoubtedly powerful and capable of intensifying life.[7]

In this cultural world of today, consequently, religious figures speaking the oracles of God cannot assume epistemic privilege as the one true revelation of the one true God, because we see without illusion their manifest feet of clay. It is their power, not putative credentials, that wins adherence. Thus here also the Word of the one true God appears as putative, a disputable human word and claim to truth (as the Scriptures, taken historically and critically, now appear), just as whatever ascents to deity that still take place in the field of natural theology aim for no more than local articulations of liberating or consoling or edifying power. In such a world the Christian claim that the particular God of the gospel is the one true God and Creator of all that is not God cannot presume a felt, cognitive need for a one true God, let alone the presumed validity of identifying a finite, human word with the Word of the one true God. And if it tries to conjure such a need or reinforce such a claim by playing on human weakness, fear, and ignorance, it makes itself doubly suspect of marketeering superstition in the sordid business of religion.

By contrast, starting with the figures of the gospel narrative—Jesus, His Father, and their Spirit—and attending to the drama of their interactions through Jesus's messianic ministry to the crisis in their life together that comes about by His innocent identification at the cross with the sin and death of the world, Christian theology can actually launch its discourse regarding the gospel's God as the one true God on today's plane of immanence. It may even succeed in gaining a hearing if in fact this discourse, to paraphrase a pungent apocalyptic parable of Jesus, "breaks into the strong man's house to bind him up and plunder his goods" (see Mark 3:27). But its gospel truth as a claim to knowledge of the one true God can in turn be demonstrated only by that one true God, hence eschatologically, in the fulfillment of His promises. Thus the oneness of God, as here being conceived, is not a rationally evident ontological implication that comes about by analysis of the ground of a

7. For this analysis of our contemporary spiritual situation, see Adkins and Hinlicky, *Rethinking Philosophy and Theology*, 87–95, 105–9.

stable and manifest cosmos. Rather, it is something posited and achieved in a fraught and contested world and thus finally demonstrated in the historical life of a particular claimant to deity by the coming, in Jesus's language, of the reign of God and, in Paul's language, the redemption of our bodies. Such is the God of the gospel. These New Testament notions regarding God's "demonstration" of God's existence, as we will see, in fact cohere profoundly with Israel's faith in the oneness of God.

Of course, that "God" could achieve and demonstrate God's deity for us in a historical life also bears ontological implications. God must be thought of as antecedently powerful enough, wise enough, and good enough to make and keep the promise of the coming of the Beloved Community, thereby demonstrating His deity in a world of His creating. That would give us a certain immanent or ontological doctrine of divine unity or simplicity, namely, a rule of faith reminding us that in all our speech about God we are referring to a singularity—the Creator of all that is not God—the One who is, strictly speaking, incomparable with the quotidian realities familiar to human beings in the world as we know it, who are not sufficiently powerful, wise, or good to give life to themselves, let alone to others. Rather, they find themselves in the thrall of many so-called gods and lords other than the God of the gospel in His claim to be the one true God. Taken this way, divine simplicity is a henotheistic or monolatrous rule of faith for believers in a contested world, namely, to have no other gods before the God of exodus and Easter, the Father of His Son, Jesus Christ, who in the power of their Spirit lays a controversial and controverted claim upon them for exclusive fidelity, one that elicits faith as a disciplined way of life that can be validated only by God's demonstrated fidelity in turn to His promise at the eschaton of judgment.

Thus the ontology of divine simplicity is eschatologically, not protologically, oriented, what Robert Jenson calls a "metaphysics of anticipation" in contrast to a "metaphysics of persistence."[8] This will be ontologically "weaker" than the classical claim to have achieved insight into how God is one by virtue of timeless self-identity. Yet it will be a doctrine of simplicity that affirms that God must be understood to be antecedently the One who is powerful, wise, and good to be the One who God promises to be for us all. In this case simplicity affirms not that the One exists but that the Three are one and will demonstrate their unity by unifying us in the coming of the Beloved Community. I will henceforth refer to the received doctrine as "protological" simplicity and the revised, rule version that I am promoting as "weak" or "eschatological" simplicity.

8. Robert W. Jenson, *Systematic Theology*, 2 vols. (Oxford: Oxford University Press, 1997), 1:108–14.

From this biblical perspective, then, one ambiguity of the received doctrine of simplicity is that it forgets the controversial, indeed polemical, nature of the gospel's claim to truth, whether as the "word of the cross" that begins Paul's First Letter to the Corinthians or as "word of the resurrection of the Crucified" with which Paul ends the same letter. It takes for granted exactly that which may not be taken for granted: that it is obvious that there is no God but God; that we are creatures of the one true God, who is all-powerful, all-wise, and all-good; that as such beneficiaries, we ought to pray, praise, and give thanks; that as such worshipers of God alone, we ought not to worship other creatures; that as creatures with others of the one and same God, we ought rather to love one another as of equal worth before Him and to honor the earth as good stewards of land not our own. Only in "baptized" form, in fact, does the received doctrine of simplicity even begin to approach these soteriological and ethical concerns of biblical monotheism.[9] The concern of biblical monotheism is to establish the claim of the first of the Ten Commandments as the practical sense of "monotheism," namely, the coming of the reign of God from God the Father through the Lord Jesus Christ in the power of the Spirit, who makes believers out of us hapless (or lethal) idolaters (1 Thess. 1:9–10). In fact, the received doctrine of protological simplicity, going back to its philosophical sources in the pre-Socratics, as we will see, has an entirely different trajectory of disestablishing *all* putative words of God, of affirming the world just as it is (and necessarily must be) and thus guiding enlightened souls to a private peace that (just as) putatively transcends the strife of embodied existence. What began in Parmenides ends in Spinoza. And what continues in Spinoza terminates in Hegel.

This philosophical doctrine of divine simplicity is fundamentally the claim that what is without parts or composition, hence what is metaphysically indivisible and self-identical, is by nature imperishable in the sense of being incapable of decomposition. It is, in a nutshell, the metaphysics of pure persistence. And this tells what is divine, the one true God, or more precisely, the truly divine nature. Ironically, this too is a putative insight, a claim—albeit in the form of a denial or negation of divisibility—to know what God is, what characterizes divinity essentially and as such by disqualifying ontologically any and all other possible characterizations. Divine simplicity, in this rendering, is a superattribute. In contrast to us mortals, the negative claim is that God is not mortal, perishable, or passible. All human speech, consequently, that attributes relationality, sociality, patiency, other-regard—in short, all passion of life—must be taken as an improper way of human speaking, as

9. Hinlicky, *Divine Complexity*, 167–79.

"anthropomorphism," not in metaphysical strictness predicating impersonal and asocial and apathetic divine being. As we will see, herein lies a great irony: the metaphysics of divine simplicity, which asserts kataphatically the putative natural insight that God is simply God, *esse ipsum subsistens*, finally succumbs to apophaticism. It can assert *that* God exists as timeless self-identity, but at the cost of denying any possible knowledge of *what* God is like—that is, knowledge of what this divine self-identity consists.

True, as we will have occasion to note, this starvation diet is frequently augmented with the (unconsciously) anthropomorphic picture of God as Mind that lends an apparent dynamism to it. The God who is simply God as timeless self-identity is pictured as thought thinking and willing itself. But, as above, on strict examination even this picture proves too anthropomorphic. And in that case, Christian theology has to ask whether the philosophical doctrine of divine simplicity is not "simply" vacuous, pointing to a No-Thing. Nor does it help before this question to say that it is precisely supernatural revelation that fills the knowledge gap with supernatural truths about God's personhood and sociality that are beyond reason's grasp. That does not help, because this cut-and-paste job does not survive the vacuity of affirming as divine a timeless self-identity—we know not what. It is betrayed by the ferocious, relentless "power of the negative," as we will see, that debunks not only the idols of the nations but also the biblical God, and in the process misconstrues what is at stake in the contest between the God of the gospel and the idols of the nations.

In reality, the classic doctrine of simplicity makes unthinkable a true incarnation along with the eternal perichoresis that the incarnate Son attributes to His relation to the Father in the high priestly prayer of John 17. It makes the drama of Hosea 11, in which the God of love surpasses wrath to achieve mercy, a soap opera on the same level of Zeus's fits of jealousy. It replaces with a putative insight into the beyond the true mystery of divine being as the self-surpassing, self-donating, self-communicating Three of the gospel narrative, who are and claim to be the eternal harmony of power, wisdom, and love that promises to bring creation to fulfillment by an act of costly redemption at the cross of the incarnate Son and the mission thence of His holy-ing Spirit to the nations. Here the oneness of the Triune God is concrete, living, and holy love: *esse Deum dare*. The proposed rule is this: so speak of the one true God as the Father of the Son, who in the Spirit infinitely gives such that we and all creatures are spoken of as gifted. "What do you have that you did not receive?" (1 Cor. 4:7). Abstractly put, in terms of a characterization of the singularity of divine nature, the freedom to love wisely is divine—the whatness of the one true God in the act of His being, also for us, when the eternal act of God's being is understood as the Father's generation of the Son, on whom He breathes His Spirit.

In this book, then, I wish to fill out explicitly the case implied in my systematic theology for this rule version of divine simplicity and against what I have just characterized as an alleged protological insight. I begin by taking up the case that the late Colin Gunton began to make in his *Act and Being* before his untimely death, and updating it with the recent manifesto of R. T. Mullins. I conclude the first chapter by recalling the strong trinitarian distinction between nature and person that Régnon, Lossky, and Hinlicky Wilson have upheld in contemporary theology. Laying that out will take up the first chapter.

From there, I will turn in the second chapter to the classical Christian baptism of the metaphysics of divine simplicity performed by St. Thomas Aquinas, though with a different focus than is usual today. I will not examine the *Summa Theologiae*, where the baptized doctrine is already axiomatically at work, but will look instead to the first book of the *Summa contra Gentiles*. I want to underscore, affirmatively, the anti-gnostic motive in Thomas's baptized version of simplicity and, critically, to dissect the complex relation of Thomas's doctrine to the Islamic mediation of Aristotelian philosophy. That study will lead to a consideration of a range of contemporary thinkers who have similarly wrestled with Thomas's legacy in this regard: the Sufi Muslim Seyyed Hossein Nasr, the British Catholic Fergus Kerr, and the American Catholic David Burrell. The chapter will conclude with the debunking executed by the Franciscan Daniel P. Horan of the au courant narrative of the fall into nihilism that begins with Scotus, having unveiled instead the aporias embedded in Thomas's unstable synthesis. The intention is to provide in chapter 2 as appreciative an account as possible of the theological (as opposed to philosophical) position on divine simplicity that this book rejects. A study of Clement of Alexandria's claim for Christian "gnosis" will be appended in an excursus as a segue to chapter 3. The reason for it lies in contesting certain claims for the *philosophia perennis* made by Nasr, as will become evident in the course of chapter 2.

In the third chapter I will point with Gavin Ortlund to the diversity of ways that notions of divine simplicity have played in the history of Christian doctrine, especially comparing Augustinian and Cappadocian appropriations of the thought in relation to trinitarianism. We will see how Paul's statement that "Christ [is] the power of God and the wisdom of God" from the opening of 1 Corinthians initiates a differentiation in the divine life that leads to the prototrinitarian confession of 1 Corinthians 8:4–6 and to the eschatological "theopanism" of 1 Corinthians 15:28. Of particular interest in this light is the fact that Augustine stumbled over just this Pauline affirmation of "Christ

[as] the power and wisdom of God" for its apparent compromising of divine simplicity. In tandem with this analysis we will also note the hyper-Arian stance of Eunomius and the ironic ways in which his contention for timeless self-identity of nature penetrated Christian theology in the thought of Evagrius and Pseudo-Dionysius. I will follow Knut Alfsvåg's rejoinder to this development in his contention for *christological* apophaticism at the conclusion of chapter 3.

In the fourth chapter I will sustain the christological critique of protological simplicity by attending to the correlative doctrine of analogy, not only of being but also (though subtly) of Karl Barth's "analogy of faith." In this connection, Barth sometimes speaks of a repetition in time of God's eternal being such that the man Jesus is to God as the eternal Son is to the eternal Father, a formulation that corresponds to his early trimodal and psychological account of the Trinity. This is but one side of Barth's ever-dialectical theology, to be sure. But in this formulation protological simplicity will be exposed as the culprit in an unfortunately Nestorian construction of a Christology of two sons, albeit in precise "analogy" to each another. In the conclusion, after a brief refutation of the analytic theologian James Dolezal's defense of strong simplicity as incoherent with divine freedom, I lay out the results of the study in a proposal for a rule version of divine simplicity structured by the first table of the Decalogue—that is, as rules applying first of all to theology itself.

1

The Simplicity
of Consistent Perichoresis

Auseinandersetzung

In this chapter we are engaged in the *Auseinandersetzung* that was just introduced. This wonderful German theological word refers to the setting out of
differing positions for comparison and contrast. In this chapter I will lay out
the case for the eschatological simplicity of a consistent account of divine
unity as trinitarian perichoresis, the mutual indwelling of the trinitarian persons. Here the unity of God, or divine simplicity, is a function of trinitarian
communion of being, not a foundation for it as in protological simplicity. It
understands divine simplicity from the "monarchy" of the Father instead of
the equality of the essence. In being denominated "weak," it is opposed to
"strong" simplicity—that is, a doctrine of the absoluteness of God's sheer
being in its awesome actuality. Or, it may be called the Christian-theological
rule version of simplicity that requires an apophatic qualification of the kataphatic revelation as opposed to the supposed protological insight of natural
theology. All of these ways of naming the simplicity of consistent perichoresis
are synonyms that differ only by aspect or connotation. At the same time,
the urgent, contemporary sense of this affirmation of consistent perichoresis

cannot fully be appreciated without some initial working knowledge of the alternative account of protological simplicity as timeless self-identity. So we must begin this chapter with a sketch of protological simplicity from the avowedly critical perspective of the notion of God's unity as consistent perichoresis.

As noted in the introduction, the classic Christian doctrine of divine simplicity (as articulated by Thomas Aquinas, to be examined especially in the next chapter) holds, in Richard Muller's definition, that "God is absolutely free of any and all composition, not merely physical, but also rational or logical composition. . . . Simplicity is the guarantee of the absolute ultimacy and perfection of God, so much so that it frequently appears in scholastic systems as the first divine attribute on which a right understanding of all other divine attributes depends."[1] In this procedure, of course, Reformed dogmatics follows Thomas's procedure in the *Summa Theologiae*. In Thomas's exposition, as we will see, God exists as the act of His own being, as the full actualization of His divine essence; that is, God is the ontological one and only, whose essence is to exist, and whose existence is wholly the actualization of His essence. Just so, the doctrine of divine simplicity takes as granted that God is one. God's oneness is axiomatic, true by definition, analytically true, if God is simple. What else could God be? Oneness constitutes the very notion of the truly divine nature as timeless self-identity in that God is never other than God, thus doubled into a multiplicity. God—taken further as a single subject, as a divine nature with agency—is, supremely is, and exists as its own actualization, we lesser beings know not how. All we do know is that the denominator, God, points simply to being perfectly, the really real, being as such. Hence we can capture the sense of this reference by saying that God is *simply*—that is, without any mediation, without any other, without any composition of parts, without any external acquisition, without any history or embodiment.

How then can this simple God be the God of the Bible, who creates, redeems, and fulfills a creation in a history with humanity? God, being perfectly, can only act externally with and as the same timeless perfection, funding the existence of all other imperfectly existing beings in a single, creative, intuitive protological act of explication of what is implicit in God's being as the absolute unity of all perfections. Thus, in creation, God thinks Himself as refracted, so to say, into the splendid multiplicity of the perfections appearing in the created world, where each thing, in its own way, by the mere virtue of existing, imperfectly but truly reflects God its Creator. Here, however, we

1. Richard A. Muller, *Dictionary of Latin and Greek Theological Terms Drawn Principally from Protestant Scholastic Theology* (Grand Rapids: Baker, 1985), 283.

encounter the complication of human being and angels, free beings, who may or may not relate themselves properly to God in their own acts of being. This proper relation, naturally, would be as His similitudes, freely fulfilling their own natures to reflect in some particular respect God's perfection. Falling short of that, the privation of being in sin leads naturally to corruption and death, just as also the amplification of being occurs in obedience that leads to life. The latter similitude, paradigmatically, is the new Adam, Jesus Christ, "man's road to God."

Especially in the baptized account rendered by the Christian tradition, divine simplicity is a metaphysical vision of no little elegance and intellectual power. It articulates the Christian gospel of the strong distinction between Creator and creature and thus specifies their proper unity by way of similitude or analogy, as ectype to archetype, in the face of new challenges beginning in the twelfth century from the West's discovery of Aristotelian naturalism as expounded by a philosophized version of Islamic unitarianism from the pens of the most able commentators, Avicenna and Averroes. Naturalism continued in new forms in the early modern period—now closer to Averroes than to Avicenna—with the rise of the natural sciences,[2] when Thomism experienced a corresponding revival in both Protestant and Catholic neo-scholastic orthodoxies.[3] Indeed, the hegemony of Thomism in both Protestant and Catholic theology did not really come to an end until the rise of Darwinian biology, which made the mutation of forms the very key to natural history,[4] profoundly questioning the idea that God's creation is a single, intuitive, creative protological act.

What matters at the moment, however, is to take note of several unwarranted assumptions that are being made in the preceding. The first is that there

2. This is the case even though the Reformation unleashed natural philosophy from the constraints of Aristotelian teleology. See Sachiko Kusukawa, *The Transformation of Natural Philosophy: The Case of Philip Melanchthon*, Ideas in Context (Cambridge: Cambridge University Press, 1995).

3. Robert D. Preus, *The Theology of Post-Reformation Lutheranism*, vol. 1, *God and His Creation* (St. Louis: Concordia, 1972), 36. Richard Muller properly traces the procedure of "principlizing"—that is, the extracting of principles from the Bible for rational reordering in a scientific system of doctrine—to Thomas, which in the present view is the chief hermeneutical fault of scholastic theology, old and new (*Post-Reformation Reformed Dogmatics: The Rise and Development of Reformed Orthodoxy, ca. 1520 to ca. 1725*, vol. 1, *Prolegomena to Theology*, 2nd ed. [Grand Rapids: Baker Academic, 2003], 92–93). See Kevin Vanhoozer's insightful critique of contemporary evangelical reliance on ahistorical "principlizing"—that is, "abstracting the [allegedly] transcultural principles from their biblical context in order to clothe these naked principles in cultural garb that is intelligible in the contemporary context"—in *The Oxford Handbook of Evangelical Theology*, ed. Gerald R. McDermott (New York: Oxford University Press, 2010), 43.

4. John C. Greene, *The Death of Adam: Evolution and Its Impact on Western Thought* (Ames: Iowa State University Press, 1996).

can be in reality only one God and that this can be known axiomatically by natural reason. To be sure, the Bible seems to say so in both Testaments, and hence Judaism and Christianity as well as Islam, following the Scriptures, say so. But what does this affirmation mean in the face of a world surfeit with many so-called gods and lords? Are these others simply illusions? Malignant illusions, idols? It is not so obvious. God may be one in heaven above, but here on the earth, gods are many. Is that what is meant? Are the gods various masks, locally adapted, of the one God beyond all the many? Are they similitudes? Icons? Or are they, as Paul blurts out, the deceptive masquerades of "demons" (1 Cor. 10:20–21)?

A second assumption is that God is one in the way of being substance, and perfectly so, hence the only true or genuine substance, of which other substances are echoes or reflections with a derivative substantiality. The precise definition of a substance has long been a matter of debate, but the concern for unity in the sense of persistence of an internally coherent entity in time or, indeed, in spite of time—that is to say, for being over becoming—is at the heart of the notion. And if we purify this concern and thus narrow the notion to the pure act of persistence in self-identity over against all temporal becoming, we get the idea of a perfect being that exists outside of time altogether: Being itself, timeless self-identity. It is, at the least, not clear prima facie how this ontological notion of divine unity would or could match with the biblical notion of God's fidelity to His promises through time, which implies an alternative ontology, often indicated nowadays by the term "relational" ontology. Here God and creatures exist as internally coherent entities by keeping faith with others in time, even if the time of the Trinity and the time of creatures are something infinitely differentiated.

A third assumption, briefly mentioned above, pertains to the (tacitly anthropomorphic) intellectuality of perfect being, Aristotle's "thought thinking itself." Anything admitting of unrealized potentiality would not perfectly be; anything admixed with accidents or external relations that become essential to its identity would not perfectly be; anything subject to others would not perfectly be; anything once composed that could come apart again would not perfectly be. Such negative stipulations for perfect being seem to price the notion right out of the earthly marketplace. In a sense, that is precisely the point. By this reflection, we ascend in thought to the notion of a timelessly eternal act of being, what simply and purely and immaterially is. Although we imperfect beings cannot know and say what this act of timeless self-identity is—if we could, we would be perfect beings—we can point to it by analogy. It exists like the minds that we are, whose ascent in thought has brought us to the cusp of this insight. God is like mind, only purely so. God is like mind, only thinking itself, not any other. God is like mind, thinking and willing itself, not any other. God is like mind, not like matter. God, then, *is*—so we may leap—immaterial Mind in relation to whom all else is mere matter as clay to the potter. God as Mind, then, is related to external, nonessential, accidental things in the flux of becoming when God thinks Himself by way of refraction in the act of creation, giving form to matter to make the world of many really existing things. Note here, as well, the highly ambiguous status of matter; while Christian theology, following the Bible, had to assert that matter is also God's creature, this claim can only amount to an obiter dictum that does not harmonize easily with the negative notion of God derived by the path of dematerialization, which tacitly presupposes the eternity of matter. The privileging of intellect as the Godlike power thinks by analogy from the laws of nature that rule things and the obedience to the law of nature that ought to rule minds. It arrives at the pure intellectuality that is God timelessly and immaterially thinking and willing God, also *ad extra* in the refractive act of creation.

The oscillation here between a seemingly kataphatic insight (God is perfect Mind) and an apparent apophatic negation (God's Mind is not discursive like any mind that creatures can imagine), or, God is Being itself but beyond the duality of being and nonbeing, is endemic. We can take it as a healthy dialectic or as an unprincipled instability, depending upon an independent variable: what we think theological discourse is trying to accomplish.

This analogical thinking, in any event, gives to us imperfect beings the celebrated "analogy of being": as mind is to matter imposing form, so the perfect being is to the chaos/matter rendering a cosmos, an order of beings organized into a system. As such, whatever exists in the world does so insofar as it is formed by, and thus participates by imitation in, perfect being—that is, its materialized form somehow partaking in and so imitating the pure form that exists in God's perfection at one with all other forms. And insofar as this materialized form exists, it is also good in analogy to the Goodness itself that created it. Its goodness in being, materialized and finite as a creature must be, gives us a piety—"cosmos-piety," we can call it—of reverence and respect for the fragile order that we imperfect beings experience, ever exposed as we are to the threat of chaos—that is, the loss of form, the reversion to mere matter. And it correspondingly gives us rational creatures an ethic, a moral teleology. Each of us is to discover our place in the order of beings as cosmos, and there to bring to consciousness and actively realize our essence as our innately given telos, becoming the best possible butcher, baker, or candlestick maker that we can be.

We are now prepared by way of the foregoing sketch to contrast this venerable metaphysic of divine simplicity with the position that I am advocating in this book. The incomparability or singularity of the being of the Triune God consists in the eternal becoming of the self-surpassing Father of the self-donating Son in the self-communicating Spirit. Nota bene: what we have just heard is a summary description, not an explanation (i.e., a theory that comprehends). It comes not as an insight but as the gift of revelation; it comes not by mind's ascent to the notion of its own perfection but by the surprising, disruptive descent of divine love for inferiors who are also enemies; it is possessed not by imitation but by self-entrusting faith; it is realized from above in our receptivity, not from below by our achievement and merit; it is active not in the self-love that aspires to security from the threat of chaos but in other-love that bears with chaos in hope of redemption—that is to say, it exists not by the suppression of chaos but by a militant hope within it for the Beloved Community that de facto disrupts with creative tension the present unjust ordering of things, as in Moses's word to Pharaoh, "Let my people go!" or Jesus's word of rebuke to the demon, "Be still and come out of him!"

It does all this by holding up one, decisive stop sign: Halt! With this prohibition, it thwarts the protological ambition of human reason to be as God, knowing good and evil (Isa. 55:8–9), which is the original false promise, the *sicut Deus eritis*, of the serpent. "For I am God, and there is no other; I am God, and there is no one like me, declaring the end from the beginning and from ancient times things not yet done, saying, 'My purpose shall stand, and I will fulfill my intention'" (Isa. 46:9–10). Here the incomparability of God is predicated on His self-identification as the redeemer of Israel, and it takes shape as its accompanying prohibition against knowing God by way of comparison with supposed earthly perfections. This prohibition is theologically the prohibition of constructivism in theology—that is, free and natural analogizing, as the veritable workshop of metaphorical idolatry. At the same time, the self-identification of God sanctifies and fulfills reason by assigning it new ambition and proper tasks for the identification of God at work in time through the gospel (Isa. 52:7), anticipating adoration in the same God of the same God to all eternity (Isa. 54:7–8; 55:13). The proper and theological rule of divine simplicity, then, is to qualify all earthly language, captured and sanctified by God to speak God, as referring to an incomparable and hence essentially mysterious divine life that can be identified but not comprehended, enjoyed but not utilized, adored but not mastered. With this christological root (Isa. 53) from the Hebrew Scriptures, that mysterious divine life is identified in Christian theology as the Father of the Son in the Spirit, who sends His Son as His suffering Servant, on whom were laid the iniquities of us all. Such is the divine life or eternal becoming for which no analogy exists in that it is eternally capable of time and space in this christological way, such that its claim to truth is "legitimated by the continuity of prediction"[5] with its "universal sweep."[6]

Here we have accordingly a very different take on what it might mean to say that God is one, namely, that a certain God who appears as a figure in history as proclaimed by His prophets is, claims to be, and will prove to be the incomparable one true God—the singularity, the zealous, jealous One who requires a corresponding fidelity. What makes God one within this biblical framework is not that God in heaven above is indivisible and hence by nature invulnerable. Rather, what makes God one is His Word, which in His Spirit returns to Him not in vain (Isa. 55:11), which for us is an exclusive claim to save. God is one for us in His *katabasis*, His philanthropic descent, not in our *anabasis*, our ascent. And God *can*—that is, *antecedently*—be thought of as one for us in this historic way, if God for God *is* His Word and God *is* His communication or impartation of this Word that He *is* to creatures, God the Spirit. Thus God is one as the begetter of His Word and spirator of His Spirit, the Father of the Son in the Spirit. In this sense, the Three of the gospel narrative are understood to be one eternal life who can be, who promises to be, and who will prove to be all things to everyone (1 Cor. 15:28).

The church has always—explicitly from the composition and reception of the high priestly prayer of Jesus in John 17—held to such a notion of God's oneness or unity as consisting in the mutual indwelling (perichoresis) of love of the Father and the Son in the Spirit.[7] But it has not consistently held to perichoresis as the divine unity simply and as such and so as the rule of faith; it has retreated into the metaphysics of protological simplicity in fear of the risks involved in consistent perichoresis, beginning with the divine risk taken in creating a world of beings such as we are, continuing in the risk of becoming one of us, and extending to the fulfillment of the divine purpose of the Beloved Community in the time and space of creatures. Such consistency, with respect to the doctrine of God, would mean to persist and follow through on Athanasius's great insight that this Father cannot be the Father that He is without the Son, nor the Son be Son without the Father, nor the Holy Spirit be Holy apart from the Son and the Father. In significant ways, the Cappadocian fathers extended this discovery of Athanasius in their battle

---

5. Gerhard von Rad, *Old Testament Theology*, trans. D. M. G. Stalker (New York: Harper & Row, 1962), 2:247.

6. Ibid., 2:262.

7. "That which is from all eternity is the unity of the Father and Son, in a 'mutual knowledge,' an 'indwelling,' of which the real character is *agape*. This is the ultimate mystery of the Godhead which Jesus revealed to the world. . . . The human career of Jesus is, as it were, a projection of this eternal relation (which is the divine agape) upon the field of time" (C. H. Dodd, *The Interpretation of the Fourth Gospel* [Cambridge: Cambridge University Press, 1995], 262).

against the hyper-Arian Eunomius, as we will see. But alongside it, the church has been tempted to think the oneness of God in the former way described above, according to the protological metaphysics of perfect being or simply timeless substance—that is, by the negative notion of an allegedly sheer, thus vacuous, indivisibility.

Indeed, this temptation to retreat from the divine self-risking told in the Bible becomes well-nigh unavoidable under two conditions. The first is that the trinitarian conception of God in the gospel narrative is forgotten or obscured. Then the doctrine of the Trinity is received on mere ecclesiastical authority as a supernatural mystery that has ceased to do actual theological work in identifying God in time for the praise of God in eternity. It becomes instead a speculative riddle, how three can be one and one can be three, a problem for academic theology to master logically. That in fact occurred in the Middle Ages.[8] A second condition has prevailed in modernity as the literal plausibility of the scriptural account of origins faded and with it the plausibility of the strong Creator/creature distinction, which previously had seemed axiomatic. Nevertheless, this second condition for thinking the oneness of God metaphysically is in fact a profound retrieval and radicalization of the medieval analogy of being, contrary to recent polemics about a fall that began with Duns Scotus. Indeed, this way of thinking the oneness of God under modern conditions may be seen especially in the thought of Hegel. By way of a brief digression, I will dwell on this second condition for a moment, since it profoundly contravenes the increasingly well-known narrative of Radical Orthodoxy that sees in Hegel's kind of atheism the outcome of the fall of Duns Scotus from Thomism's analogy of being.

In Hegel we find a remarkable philosophical account of the rise of self-consciousness in the life of the mind by a process of self-diremption and self-recovery in self-affirmation. This account of consciousness displaces the dramatic gospel narrative (its religious "representation"); it does so by robbing God of the freedom the biblical narrative presupposes in the achievement of philosophical comprehension of it (*fides quaerens intellectum*, indeed). Now, in philosophical comprehension, the cosmos becomes the project of God's self-realization, the necessary unfolding of His own being as essentially creative. Hegel attacked the abstract, eternal idea of God in and for himself "prior to or apart from creation"; he even understood that in Christian theology this is "expressed in terms of the holy Trinity." The function of the doctrine of the

---

8. Of course, that is not all that occurred. See the wonderful survey in Pekka Kärkkäinen, ed., *Trinitarian Theology in the Medieval West*, Schriften der Luther-Agricola-Gesellschaft 61 (Helsinki: Luther-Agricola-Society, 2007).

eternal or immanent Trinity had been to account for God's transcendence of creation as its free author by virtue of the Trinity's antecedently fulfilled life as the eternal love of the Father and the Son in the Spirit, what I am calling "consistent perichoresis." Yet in criticism of this very theological function of the immanent or ontological Trinity, Hegel argued that "insofar as [God] is not the creator, he is grasped inadequately. His creative role is not an *actus* that 'happened' once; [rather] what takes place in the idea is an eternal moment," since "it belongs to his being, his essence, to be the creator."[9] In that case, as well, the Trinity will be radically revised to express divine self-creativity as the coming of the cosmos to self-consciousness.

Thus the becoming of the cosmos is embraced and interpreted in a dynamic way. God had been classically thought of as pure Mind thinking itself and loving itself timelessly above, drawing all others to imitation by the worship that God's perfect being inspires. Now this same tradition of natural theology (which appears in Christian theology as the psychological model of the Trinity) turns the conviction that the real is the rational and the rational is real against its classical synthesis with trinitarianism in Thomas. The vulnerability, however, was already there in Thomas (as will be argued in detail in the next chapter), the Aristotelian who had a difficult time rejecting the eternity of the world. In order to affirm the freedom of God's act of creation against the more natural inference from his presuppositions of an eternal creation by a timelessly eternal Creator (over against equally eternal matter), he had to resort to revelation of a supernatural truth. Christianly speaking, this was needed to fend off the necessitarian thought that God, as the timelessly perfect being, must be *ever* creative, just as Hegel would later think (and as Origen had earlier thought). Truth be told, however, if God is not understood robustly as *freely* creative of a world other than God because of His own eternal life of becoming in love as the Father of the Son in the Spirit, then we are driven at length by the reality of our world's becoming, in which we live, move, and have our being, to the idea that God necessarily creates a world as the natural act of God's own being, God's own self-realization.

With the way for this modern move long prepared by the Neoplatonic trinity of mind thinking and willing itself and emanating this self-thinking outward by refraction in the great chain of being, the modern this-worldly turn of thought exemplified in Hegel decisively displaced the social Trinity of the gospel narrative and, as we will see, virtually required a Nestorian account of

9. G. W. F. Hegel, *Lectures on the Philosophy of Religion: The Lectures of 1827*, ed. Peter C. Hodgson, trans. R. F. Brown et al., one-volume ed. (Berkeley: University of California Press, 1988), 417.

Christology: the earthly son of Mary who corresponds to the eternal Son of God, a Jesus who (merely) shows us what God is like, a kind of supersaint, the paradigm in a world composed of analogues of God. If this narrative of the Platonic line through (Origen and Pseudo-Dionysius and) Thomas to Hegel via Spinoza holds, we will see in Scotus not Radical Orthodoxy's fall from Thomas that leads to disaster but rather an (ambiguous) attempt, Christianly speaking, to preserve the freedom of God and prevent the disaster for Christian theology that follows from treating divine nature as the true subject or agent in God rather than the trinity of persons.

In a nutshell, then, the venerable protological doctrine of divine simplicity is the insight of the ascending mind to the thought of perfect being as timeless self-identity. On this putatively rational foundation, the revealed truth of the tri-personhood of the God of the gospel was appended and thus could also be jettisoned as a nonessential superstructure under the duress of the modern rediscovery of Heraclitus's stream of becoming. Or, as in Hegel, the dynamism of the psychological trinity of thought thinking and willing itself could be retrieved for an account of the cosmos as history coming to self-consciousness. Between the medieval theologians and Hegel, however, stands the peerless Spinoza, the purest thinker of the thought of divine simplicity, who had taunted theists with the embarrassing question of how a perfect being could ever be conceived to begin to create—that is, to create freely.[10] This is the very conundrum that Thomas already faced but dodged by appeal to special revelation over against the plain implication of his own natural theology. Such a beginning by God being simply inconceivable, if God is timelessly eternal (in spite of Gen. 1:1), the fatal step was taken after Spinoza's taunt in the direction of Hegel's conviction that deity is *essentially* creative, simply *natura naturans* in Spinoza's reconceptualization of divine simplicity.

In the proposed theological rule advocated in this book, by contrast, divine simplicity is a divine command to qualify speech and understanding of the tri-personhood of the gospel's God—namely, that the Three must be thought of as one incomparable life for time, in time, and in fulfillment of time, the Beloved Community. This divine life is a singularity; the theological account of God's unity as such is a description that serves to identify and adore, not *theoria* that claims comprehension. Qualifying all speech regarding the divine life as "simple" and thus ineffable in obedience to divine command means that this life of the Father, the Son, and the Holy Spirit is eternally mysterious,

10. Baruch Spinoza, *The Ethics; Treatise on the Emendation of the Intellect; Selected Letters*, trans. Samuel Shirley, ed. Seymour Feldman, 2nd ed. (Indianapolis: Hackett, 1992), 58–59. See the discussion in Brent Adkins and Paul R. Hinlicky, *Rethinking Philosophy and Theology with Deleuze: A New Cartography* (London: Bloomsbury Academic, 2013), 161–62.

the eternally fascinating mystery of the world on the way to its redemption and fulfillment. Credit for initiating this analysis of the present "crisis" of Christian theology—in contrast to Radical Orthodoxy's diagnosis of the same malaise—in understanding the oneness of God in Euro-America today belongs to the late Colin E. Gunton, whose pioneering but incomplete final book, *Act and Being*,[11] I will now summarize and analyze.

Are Divine Attributes Projections?

Gunton's exploration is indicated in the book's subtitle, *Towards a Theology of the Divine Attributes*; his accent on the divine attributes, by account of which properties any notion of a substance (or substantial subject) persisting in time is rescued from vacuity, has a backstory. It consists in Gunton's reception of Robert Jenson's brilliant case at the opening of his *Systematic Theology* for the priority of the "who" question in Christian theology over the questions of what and how. Indeed, so drastic was Jenson's effort by way of this prioritization to purge Christian theology of the Trojan horse of an alien metaphysics—that is, of the axiomatic force of protological notions about the what and the how of God—that he intentionally dispensed with the classical topic of the divine attributes altogether. It is knowledge of *who* God is that is consistently to govern thinking about what and how God is. Jenson thus treated questions of divine "nature" ad hoc, as the topics in his system of theology variously required.

The deep justification for this procedure was Jenson's historicist claim that metaphysics is myth that has forgotten itself in the process of its own rationalization. This exposé levels the playing field for Christian theology, whose narrative ("myth") tells as its priority who God is as the God of the gospel for us in Jesus Christ. It is not a matter, then, of theology being mythical and metaphysics being sober and rational. Rather, myths (narratives) taken on faith (as powerful and plausible) are rationalized theologically or philosophically, as the case may be. Gunton summarizes this decisive stimulus from Jenson at the outset of his book:

> [Jenson] points out that Greek philosophy and its descendants have no more claim to universality than any other set of doctrines. The various accounts of the structure of being in the Presocratic and classical Greek philosophies are

11. Colin E. Gunton, *Act and Being: Towards a Theology of the Divine Attributes* (Grand Rapids: Eerdmans, 2003). Henceforth, citations from this book are followed by page numbers in parentheses in the main text.

in point of fact theologies, attempts to conceive the world in relation to the divine. . . . Greek philosophy begins as an attempt to provide a rational version of the ancient world view those gods represent. It is a demythologization (*Aufhebung?*) only as a translation or transposition, not a displacement or abolition. (5–6)

The parenthetical allusion to Hegel's *Aufhebung*, as we have seen, is spot-on. Metaphysics works the denarrativizing of religious figures, as given in their myths, and in this way brings the figure or representation to comprehension, supremely in abstract accounts of divine nature.

Gunton, however, resists "the fashionable assumption that we may simply reject certain of the ancient attributes—for example, impassibility," because "no victory can be won simply by bombing the opposition out of existence" (22). This is a veiled criticism of Jenson's (deliberate) neglect of the topic of divine attributes, all the while passionately affirming the suffering of God. Of course, suffering is also an attribution. Stepping back from the highly fraught discussion of possibility, Gunton sees that in fact a who without a what and a how would be equally vacuous—a ghost, really, a subject without a body. Some ontological account of the divine "nature" is required of any theology that wants to sustain the Creator/creature distinction (christologically, the doctrine of the two natures) as the very presupposition of difference in kind that renders intelligible the coming of the Beloved Community from above as gift, a free grace that unifies persons in love.

Attributes, we may say modestly to begin with, are qualities by which we identify a class of beings by its characteristic possibilities. If it quacks, flies, and feeds in the water as well as on land with a bill-shaped beak, it probably is a duck, a member of the class *Anas platyrhynchos*. Attributes like flying, quacking, and bill-shaped beaks combine into sets that help us to classify entities—that is, to group entities of experience in virtue of shared characteristics as discerned from some particular angle of vision (e.g., to the human being the wooden structure on which she sits is classified as a chair, though to the termite it is a potential meal). It is a means of efficiently if roughly processing the infinitude of the stream of perception. In Christian theology, such attribution helps us classify what is creaturely and what is creative from our perspective as redeemed creatures of God destined for His Beloved Community. This distinction of natures, as by sets of characteristic attributes, is an inalienable legacy of biblical faith. To know what is God and what is not God is to know what God can be and do for us and what we must in turn suffer and do. Theology must be able to know and to say what is God and what is not. Melanchthon wrote, "In earnest invocation of God it is necessary to consider *what* one wants to address, *what* God is, how he is known, where and how he has revealed himself, and both if and why he hears our pleas and cries."[12] Theology does this cognitive work by way of classes of attributes that serve generally and abstractly to distinguish God as Creator from His creatures.

Yet the one and only God, we might object, is *non in genere*; that is true, if we mean by this denial that God belongs in a genus to affirm that God is in fact a singularity, *sui generis*, in a class by Himself. That is indeed one way, ontologically, of understanding God's oneness. God, taken as a single subject, is the one and only member of a set of characteristics that identifies divinity. Otherwise, this worry is concerning only if we think that our classifications of attributes have extramental reality as such rather than being merely finite conceptual devices, variable with our perspectives, serving to identify extramental realities for the efficient processing of information in our earthly journeys. If classes of attributes are but conceptions of our minds by which we organize the chaos of data into useable sets, we do not in reality capture God in any of our ideas of divinity or creativity, even classifications adequate to God's reality as subject of them, thus subordinating God in reality to some idea that is itself regarded as real. All we do is point in a general way to what is God and what is not God, though always on the basis of assumptions, borrowed from some revelation, about who God is. If I say that God is the Father almighty, Creator of heaven and earth, then I classify as divine what can create all that is not God. Or, if I say that God is the ontological One, then I classify as divine all that is not multiple.

As a safeguard against presumption, we might then designate that singularity of genus, namely, that God is in a class of His own, as the "holiness" of God, as Gunton argues (against Barth [117]). This stipulation of holiness in regard to attributions made concerning God comports with the rule theory of simplicity for which I am arguing as a kind of qualification of all our qualifications of God. The import of it is that we should not presume to know a priori what is divine but rather should discipline ourselves to learn what a class of divine capabilities is from God's self-revelation, learning the what from the who. If God is revealed as the Creator of all that is not God, then, God's divine being must be understood in terms of such capabilities that would attend such an all-creative subject: the power, the wisdom, and the goodness that are able to make this world, on the way to the coming of the Beloved Community, the best of all possible worlds (as Leibniz and I, not Gunton, would put it).

12. Philip Melanchthon, *On Christian Doctrine: Loci Communes, 1555*, trans. and ed. Clyde L. Manschreck (Grand Rapids: Baker, 1982), 3.

Refining Jenson's position, then, Gunton argues that a theological account of divine nature by a consideration of the attributes of the God of the gospel requires, not doing away with attribution, but what he calls a positive rather than a negative derivation of divine attributes. He is not simply preferring the philosophical way of eminence to the way of negation. The way of eminence in a "positive" account learns what God is from who God is; it is an exercise in revealed theology. By contrast, a "negative" account achieves by way of natural theology a definition of God by negation of worldly attributes (as also the philosophical way of eminence, by removing imperfections to come to God's perfection, is also an eliminative—that is, a negative way—in natural theology). So if Christ is the power of God, and the wisdom of God, and the righteousness of God, and so on, the theological problem of attribution in a positive account becomes the question of how to conceive the relation of these multiple divine attributes to one another in view of the unity or simplicity of God as one subject. The problem is not how our earthly language attributes to God as in natural theology; it now becomes how various attributions to God cohere with one another as a single or at least unified subjectivity. Gunton comes to this formulation of the problem of positive attribution from statements of Karl Barth in the *Church Dogmatics* (*CD* II/1, 327–28),[13] where Barth maintained that "the very unity of [God's] being consists in the multiplicity, individuality and diversity of His perfections" (31). A *via negativa* that would regard the attributions as merely human ways of speaking corresponding to nothing real in God in "pure simplicity" is "rightly" rejected by Barth, so Gunton argues, in favor of a "positive" articulation of the God who gives and communicates Himself (32) in the unity of His multiple perfections.

The "real" problem is thus intensified. Indeed, if we wish to "hold on to a doctrine of the unity and coherence of the divine being, . . . our question remains, How are the various attributes related to one another, and to their common centre in the being of God?" (32). We do, Gunton presumes, want to hold on to the unity and coherence of the divine being. Divine simplicity, then, is to be affirmed. But it is to be affirmed positively rather than negatively—that is, not by the protological definition of perfect being as indivisible (by the "absence of composition") but rather as the theological qualification of the revealed God as unified in the diversity of His attributions. Divine simplicity in this sense safeguards in principle the irreducibility of God not in spite of but in accounting for God's relations to His creation.

13. Karl Barth, *Church Dogmatics*, trans. G. W. Bromiley, ed. G. W. Bromiley and T. F. Torrance, 4 vols. (Edinburgh: T&T Clark, 1975). Henceforth, citations from this book are referenced in the main text by parentheses with "*CD*," followed by volume and part and then page numbers, as in the present instance.

Agreeing with Steve Holmes, Gunton says that "to describe God as 'simple' means that God is ontologically basic" (122), or "substantial," in the popular sense of the word. The agreement here, it may be noted, corresponds to Christopher Stead's assertion that divine substantiality (in the popular sense of something existing apart from my knowledge of it, not in the specialized usage of trinitarian doctrine) is but the affirmation that God is *a se*, not reducible to His relations with creatures.[14] In any event, thinking along these lines, Gunton argues that his positive account of the simplicity of the revealed God's being safeguards God from reduction while avoiding the construction of a concept of God's irreducible reality by means of a "process of negation" that makes the account of the Creator's being antithetical to the creation—ultimately the reification of No-Thing. Instead, he argues that a positive account of divine simplicity thinks in terms of "perichoresis, of the relations of persons," which, in the case of the Trinity as the one true God, would require that we think of the Father, the Son, and the Holy Spirit as "one God without remainder because their communion is perfect and unbroken . . . entirely from being who they particularly are in relation to one another" (122).

The test case for any proposal to maintain the unity and coherence of the divine being in the multiplicity of its attributions is a Christology that takes Jesus's cry of dereliction (Matt. 27:46; Mark 15:34) with utmost seriousness, as implicating divine being. Here too Gunton displays the advantage of a positive rather than a negative notion of divine impassibility as an implication of the holiness or singularity of God in being as the perichoresis of the Three. Against the sentimentalism current in popular theology of divine suffering, he writes, "To say, 'I feel your pain' is not much of a help. . . . [It] runs the risk of affirming suffering, making it in some way the will of God" (130). This is surely right so far as it goes, though the call to bear the cross in following Christ surely does make *some* suffering the will of God. Precisely so, however, the cry of Jesus from the cross is to be taken not as a "breach of perichoresis . . . a rift in God" but rather as indicating "the final episode in the incarnate Son's total identification of himself, through the Spirit, with the lost human condition" (130–31) (as in 2 Cor. 5:21; Gal. 3:13–14) at the Father's own behest. This is more easily affirmed than understood, but theology is about understanding God according to the gospel. What, then, provides for affirming living and divine unity in the case of the most extreme *personal* disjunction in the life of the Father and the incarnate Son, so Gunton argues (retrieving the social trinitarianism of Eastern theology), is the sharp differentiation between nature (*natura, ousia*) and person (*persona, hypostasis*).

14. Christopher Stead, *Divine Substance* (Oxford: Clarendon, 1977).

This classical distinction, though often underappreciated if not forgotten in the Western theological tradition, bears decisively on the entire problem of a descriptive account of God's irreducible substantiality by way of a positive theology of the divine attributes. It will not do, Gunton argues, to turn "properties, defining characteristics, into things . . . to treat natures as things which have attributes. But natures are not hypostases, and so do not have attributes; in a sense, they are attributes, ways of speaking" (149) that serve to classify real things or persons. It is persons or things that bear attributes, whereas "natures" are conceptual classifications of characteristic possibilities that serve to sort experience from some particular perspective for some particular purpose. Against the modalist tendencies of Western tradition toward reifying natures as quasi-agents, then, Gunton sees the gravest threat to robust trinitarianism in thinking that natures are something extramentally real rather than mere concepts. But it is the knowing subject that employs attributes in order to grasp things and manipulate them. Inevitably, as a result, one creates the double-subject Christ in which divine and human natures do their own thing in varying measure and mysterious coordination. On the other hand, if we observe the strong trinitarian distinction between nature and person, we know that natures are nothing but mental classifications of attributes, and that only things or persons are real. In that case, christologically, "everything Jesus does is both fully divine and fully human action. The person who acts is the eternal Son of God, become truly human without loss of his divinity" (149–50). The unity of the incarnate divine Person, in His true and fully human and divine properties, gives us the singularity and mystery that is the one Lord Jesus Christ "through whom are all things and through whom we exist" (1 Cor. 8:6).

The positive account of the divine attributes, then, gives as the God not reducible to His relations to creatures the God of the gospel, the Father who freely sent His Son in the Spirit to find us at the depth of our helpless alienation, to the cry of dereliction. This is the positive account of the singularity of divine nature that, as revealed, is capable of the creature's time and space; as such, it will ask about the power, wisdom, and goodness of God, according to its truthful self-expression in Christ crucified, and probe the harmony of these attributes as the very sense of divine unity—especially as it seems imperiled and at risk in the Son's incarnate life "in the likeness of sinful flesh" (Rom. 8:3). It should be further carefully noted at this juncture how this christologically normed, positive account of divine being and attributes differs from the metaphysical account: it declines the corresponding doctrine of analogy in favor of univocity.

The reason is that analogy from complexly existing things of the visible world to the perfectly existing Source of things proceeds, as Gunton indicated, by natural theology's way of negation; that is, as things exist imperfectly, so God exists perfectly. Christologically, such a procedure is not able to say, as above, that "the person who acts *is* the eternal Son of God, become truly human without loss of his divinity." Rather, it would have to say christologically that the imperfect creature, Jesus, is to God as the perfectly eternal Son is to the perfectly eternal Father, making an absolute claim for the creature Jesus as the one true human image of God (rather than God's own putatively saving claim for creation in His Son's once for all descent *ad infernos*). In the former case of univocity, we can know God in time as Creator of this creation, as incarnate in Jesus Christ, as the Spirit making of believers a living temple, and so on. In the latter case, we cannot say, for example, as Gunton does, that "the love of the man Jesus *is* the love of God in action, just as his anger at the sickness which disfigures the creation is the wrath of God against evil" (70 [emphasis added]), but only that it is *like* the transcendent love of God. If we do affirm, however, that "the love of the man Jesus *is* the love of God in action," Gunton asks, "is not that, inescapably, a form of univocity?" (70).

Indeed so. In the christologically normed discourse about the one true God we have the *est* of univocity, not the *significat* of analogical equivocation. As Rowan Williams put the matter in a splendid essay that followed up in this precise connection on Gunton's probe,

> God is what is constitutive of the particular identity of Jesus: that is what can be said of him, and it is what the *homoousion* of Nicaea endeavored to say: If we say less than this, the identity of Jesus becomes external to God and so "parabolic" in its significance: it is one determinate thing pointing to another. Jesus is "like" God in certain respects, and presumably not in others, which licenses us to leave out of account in our theology what in the story of Jesus is held on some prior grounds to be unassimilable for language about God. Thus we are swiftly brought back to the question of the authority by which we may say anything at all of God. Christ as parable relieves us of Christ as paradox; and it pushes back towards the purely negative characterization of God once more, as that which is not involved in the world's discontinuities.[15]

Involvement in the world's "discontinuities," of course, is christologically emblematized in Jesus's cry of dereliction. It is the very touchstone of the particular identity of the God to whom Jesus in His history with us is internally related. Paul's shot across the bow in 1 Corinthians 1:18–2:5 not accidentally

---

15. Rowan Williams, *On Christian Theology*, Challenges in Contemporary Theology (Oxford: Blackwell, 2000), 157. Thanks to Derek Nelson for reminding me of this connection.

connects the *folly* of the word of the cross, then, with Christ as the *power and wisdom* of God.

As we will examine in greater detail in coming chapters, Paul's statement at the beginning of 1 Corinthians that "Christ *is* the wisdom of God" (1:24) greatly troubled Augustine, as it seemed to imply that God the Father had no wisdom of His own, but had wisdom through His Son, and that consequently the attributes of God would be divided and as a result God's protological simplicity would be compromised. Gunton finds this same Augustinian worry in a recent treatise defending protological simplicity by Stephen Carnock, whom he quotes as follows: "If the Son were the wisdom whereby the Father is wise, the Son would be also the essence whereby the Father is God"—in impossible contradiction to protological simplicity.

But is it not the case with Nicaea's *homoousios* that the Son *is* (also) the essence whereby the Father is God, just as the Father (too) is the essence whereby the Son is God? It is the same essence—that is, the same set of divine characteristics equally accessible to the Father and the Son, though it is accessed by each according to their own personal way of being, so that the Father is God in the way of being Father of this Son and the Son is God in the way of being Son of this Father. Thus, the correct distinctions are not natural but personal. Gunton immediately rebuked Carnock's worry: "But is a Sabellian [i.e., modalist] conflation of the Father and the Son the only alternative?" (91). Such a modalist conflation would be, in place of consistent perichoresis whereby the persons share their personal lives in equal access to one and the same divine essence, the invention of a divine fourth—that is, of a self-standing divine substance underlying the three persons, resulting in a quaternity. Underlying the worry, one fears, is the (unbaptized) thought that to be divine by nature is to be ingenerate or unbegotten as such, when to be the unbegotten begetter is rather to be the person of the Father of the Son in the Spirit. This (unbaptized) thought expresses the hyper-Arian position of Eunomius, a "rationalism," ironically enough according to Gunton, "which Cappadocian assertions of the unknowability of God are designed to refute" (82 [but see also 54]). What a cruel irony, then, so far as modern theologians appeal to the Cappadocians' specific take on the unknowability of God, not for trinitarian but for Eunomian purposes!

These themes from Gunton—two versions of the simplicity doctrine, a christologically normed "positive" version that is able to account for God's irreducible and therefore free grace, and the necessity of univocity in making trinitarian Christology intelligible—will accompany us throughout this book. In the decades ensuing since this seminal work, the debate about divine simplicity has broadened and deepened, such that a comprehensive review of the literature would vastly exceed what is necessary for the present purpose of an intervention in this debate on behalf of a rule version of simplicity that can incorporate important concerns of the metaphysical doctrine for the irreducibility of God without succumbing to its subversion of robust trinitarianism. Recalling that Gunton wanted, as does the present proposal, to affirm one version of simplicity and to reject another, it will serve to sharpen my proposal to continue in this chapter by recounting a particularly pungent critique that denies that protological simplicity is whatsoever a possible perfection of the Christian God.

Not a Possible Perfection of the God of the Gospel

R. T. Mullins makes this case because protological simplicity is a truly radical stance that regards and must regard extrinsic change as accidental and thus improperly attributed to God. But this stance is in impossible contradiction to the witness of Scripture. According to protological simplicity, "When a human worships God and says, 'You are my Creator and Redeemer' she is predicating an accidental property of God . . . [that strictly speaking does] not apply to God but only befall[s] the creature" (183).[16] To affirm this of the God of the gospel, who freely becomes Creator of a world of creatures, then forever and ever becomes incarnate as one of them in order to make of creatures an everlasting temple of divine dwelling, would be the opposite of perfection, according to protological simplicity.

Mullins describes the doctrine of divine simplicity in current literature as consisting of four theses: (1) God cannot have spatial or temporal parts and (2) cannot have intrinsic accidental properties; (3) there can be no real distinction between essential divine properties and (4) also no real distinction between the essence and existence in God. The medieval philosophy in the background here typically contrasts what is really distinct from what is conceptually distinct, where the latter says that there is no extramental reason to distinguish things so that a conceptual distinction exists only in the mind. Thus attribution to God of complexity exists in the mind only, not really in God, according to the protological metaphysics of divine simplicity. Intriguingly, Mullins introduces John Duns Scotus at this juncture, since Scotus further postulates beyond real and conceptual distinctions a further, "formal

---

16. R. T. Mullins, "Simply Impossible: A Case against Divine Simplicity," *Journal of Reformed Theology* 7 (2013): 181–203. Here and below, citations from this article are followed by page numbers in parentheses in the main text.

distinction."[17] This notion of formal distinction is said to bridge between real and conceptual distinctions in asserting that "there is some extramental feature in reality that makes [some things] distinct, yet they are coextensive and inseparable" (184) in reality—an almost perfect characterization of the personal distinctions in the Trinity (which is, perhaps, Scotus's inspiration). As we will see down the road, Scotus's "formal distinction" makes it possible to say that God is by nature (as per the dictum *esse Deum dare*) disposed in one way rather than another, yet not necessitated, by His "nature," on the one side, and on the other to deny that God is a *deus exlex* of sheer arbitrary willfulness. It makes it possible to think of God as inclined by the divine harmony of power, wisdom, and love to freely create the best of all possible creations on the way to the Beloved Community (as Leibniz in early modern times retrieved and reformulated Scotus's legacy).

Mullins begins his frontal assault on protological simplicity by showing that even conceptual distinctions are "repugnant to divine simplicity," as is clear in the case of denying, even conceptually, temporality to God (think, for instance, of Paul's "in the fullness of time God sent forth His Son" [Gal. 4:4]). "God has no before and after in His life because He has no moments in His life at all. On [this] understanding, this makes God a truly permanent entity." That is to say, God certainly does not in reality send forth His Son once for all or once upon a time. If God sends Christ, then God timelessly sends Christ, as required by definition of God's simplicity. As a result, Paul's anthropomorphic way of talking does not even conceptually clarify God but rather obscures God. The result, as Mullins puts it, is that if "conceptual distinctions cannot even be applied to a simple God, it would seem that Christian theology [at least on Paul's model] is a non-starter" (185). An embarrassed theologian would have to fess up that all her logic chopping and word crafting produces "distinctions" that "exist in her mind only. They do not apply to God at all."

Moving on to extrinsic accidental properties, such a being referred to as Creator, Redeemer, and Lord by creatures because God truly becomes their Creator, Redeemer, and saving Lord, Mullins next shows that these attributions, if taken realistically, would "entail that God came to have them, and thus He would be mutable, temporal, and not simple." The truly "radical" doctrine of divine simplicity disallows such mutation of God in the acquisition

17. The definition provided by Yann Schmitt is helpful: "X is formally distinct from Y if and only if 1) X and Y are inseparable even for an omnipotent being, 2) X and Y do not have the same definition, 3) the distinction exists *de re* (it is independent of its conceptualization)" ("The Deadlock of Absolute Divine Simplicity," *International Journal of the Philosophy of Religion* 74 [2013]: 118).

of external and "accidental" properties, even as its Christian defenders fail to realize the "systematic connections between simplicity, immutability, and timelessness." Simplicity is a "determinate concept that cannot be weakened" from its necessitarian implications (186) (note that I will disagree with Mullins here). To make the same point from the opposite direction, Mullins writes, "If we allow for God to have an accidental property we have (i) said that God has properties, (ii) said that God has accidental properties, (iii) introduced diversity in God, and (iv) introduced potential into God since there are other ways He can be" (187) than He simply is. Thus divine simplicity is reduced, Christianly speaking, to absurdity if it implies that God cannot truthfully be worshiped as our Creator, Redeemer, and saving Lord because He has chosen freely by grace to become so to us.

What is noteworthy in the previous citation is the seemingly obvious affirmation that "God has properties." What else would a theology of divine attributes want to affirm? But to *have* properties is to have capabilities subject to a subject's disposal. Strictly speaking, the metaphysical doctrine of simplicity, in affirming that in God essence and existence are identical, denies this notion of a person or subject having properties at free disposal in favor of a notion of divine nature that simply is and thus is timelessly identical to whatever various perfections are (misleadingly and anthropomorphically) ascribed to it. As Mullins puts it, "On divine simplicity, anything that one might predicate of God should be understood as signifying the divine substance. You could say that God is eternal, immortal, incorruptible, unchangeable, living, wise, powerful, beautiful, and so forth. Yet all of these terms signify the divine substance. They are not qualities or properties that God has because they are identical to God" taken as divine nature, perfect being, properly timeless and immutable self-identity (188–89). So if God, taken as a nature rather than a person, is lacking any potentiality, He must be pure actuality—that is, not a free subject enacting His identity according to His divine disposition. In this light, the Thomist paraphrase of God as the act of His own being contains a subtle but illicit anthropomorphism. Rather God is, so to say, impersonally actual, unchanging, simple, without properties, "who does all that he does in one timeless present. He simply is His act of thinking, willing, creating and so on" (190).

At this point, Mullins wisely introduces a word of caution against know-nothing biblicism playing the Greek metaphysics card too hastily. To be sure, the metaphysics of simplicity has its historical origin in the "time of Parmenides and found its fullest expression in the Neoplatonic system of Plotinus" (190). Yet in a way that recalls Lewis Ayres's important argument about Origen's contribution to the rise of the doctrine of the Trinity, Mullins notes, "Any theologian wishing to maintain the eternal generation of the Son ought not to use the Greek card." What decides the matter, he says, is not the pedigree of a doctrine (what pragmatism calls the "genetic fallacy") but rather its "compatibility with Scripture" (191). And in this respect the orthodox consensus, which protological simplicity intends to defend, is that God, possessing all perfections, "is not dependent upon anything or anyone outside of Himself." This Mullins calls the "Sovereignty-Aseity Conviction": "God's will is self-determined. There is nothing outside of God that determines His will. God is thus perfectly free."

Yet therein lies the rub: free even, if not especially, from a divine "nature" that would make God's grace either some kind of default policy set on automatic or an arbitrary, even reckless geyser of spontaneous emoting? What goes missing in the account is the personal freedom of God. To be sure, Mullins quickly denies that the God who is free in His grace is free to be or to do nonsense. The way to test for this is to see whether "the attribute is metaphysically compossible with who God is. Can God lie? No (Titus 1:2)." By giving precedence to the who of revelation over the what of metaphysics in theological knowledge, theology can establish "what can be meaningfully said of God based on rational reflection of God's self-revelation" (193); that gives us an account of the divine properties as a disposition of freedom to love wisely. In this way, divine self-revelation—Jenson's priority of the who over the what and the how—provides a better way to sustain the Sovereignty-Aseity Conviction than a naturalistic metaphysics that makes grace a divine and impersonal habit rather than a costly and fitting decision. Just so, however, if grace is the costly decision at the heart of God's self-donation in Christ, divine simplicity is "not compossible with who God is" (194) because God, who genuinely decides one way rather than another, is thus taken as a subject or person who therewith has as such unactualized potential. Indeed, taken as person, God the Father almighty, to whom all things are possible, perfectly possesses all unactualized possibilities as at His own disposal.

Consider once again, at this juncture, Spinoza's taunt to the befuddled theist who cannot account for why God, as Scripture attests, *began* to create, since God timelessly has eternally fully actualized all possibilities yet is said in the act of creation to have enacted this particular set of possibilities that is our world. How did God "decide" that? How did God determine Himself to be Creator of this particular world, with His lamb slain before its foundation, with His mystery hidden from the ages but now revealed as the coming of the Beloved Community? A decision is inalienably some kind of temporal act, as Spinoza knew, thrusting this dagger at the heart of the Christian Platonist attempt to domesticate the radical doctrine of simplicity.

Mullins amplifies the taunt: "Divine simplicity should push one to say that God created an infinite number of universes. Otherwise God would not be pure act," because in deciding upon one world in particular God forgoes others, thus betraying a host of unactualized potential in God (195). The alternative to the multiverse is Spinoza's "modal collapse": "Necessarily, there is only one possible world—this world. Necessarily, God must exist with creation. There is no other possibility" (196)—what is, is necessarily. What an irony, then, if a major Christian motivation in the protological doctrine of simplicity has been to safeguard the "absoluteness" of God, if God is thereby made prisoner of His own perfection, and finally codependent with creatures in the necessitarian system of an eternal creation!

We note once again an allusion to Scotus, and perhaps also to Leibniz: modal arguments, Mullins affirms, can "flesh out Christian doctrine . . . how we think about the necessity and aseity of God, the contingency of creation, the freedom-foreknowledge problem, the distinction between the immanent and economic Trinity, and so forth" (197) so that we may steer between the Scylla of divine determinism and the Charybdis of divine voluntarism in the direction of a dispositional divine ontology. The deeper point, then, is that "if it is possible that God does anything other than what He in fact does do, He has potential that is unactualized" (198). Put otherwise, "All that is needed—to show that divine simplicity is false—is the claim that God is free" (199). An ontology of divine being as the freedom to love wisely disposes God to create from the origin a world for redemption and fulfillment, though it does not necessitate it. This approach staked out by Mullins in his impressive article has major implications for the interpretation of Christian doctrine, in that it vindicates "the Bible [for having] no qualms predicating accidental properties of a God who is intimately and radically related to creatures."

This is preeminently the case in regard to the incarnation, especially when the incarnation is understood according to the doctrine of the *communicatio idiomatum*: "Defenders of divine simplicity must explain how a divine person who is simple can have properties and remain simple." That christologically Christ is made to be sin so that sinners can be made to be righteous collapses into nonsense if taken as a natural mutation; but it is good and saving news if it is taken as a personal exchange. Thus the evacuation of the saving Christology of the patristic church into the toothless similitude, "Jesus shows us what God is like," as Rowan Williams explained, is but the flip side of the modalist confusions bundled up with protological simplicity. Mullins asks pointedly, "How can a person be an act?" He answers, "It is obvious that an act is something that a person *does* and not something that a person *is*." By the same token (once again invoking Scotus), Mullins asks defenders of divine simplicity to account for "how the divine perfections apply to God without being synonymous with each other" (and thus becoming vacuous), since something like the passage from the wrath of love to the mercy of love seems essential to the biblical narrative of the coming of God for us. In sum, "What is at stake in this issue is the ability to know anything at all about God. If none of our concepts apply to God at all, divine revelation is impossible" (202). But that is precisely Mullins's radical point about the radical doctrine of protological simplicity: "Simplicity is not a possible perfection because it is not compossible with who God is" as revealed in the gospel (203).

The Régnon Thesis

The question about who God is as revealed in the gospel narrative is answered not simply but complexly: Jesus and His Father and their Spirit. Thus the Christian meaning of the most basic term in theology, "God," is gained by following in thought after these Three and so coming to their divine unity by way of their dramatic history with one another on account of their even more dramatic engagement with creatures. This claim for the knowledge of God is known as the "Régnon thesis," after the French scholar Théodore de Régnon. In John Meyendorff's translation of Régnon's own words, "It would seem that in our time the dogma of the divine unity had, as it were, absorbed the dogma of the Trinity of which one only speaks as a memory." The critical thrust of the observation is directed against the "Latin" tendency to "consider the nature in itself first and proceed to the agent [rather than to] consider the agent first and pass through it to find the nature. The Latins think of personality as a mode of nature; the Greeks think of nature as the content of the person." Meyendorff built on this critique by Régnon to exposit the Eastern doctrine of the Trinity: "The incarnate Logos and the Holy Spirit are met and experienced first as *divine agents of salvation*, and only then are they also discovered to be essentially one God."[18]

Meyendorff's elder contemporary, Vladimir Lossky, had similarly explicated the strong distinction between nature (*ousia*) and person (*hypostasis*) stemming from the Eastern identification of Father, Son, and Holy Spirit first as "divine agents of salvation" by applying the nature-person distinction to theological anthropology.

> Man created "in the image" is the person capable of manifesting God in the extent to which his nature allows itself to be penetrated by deifying grace.

18. John Meyendorff, *Byzantine Theology: Historical Trends and Doctrinal Themes* (New York: Fordham University Press, 1979), 180–81.

Thus the image—which is inalienable—can become similar or dissimilar, to the extreme limits: that of union with God, when deified man shows in himself by grace what God is by nature . . . or indeed that of the extremity of falling-away . . . [to] the place of dissimilarity.[19]

In this application to theological anthropology, Lossky "assumes that both the Trinity and the incarnate Christ will illuminate human being . . . [in that] the human hypostasis [becomes] equally irreducible to the human ousia. . . . Instead of focusing on natures, which so often turns into stereotypes and essentialism, Lossky focuses on the person."[20]

It is evident by now that the critique of strong simplicity outlined in this chapter is the critique of the "Latin" approach that privileges nature over personhood under the speculative assumption that we already know what divine nature is apart from the cognitive encounter with the Father, who sends the Son to and for us, on whom He breathes His Spirit that we may believe. This speculation trades on the equally speculative presumption that we already know what it is to be creatures of this God and can apply that knowledge *tout court* to the divine by the analogy that ascends from imperfect to perfect being. But this delivers no more than the projection of our alleged perfections onto the empty screen of the ineffable and thus sacralizes idolatry rather than liberates from it.

Sarah Hinlicky Wilson, building on Lossky's application of the strong nature-person distinction from the Eastern doctrine of the Trinity to theological anthropology, has exposed the cost of the Latin approach, not only in how it obfuscates the trinitarian knowledge of the God of the gospel, as Régnon and Meyendorff urge, but also in how it illicitly sacralizes a gender essentialism that squanders the liberating insight of the nature-person distinction: "A male person and a female person will always exceed and transcend his nature and her nature, however distinct those natures may be from one another. What makes him or her the same, in the end, is their common ability to transcend themselves, that neither is reduced to the respective natures." In that case, being gendered as masculine or feminine as a reflex of biological heterosexuality is a flexible matter of personal existence, while nature, as male or female, is neither "alien" to the person nor yet does it "contain" him or her. "Gender does not exist as such, but gendered humans do. They are hypostases of the shared human ousia, whether they are male or female. . . .

19. Vladimir Lossky, *In the Image and Likeness of God*, ed. John H. Erickson and Thomas E. Bird (Crestwood, NY: St. Vladimir's Seminary Press, 1985), 139.

20. Sarah Hinlicky Wilson, *Woman, Women, and the Priesthood in the Trinitarian Theology of Elisabeth Behr-Sigel*, T&T Clark Theology (London: Bloomsbury, 2013), 161, 163.

The hypostasis must be the person, not the person's gender. That is the proper trinitarian analogy."[21]

But the "reduction of person to nature" is precisely the Latin error in trinitarian theology as in trinitarian anthropology. It turns the liberating gospel on its head, exchanging the freedom for which Christ has set us free (Gal. 5:1)—that we be one in Him, neither Greek nor Jew, slave nor free, married nor single (Gal. 3:27–28)—for the straightjacket of allegedly natural class, race, or gender teleologies. In this way, it renders the personal distinctions between the Father and the Son—by which the Son suffered the curse for others in filial, not servile, obedience to His Father's will—nugatory, as the same Pauline epistle to the Galatians teaches (Gal. 3:13). Little wonder, then, as Régnon observed, how the exuberant shout from the life of the new creation (Gal. 6:15), "God has sent the Spirit of his Son into our hearts, crying, 'Abba! Father!'" (Gal. 4:6), has been muted into a fading memory in the funeral societies today that still bother to call themselves Christian.

One can hardly impute this deleterious outcome to the Latin tradition as an intention. To the contrary, at its best it wants to defend the reality of God as irreducible to His relations to creatures and so to preserve us in our thinking about God from a reduction of God's *substantia* into His external relations. And in the popular sense of this term, "substance"—that is, for something substantial that exists apart from my relating to it—this intention is surely right. Likewise, the doctrine of simplicity is right in the vague sense that God is to be thought of as singular—that is, other in divine being than His many creatures and, moreover, one and only in this otherness of being. In what follows here, I follow the lead of the Régnon thesis, seeking a way to honor and incorporate these legitimate Latin concerns without losing the Trinity or squandering the liberating distinction that it brings between nature and person. That way will require a more precise account of divine simplicity as a divine command to honor divine holiness in all that we say about God and do in God's name.

21. Ibid., 163–64.

2

The Unstable Synthesis of St. Thomas Aquinas

Ground Clearing

I begin this chapter with a confession (of what may well already be obvious to my Thomist friends). I have spent a theological career avoiding direct engagement with Thomas Aquinas. This was not for lack of effort on the part of my teachers, nor even of myself. Rather, I have always felt in reading Thomas that I was on exotic turf, disoriented, with maps that were not user-friendly and did not appear to match the terrain. This has not been the case with many others. Appreciation of the Greek fathers, and the Westerners Augustine and Anselm, and even Protestant scholastics such as Johann Gerhard is well documented in my writings. I have come lately to see, however, how I have been blocked by the confessionalization of Thomas—that is to say, confused about how what I was reading cohered with what others, particularly self-identified Thomists (as well as their antipodes, self-identified anti-Thomists), were saying about the material. But I have come to recognize this phenomenon of confessionalist distortion from labors in my own theological tradition; my first major book was dedicated to liberating Luther from the distortions of Lutheranism.[1]

---

1. Paul R. Hinlicky, *Paths Not Taken: Fates of Theology from Luther through Leibniz* (Grand Rapids: Eerdmans, 2009). Recall here the opening notation of N. T. Wright's reading of 1 Cor. 8,

Therefore theologians like myself of other confessional traditions may take heart, as I have, in the observation that Fergus Kerr made in launching his rich and insightful study:

> Current readings of Thomas's works are so conflicting, and even incommensurable, that integrating them into a single interpretation seems impossible. Some readings are deeply misguided; but even these, since they issue from respectable theological and philosophical presuppositions, demand and deserve attention. We need to ask what it is, in Thomas's work, and in the uses to which it has been put by opponents as well as disciples, that makes certain misreadings attractive, and almost unavoidable.[2]

I would happily venture the same observation regarding Luther, who similarly stands at the head of an inwardly conflicted theological tradition. Kerr's work is invaluable for exemplifying this hermeneutical self-awareness from within theology in the tradition of Thomas and bringing it critically to bear on a tradition that accidentally, as it were, may be inclined to think in the rarified atmosphere of contextless propositionalism,[3] unaware of its own sources, occasions, circumstances, contingencies, and continuous, often unconscious, development under transformed conditions.

For a pertinent example, Kerr points to Thomas's lifelong battle against recurring gnosticism (4) and in this connection cites *Summa contra Gentiles* (hereafter *SCG*) I.7–8: "The truth that human reason is naturally endowed to know cannot be opposed to the truth of the Christian faith" (*SCG* I.7.1).[4] He shows that this embrace of the natural endowment of human reason is part and parcel of an affirmation of the inalienable goodness of creation over against the counterthesis of gnostic dualism with its corresponding plunge into irrationalism. Kerr is thus able to resolve the often puzzling optimism about the human condition that current readers, not only Protestants, find in Thomas. As a result, we can understand that we are dealing with the affirmation by the Christian theologian—going back to the great treatises of Irenaeus—of the goodness of God's creation in spite of its corruption by sin. I could make

---

which includes his familiar assault on the Lutheranization of Paul; suffice it to say, Wright's real target is in fact the existentialization of Paul, to which I would apply a parallel critique of the existentialization of Luther in neo-Protestant scholarship.

2. Fergus Kerr, *After Aquinas: Versions of Thomism* (Malden, MA: Blackwell, 2002), 15–16. Further citations from this book are followed by page numbers in parentheses in the main text.

3. For this reason, I found valuable access in St. Thomas Aquinas, *Summa Theologiae: A Concise Translation*, ed. Timothy McDermott (Allen, TX: Christian Classics, 1991).

4. Quotations of this work are from Thomas Aquinas, *Summa contra Gentiles*, trans. Vernon J. Bourke, 5 vols. (Notre Dame, IN: University of Notre Dame Press, 1975).

the same observation about another of my intellectual heroes, Gottfried Leibniz, who often argued in the same vein against the neognosticism of Pierre Bayle, the disillusioned Huguenot who openly embraced neo-Manichaeism.

"Many people, certainly philosophers," Kerr contemporizes, "regard the world as inherently hostile or at least indifferent to human beings: unsurprisingly they have no difficulty in postulating some kind of screen between the mind and the world, a confrontation, perhaps a voluntaristic imposition of concepts on raw and hopelessly unreachable objects" (32). But for Thomas, "human beings are created in God's image and likeness, and, more particularly, are born such that our minds are connaturally open to the world that reveals itself to us and even reveals itself as created. . . . [It is a] perhaps optimistic and anthropocentric sense of how creatures of every kind, and certainly creatures of the human kind, are at home as participants in the world that is God's creation" (33). It was polemic against the gnostics of his day, then, when Thomas held that "sin cannot destroy the ontological structure of human nature, or change the created subject's species-specific nature—but it certainly restricts, wounds, and disorders the human creature" (144).

Thomas's is actually, then, the classical double-sided stance, following Augustine's own balancing act between Manichaeism and Neoplatonism. "Thomas is indebted to the Augustinian tradition: Christian salvation is redemption, restoration of a disordered nature, deeply wounded by the Fall. . . . But he is even more indebted," Kerr adds, "to the Dionysian or Greek patristic tradition: salvation as elevation of nature, as divinization, rather than healing" (145)—though this too recalls a certain anti-gnostic line of thought: *bona naturalia manent* (144 [citing Pseudo-Dionysius at *Summa Theologiae* I-II.63.1]). Thomas's axiom "The gifts of grace are conferred on nature in such a way that they do not destroy it but rather perfect it" (*Summa Theologiae* I.1.8.2) is, according to Kerr, nothing other than the patristic stand, with the help of Platonism,[5] against the gnostic denigration of creation and the misconstrual of redemption as escape from, rather than the healing and perfection of, the creature.

Such helpful contextualizations of Thomas's thought are critical to the hermeneutical endeavor made in this chapter to appreciate the classical

---

5. This aid in the battle against gnosticism is still poorly understood by contemporaries who, following Harnack, regard gnosticism as "extreme Hellenism" rather than the deep historical opposition to Hellenism that originates largely in circles of disillusioned Jewish apocalypticism. For Platonism's opposition to gnostic alienation, see Margaret R. Miles, *Plotinus on Body and Beauty: Society, Philosophy, and Religion in Third-Century Rome* (Oxford: Blackwell, 1999); Paul R. Hinlicky, *Divine Complexity: The Rise of Creedal Christianity* (Minneapolis: Fortress, 2009), 160–61.

Christian adaption of the protological metaphysics of divine simplicity. The effort undertaken to appreciate the Christian concern in Thomas's formulations will not only nuance the counterproposal regarding eschatological simplicity advocated in this book; it will also, if successful, move the ecumenical argument forward. I will accordingly expend further effort at the outset on Kerr's interpretation of this web of issues, then further refine the alternative account of the act of God's being in patrology, before turning to *SCG* I. There we will detect how Thomas, the Christian theologian, had also to do covert battle with erstwhile allies, namely, the philosophical antignostics in the form of the Neoplatonic Islamic commentators on Aristotle. For their optimism concerning the powers of unaided reason, over against gnostic pessimism and what they regarded as fideism, could spill over in the opposite direction of subverting the need for the redemptive graces of Christ and the Spirit. Indeed, it was just this appearance of undermining the need for redeeming grace that accompanied the new Aristotelianism that brought on the condemnations in 1277 of a "sort of polymorphic naturalism stressing the rights of pagan nature against Christian nature, of philosophy against theology, of reason against faith . . . to the effect that the philosophical way of life is vastly superior to that of theologians" (12–13 [cited from Gilson]). For reasons good and bad, then, it has been ever since hard to apprehend and appreciate, especially through the lenses of later Protestant criticism, the double front on which Thomas in fact battles.

Kerr attends to such tone-deaf Protestant criticism; we can begin with his rejoinder to the theologian who guided our path in the previous chapter. Kerr takes up Colin Gunton's critique of divine omnicausality in Thomas and characterizes it thus: "The fear clearly is that, for Thomas, there is only one real cause and all other 'causes' are spurious" (41). This is a view of God as cause of all causes that could seem monstrous from the perspective of the gnostic sufferer, telling of a demonic warden causing imprisonment in this world of matter; or it could appear delightful in the eyes of the optimistic, progressive, world-affirming Neoplatonic cosmopolitan, seeing in the world's order the very expression of self-diffusing deity. In Gunton's case, however, Kerr traces the precise objection to Barth's critique of natural theology. Thomas's natural theology conception of God as sheer existence subsisting in its very nature and as such the all-embracing cause of beings is said to be abstract and merely monotheistic, unbaptized by the doctrine of the Trinity. As we will see, in a deep and not superficial way, that is the question. More precisely put, it is the question of whether the act of God's being entails the action of creation in a necessary way, insofar as strong simplicity allows no distinction between what God necessarily is and what God correspondingly does.

Thomas the Christian, of course, resists any such implication. Thus, on the surface, Kerr corrects the impression of determinism with pithy citations from the *Summa Theologiae* (hereafter *ST*), for instance: "We exclude the error of those who claim that God produced things *ex necessitate naturae*" (39 [citing *ST* I.32.1]), thus "curing Christians of the temptation to think that the world (as he would put it) might be the result of some external pressure on the creator or some compensatory expression of the creator's need" rather than being "simply an expression of love" (39) that gives freedom to creatures also to be. God is not omnicausal by sheer nature, since a free act of creation is affirmed. "A theological account of the world as created which could count as Christian must involve a conception of God as a personal agent: the existence of the world has to be attributed not to chance or necessity, but the creation of the First Cause to which must be attributed knowledge and will" (40 [cf. *ST* I.2–26]). Though there are tensions inherent in this combination of Christian dogma and the metaphysics of the First Cause to which we will return, Thomas's point, charitably interpreted, is that, as God is by nature the act of His own being, God creates not in order to achieve something (lacking) for Himself but instead out of "sheer divine generosity" (42). Creating all that is not God generously, God is omnicausal *in relation to* creation; just because God remains unchanged in His own all-actual and thus perfect nature, God is capable then of the radical generosity of giving existence to creatures. Surely that is right, Christianly speaking: *esse Deum dare*.

The tension inherent in Thomas's view, Kerr acknowledges, is that "the God-creature relationship is not a real relationship in God, whereas the creature-God relationship is a real relationship in the creature" (43 [cf. *ST* I.13.7]). The asymmetry here seems strange in denying that God can have or acquire extrinsic properties, even when they are not understood to change God's being. But Kerr's formulation confirms Mullins's claim that even extrinsic or relational properties violate strong simplicity in allowing God to acquire properties that God could have but does not already have. Then God has unrealized potential. And God adds to God in acquiring extrinsic relations and therewith relational properties. Yet, charitably interpreted, it is once again in its own idiom making a classical and very Protestant point: "Creatures are utterly and totally indebted to God for their existence, whereas God is in no way dependent on or indebted to creatures" (43). Still, Gunton worries about "how near Thomas comes here to pantheism"; "God is in every thing, not indeed as part of its nature or as a property, but as the agent is present in what he does" (43 [cf. *ST* I.8.1]).

In fact, this view of *Deus actuosissimus* might profitably be compared to what de Lubac called, not approvingly, Luther's "theopanism" in the latter's treatise on bound choice.[6] "For Thomas," as Kerr rejoins Gunton, "God is the cause that enables all agents to cause what they do" (43 [cf. *ST* III.67.1]). If one does not exempt God from the Pauline abandonment of the idolater to the consequences of their own sin (Rom. 1:24, 26, 28), then Luther holds substantially to the same:[7] "Pharaoh cannot escape being hardened, even as he cannot escape the acting of Divine omnipotence and the perversion and villainy of his own will."[8] If the woodcutter swings an axe with a jagged edge, the ragged cut will be the fault not of the swing but of the edge. This is omni-causality not monocausality, *Alleswirksamkeit Gottes* not *Alleinwirksamkeit Gottes*, following the Augustinian mantra "God is the cause of all causes, not the maker of all choices." Kerr rightly tags this doctrine of double agency "compatibilism" (cf. *SCG* III.65.10), since "the same effect is produced by a lower agent and by God—and thus by both immediately—though in different ways. . . . It is a result of God's bountiful goodness that creatures are really and truly agents of their own activities [even in sin]. We do not live under a regime of endlessly repeated miracles" (45). Kerr rightly notes in this connection that this accent on divine omnicausality funding human agency strikes a very Barthian note. "We must have no truck with theological occasionalism, playing down or excluding genuine created efficacy" (45) (although, as we will see, Barth may have already been responding to Przywara's challenge in maintaining the compatibility of God's sovereignty and human agency).

I have proposed that one way, theologically, to articulate more clearly this embeddedness of human agency in divine omnicausality is to speak of "patiency," so that the divine-creative enabling conditions of human agency in God's *creatio continua* are not taken for granted—as if we were born full-grown adults at the peak of our powers, as if as adults we become somehow self-caused. My source for this proposal is Luther's thought that it is "the person who works." In its own idiom, as I understand Kerr, Thomas wishes to affirm precisely the same: "*agere sequitur esse*. Action, activity, inward and external, is the normal manifestation of being. Far from having a 'substantialist' ontology of self-enclosed monadic objects, occasionally knocking up against one another, Thomas's cosmological picture is, rather, of a constantly reassembling network of transactions, beings becoming themselves in their doings" (48) (of course, that is precisely not what Leibniz meant by "monad,"

6. Oswald Bayer, *Martin Luther's Theology: A Contemporary Interpretation*, trans. Thomas H. Trapp (Grand Rapids: Eerdmans, 2007), 199–201.

7. Paul R. Hinlicky, *Luther and the Beloved Community: A Path for Christian Theology after Christendom* (Grand Rapids: Eerdmans, 2010), 139–74.

8. Martin Luther, *The Bondage of the Will*, trans. J. I. Packer and O. R. Johnston (Old Tappan, NJ: Revell, 1957), 207.

which is a principle of individuation, not isolation). "Thomas' concept of the human person," in any case, is "not as an isolated self-enclosed individual but as intrinsically ordered toward community, friendship, others"; thus his "account of primary and secondary causalities [is] an account of the entirely non-competitive relationship between uncreated/divine and created/human agencies" (50) that provides the kind of distinctions that are the necessary presuppositions of friendship and, indeed, Beloved Community.

Kerr acknowledges, in passing, that the problem raised here of "the co-operation between the graceful God and the graced creature . . . is a herme-neutic crux" (142–43). Kerr's own solution draws out explicitly the missing key of the nature-person distinction from trinitarianism: "the interplay of *agents* who are implicitly modelled on *persons*" (143). To this explication, Kerr immediately adds this reflection:

> Whether co-operation is necessarily competition is an interesting question. It takes us right to the heart of Thomas's theology. He often quotes Isaiah 26:12: "Lord, thou has wrought all our works in us"—which he takes (e.g., at ST I.105.5), precisely as *excluding* all competitiveness between divine and human agency. . . . He almost always rules out the picture of two rival agents on a level playing field. . . . God "causes" everything in such a way that the creature "causes" it too. . . . It is always by divine power that the human agent produces his or her own proper effect: that is the doctrine of creation. (143)

The Reformation theologian may hasten only to add that, according to Romans 8, the Christian doctrine of redemption—as opposed to gnosticism—is precisely the redemption of this groaning earth, the redemption of our bodies, the fulfillment in us of the image of God, of the glorious liberty of the children of God through Christ Jesus in the new agency of those now led by His Spirit, also in their sufferings. So Luther explicitly states, "If we meant by 'the power of free-will' the power which makes human beings fit subjects to be caught up by the Spirit and touched by God's grace, as creatures made for eternal life or eternal death, we should have a proper definition. And I certainly acknowledge the existence of *this* power, this fitness, or 'dispositional quality' and 'passive aptitude.' . . . As the proverb says, God did not make heaven for geese!"[9] Hence the "person" is the patiency that gives rise to a specific agency within the whole, greater than the sum of its parts—that is, the community in the making, creation on the way to the best of all possible worlds.

Kerr has George Hunsinger enunciate the classical Protestant complaint that Thomas takes neither sin seriously enough as sin nor grace as grace but

---

9. Ibid., 105.

instead sees the creature as partly sinful and partly graced, making salvation into a process that progresses depending on how well the redeemed sinner cooperates with grace. The notion of cooperation in the work of redemption thus becomes suspect as a front for a de facto Pelagianism; to this sneaky form of pious self-justification, the Protestant opposes the "existential appropriation"—that is, faith, thus the justification of the unrighteous as event, indeed as miracle (140–41), that ever attends the Christian life, above all in its apparent "progress."

But according to Kerr, Thomas denies that justification is miraculous, like the resurrection of the body, since "'the soul is by nature open to grace' (*naturaliter anima est gratiae capax*)" (142). Yet, Kerr continues, Thomas is careful to qualify this defense of the goodness even of fallen creation, whose natural goods remain *capax Dei per gratiam*; that is, it is by grace that the soul is naturally open to God. "Paradoxically, fallen human beings are open to grace *naturaliter* but this is in virtue of their being open to grace *per gratiam*" (142). At bottom, then, of the Protestant complaint against Thomism is that it overlooks Thomas's own resort to paradox; the assumption, or rather suspicion, at work in this oversight seems to be that "Thomas has a doctrine of 'pure nature': human beings who are able, independently of divine grace, to bootstrap their way to God. . . . [But] nature is open to grace *by grace—only* by grace, as we now have to insist, to rule out any idea of 'pure nature'" (142). (Again, if Kerr is right here, let it be noted that we would have nothing different from Luther, citing Augustine: "Yet God does not work in us without us; for He created and preserves us for this very purpose, that He might work in us and we might cooperate with Him, whether that occurs outside His kingdom by His general omnipotence, or within His kingdom, by the special power of His Spirit.")[10]

Yet the Protestant "misreading" of Thomas as an almost "pure naturalist" is first of all a Catholic misreading that Kerr, via de Lubac, traces to Suarez and Cajetan (who played no little role historically in permanently alienating Luther from Thomas). According to de Lubac,

> Cajetan assumed that Thomas was an Aristotelian, working with a definition of nature from Aristotle's Physics, which effectively turned human nature into a reality essentially closed in on itself, with its own intrinsic powers, desires and goals. . . . [This] opened the way for post-Reformation Catholicism to insist so much on the value of nature [against Calvinist depravity] that they ended with a two-story model of nature and grace, juxtaposing the two, as it were, treating grace in relation to nature as essentially extrinsic and adventitious. (136)

10. Ibid., 268.

And Molinism at length slid into unitarianism. Karl Rahner, as Kerr reports, thus correlated this Catholic misreading of Thomas's anthropology as almost pure naturalism to modern Catholic sensibilities: "It looks as though everything important about God which touches ourselves has already been said in the treatise *de Deo Uno*. The result, anyway, is that the average Catholic accepts 'monotheism' (Rahner's scare quotes), a non-Incarnational and non-Trinitarian 'cult of the supremely one, undifferentiated and nameless God'" (183) corresponding to modernity's healthy natural soul, which appreciates the occasional help but does not need redeeming grace.

It is, again, quite striking to compare this critique of the Catholic misreadings of Thomas to the young (still "Catholic") Luther's case against the "modernist" (Luther is thinking of the later medievals Biel, Occam, and Scotus) view of unaided natural powers—for example, in his early *Disputation against Scholastic Theology*[11] or, for that matter, in his late formulations of anthropological doctrine in the Genesis lectures, where Luther regards the loss of God as object of the heart's desire as the loss of the Spirit, and just this loss of the Spirit as *the* corruption of human nature brought about by sin that leads to spiritual death. Luther correspondingly prophesied the future loss of the Trinity and Christology, as per Rahner's observation, that must come with the victory of this modernist anthropology of natural powers. If Kerr is right, then, Luther and Thomas ally against pure naturalism, even if Thomas on the whole is contextually more concerned with the danger of gnosticism than of the Pelagianism that troubled Luther.

In any event, Kerr has to explicate what is unsaid in Thomas's doctrine of agency (*agere sequitur esse*) by introducing the trinitarian distinction between nature and person, which on its own terms would rather say that "works follow *the person.*" I have in this vein proposed that the typical Protestant-Catholic clash about how to parse the compatibilism of nature and grace should be recast theologically in terms of trinitarian operations in creation, redemption, and fulfillment, taken together as an ordered or narrative sequence.[12] Called in creation as image of God to become the likeness of God in the lived history of the obedience of faith active in love and hope, the fallen human remains image (remains called by God) even in sin—that is, as they become unlike God (become caricatures of God). The new Adam, Jesus Christ, is the likeness of

---

11. "The good law and that in which one lives is the love of God, spread abroad in our hearts by the Holy Spirit" (*Luther's Works: The American Edition*, ed. Jaroslav Pelikan and Helmut T. Lehmann, 55 vols. [St. Louis: Concordia; Philadelphia: Fortress, 1955–86], 31:15), citing Augustine's favorite Bible verse, Rom. 5:5.

12. Paul R. Hinlicky, "Anthropology," in *Dictionary of Luther and the Lutheran Traditions* (Grand Rapids: Baker Academic, forthcoming).

God for us in our sinful unlikeness. Incorporated into Him by the same Spirit that led Him into battle with demonic powers, we too arise from the utter patiency of baptism into Christ's death for new agency in Christ (Rom. 6:3–4).

If we thought through the problem of compatibilism within this more biblical-canonical narrative framework, we would grasp that our clashing has been due to a shared trinitarian deficit: Protestants have contended for a monergism of the Word alone, Catholics for a monergism of the Spirit at work in the sacraments. Both contend for salvation by grace, but in these opposing ways. To sustain these equally undialectical monergisms, Protestants have had to denigrate creation as impotent, and Catholics have had to minimize sinful corruption as superficial. Neither side sustains the trinitarian dialectic of Word and Spirit adequately. But the Word incarnate who justifies the sinner by the grace of His loving solidarity "to the point of death—even death on a cross" (Phil. 2:8) points to the Spirit to receive His self-donation, just as the Spirit who bestows the gift of faith for new obedience ever grounds faith in recalling the Word concerning the *Christus crucifixus pro nobis*.

Thomas's Theology of Divine Nature

So much, in any case, for clearing the ground of stale and outdated polemics.[13] Today the issue is much more Thomas's doctrine of God. The question is indeed whether it is *deeply* trinitarian, or, otherwise put, whether the unitarian tendency of the protological doctrine of simplicity properly qualifies or radically subverts Thomas's manifest Christian trinitarianism. Kerr has a rich and thorough discussion of it worthy of extended consideration. Our segue into it may be the just-discussed doctrine of desire. Since a natural or philosophical theology can give us only a first cause or necessary being—not yet the Creator ex nihilo who promises redemption and fulfillment as the proper object of the creature's desire—it is critical, so Kerr urges, to see that for Thomas what tips the scale toward the latter notion of the free and personal God is a "certain awareness of God [that] is implanted in us . . . in the sense that we naturally desire beatitude . . . [although] we are easily mistaken or deceived about where our beatitude is truly to be found. Human beings desire to be with God, we may say, but which God, whose God?" (59 [cf. *ST* I-II.2]). This desire for beatitude is the truism that opens Aristotle's *Nicomachean Ethics*, "All by nature seek the good."

13. See the exploration of the Lutheran-Catholic Joint Declaration on Justification in William G. Rusch, ed., *Justification and the Future of the Ecumenical Movement: The Joint Declaration on the Doctrine of Justification* (Collegeville, MN: Liturgical Press, 2003).

Thomas's Christianization of Aristotle's doctrine of desire has been attacked by Kantians (and Lutherans who no longer know the difference between Luther and Kant) as "eudaimonism."[14] In this view, it must have been at bottom Jesus who misled us when He spoke the Beatitudes. But such criticism of the very desire for beatitude is in fact an inhumane puritanism that in its zealotry systematically confuses created desire with corrupted lust, commanded love for God with forbidden envy of God, blessed joy in God with incurvation into self, projected onto the idol; and in this series of systematic confusions it exemplifies Barth's dictum that the crooked man thinks crookedly and speaks crookedly even about his crookedness. This crookedness, above all in modern times, appears in the sublime name of the ethics of duty put forward historically as the thin and ascetic substitute for the theology of the Beloved Community. Because it does not know God as the Father who loves the Son in the Spirit that in the Spirit the Son may return, bound up with us, the praise of His deity to the Father—because, if you will, it does not know the good pleasure and holy eros of the Triune God—the ethics of duty systematically disdains the bonds of natural affection that bind persons together in love as persisting natural goods in, with, and under the sinful corruption. It regards such natural bonds as the source of bias, of "inclination" for one's own. And this natural love that inclines toward one's own is said to corrupt justice, which ought to be blind. As a result, justice itself is now conceived of as a blind leveling of all human difference rather than as the extraordinary social work of love that embraces difference by creatively justifying the unworthy. What cruelties have been done on the soil of post-Christendom in the name of such leveling! What hardness of heart it has worked into those made suspicious of their own concrete loves! What repression it effects in those who endeavor to live this way, as if they were universal beings and disembodied spirits rather than finite beings of flesh and blood!

When Luther writes that the solution to concupiscence is not to satisfy it but rather to extinguish it, he speaks of *corrupted* desire—lust that uses the other and the will to dominate. These corrupt desires have become second nature in Adam, but they are now to be crucified with Christ in baptism and daily mortified so far as they try to revive. It is precisely his view that only faith fulfills the holy law of God because only faith loves God as God and wants God to be God—"wanting" is desire, now rightly ordered by the impartation of the Spirit, who sheds the love of God abroad in human hearts, the love of God above all and therefore of all creatures in and under God. The Beloved

14. Anders Nygren, *Agape and Eros*, trans. Philip S. Watson (New York: Harper & Row, 1969).

Community is true blessedness and the true object of the creature's desire. By the same token, if Kerr is right that Thomas's "eudaimonism" begs the theological question "Which God, whose God?" then "natural theology" in Thomas is in fact more a tacit Christian theology of nature than a pure rational ascent from imperfect nature to the intellection of perfect nature as the object of sublime envy—an eminently natural and rational retracing of the supposed divine emanation from its nadir back to its source.

And indeed, no less an interpreter than David Burrell has recently advocated this rereading of Thomas. He calls "the distinction" of Creator from creature a "pre-philosophical stance which marks the thought and practice of all Abrahamic faiths, though each in a distinctive way, [which] becomes especially acute in Christian life and practice."[15] Burrell calls the injection of this distinction into philosophy the "hidden element" in Aquinas's thought, although today it demands unveiling. As Burrell wrote elsewhere, Thomas's secretly interjected "distinction" from revealed religion can no longer be taken for granted, because on strictly philosophical grounds "the abiding danger is that the creator will be mindlessly assimilated to creatures, which Islam rightly condemns as *shirk*, that is, so eliding the foundational Creator/creature distinction as to 'associate anything created with God,' which Maimonides identifies as idolatry. Any piece of writing which proceeds to talk about 'God' without adverting to this 'distinction' cannot help but speak about an item in the universe, better called 'god.'"[16] That identification of a being with Being itself would be "ontotheology"—an idolatrous conception of the one true God as a "being alongside other beings."[17]

One wonders immediately, however, whether Burrell's argument for the crucial, albeit veiled, interjection of "the distinction" in Thomas tells but half the story in his earnest desire to align Judaism, Christianity, and Islam. Certainly from the side of Christian theology, the claim to truth of the God

15. David B. Burrell, "Analogy, Creation, and Theological Language," in *The Theology of Thomas Aquinas*, ed. Rik Van Nieuwenhove and Joseph Wawrykow (Notre Dame, IN: University of Notre Dame Press, 2005), 78.

16. David B. Burrell, "Creator/Creatures Relation: 'The Distinction' vs. 'Onto-theology,'" *Faith and Philosophy* 25, no. 2 (April 2008): 179–80.

17. Heidegger's conception of ontotheology as the identification of God with causality in the philosophical quest for the *archē* or *principium* of the universe has its roots in Kant's lectures in philosophical theology, where Kant invented the term as he undertook the purification of the ideas of God, freedom, and the immortality of the soul. In this respect, Heidegger continues in Kantianism, as Brent Adkins and I argue in *Rethinking Philosophy and Theology with Deleuze: A New Cartography* (London: Bloomsbury Academic, 2013), 37–52. See further Hinlicky, *Paths Not Taken*, 60–66. The pejorative use of "ontotheology" in contemporary theology has become promiscuous: whatever one does not like is ontotheology. Heidegger replaces Aristotle with as much success as Aristotle had in speaking in his own voice amid the quarreling theologians.

of the gospel appears on the scene as "a being alongside other beings" in the Easter speaking of the resurrection of the Crucified One. Here on the earth, creatures tell about the "association" of the creature, Jesus of Nazareth, with God, not to mention the association of the almighty Father with the creation of heaven and earth, or of the Holy Spirit with the forgiveness of sins, the holy catholic church, the resurrection of the body to life everlasting, and so forth. It is not without cause, moreover, that in the name of the Creator/creature distinction Jews found and continue to find such Christian claims about Jesus blasphemous, and that Mohammed, upon hearing such Christian claims, affirmed instead that God "neither begets nor is begotten." This raises the question of whether in Christianity the Creator/creature distinction is made only in order to come unraveled. If not, what kind of union of the really distinct Creator and creature is christologically in view? Can this union be articulated without violence to "the distinction" but rather as a true expression and conceptual clarification of it? We will return to these christological questions in chapter 4.

For the moment, then, as Burrell has taught us, the point is that Thomas learned the essence/existence distinction from the Muslim philosopher Avicenna, who originated these concepts from consideration of Aristotle's questions, "What is it (essence)?" and, "Is it actual (existence)?" Further, Thomas revised these concepts to prioritize actuality over potency in order to secure, against Avicenna's Neoplatonic (note, not strictly Islamic) emanationism, a place for being as the actual and on this basis a stronger distinction of Creator from creature.[18] For Thomas, there are not essences (Platonic ideas or forms) hanging in the air or filling the mind of God, waiting to be manifested. It is an equivocation to assert the *being* of something that only *can* be (i.e., an essence); it is a dangerous equivocation that can carry us into flights of fancy regarding possible, indeed infinite worlds. Thought must be tethered to what is actual, to beings that presently we apprehend in the world by our senses, not to what in the imagination is possible. Essence is potential to be; it is the idea of a being, not its realization. But existence is, so far as it is, realized, actual, no longer mere essence or pure potential, an idea of the imagination about a possible being, but something there in the world, something real.

Thus, despite the utility of modal speculation about ideas or possibilities in the infinite mind of God—as in a Scotus or a Leibniz—to articulate the freedom of God in choosing to enact this particular creation instead of some other, Burrell regards Thomas's prioritization of actuality over possibility "better" for "express[ing] the relation of creator to creatures, so that the

18. Thanks to Hans Zorn for clarification on this point.

so-called 'divine ideas' are to be understood on the model of practical and not of speculative reason."[19] Thus, while Burrell expresses some hesitation in the direction of possibility at this point—"alternative designs remain a penumbra, a virtual component of an artist's creative act of making"—his account of Thomas's revision of Avicenna here is consistent with the broader thesis that Thomas in fact offers a Christian theology of nature. "Rather than import a philosophical idiom into a scriptural domain, it is the exigencies of revelation that transformed the metaphysics Aquinas received into one properly his own."[20] Thomas utilizes the metaphysics received from Aristotle via Avicenna to conceptualize this distinction, received from revealed religion, between the being of the Creator and the being of creatures, where being is assessed in terms of actuality, not potentiality. Thus he articulates the difference: in their existences creatures are never fully identical with their essences, never fully what they could and should be, but rather are composites of the real and the ideal that exist imperfectly. The One who creates, who gives essences existence, is the One who by contrast exists as fully identical to His essence, hence not composite but simply the act and actuality of His own being, existing perfectly.

We return now to Kerr. Thomas's famed account of simple divine being in *ST* I.3.1–8 as without body, not composed of matter and form, not differing from its own nature as individuals do, not differing from its existence, not a thing with properties, not a substance with accidents, in no way composite, but "altogether simple" leads, Kerr acknowledges, "to a conclusion some readers find bizarre" (77). Recalling the critiques of Gunton and Mullins from the previous chapter, that is to say, it seems to leave us speechless (not to say thoughtless) regarding God. "In particular," Kerr acknowledges, "since God is not a being with properties, we cannot say that God is, for example, wise or just, as if wisdom, justice, and so on, are qualities that God might or might not have. . . . No doubt, we may go on picturing God as a being with virtues; but that remains an anthropomorphic conception" (77). Such attributions only befall us who make them, not God to whom they are addressed,[21] rendering the praise of God into a human soliloquy in a kind of odd anticipation of

19. David B. Burrell, *Freedom and Creation in Three Traditions* (Notre Dame, IN: University of Notre Dame Press, 1993), 34.

20. Ibid., 33.

21. An alternative to this binary reasoning, as Dennis Bielfeldt has pointed out to me, is to regard God as the "truthmaker" who causes such creaturely predications as wise or just to be true of Himself, without submitting to analysis of supposed properties that would bind God to a human understanding of His nature. That would be akin to the weak doctrine of simplicity for which I am arguing, holding that God has properties in the sense that God can instantiate from the treasury of infinite possibilities according to divine freedom in its self-determination.

Feuerbach. Simplicity, rather than making the really distinct Creator of creatures speakable, thinkable, predicable, and so forth, seems instead ultimately to resolve in pure apophaticism—a blank screen onto which God-talk projects human ideals and aspirations. God preached (Latin: predicated) in Christ the power and wisdom of God becomes, strictly speaking, impossible: a way of talking but not of being.

Yet that appearance is not quite right. Kerr recounts Wolfhart Pannenberg's account, which "tells a different story," more sympathetic to Thomas than those of Gunton or Mullins. He takes the analysis of God as First Cause of the world, articulated metaphysically as the perfect and necessary being, to yield important truths. There is (1) one cause (not many) of the world; (2) this one cause is itself not caused (blocking an eternal regress and yielding the absoluteness, simplicity, perfection, and spirituality of the uncaused First Cause), (3) allowing the inference of knowing and willing in the First Cause in analogy to the agent causality of creatures, and so (4) coming to a psychological model of divine triunity as being with mind and love that can as such be a person-like First Cause of all else that is.

> This, Pannenberg clearly thinks, is a wonderful achievement; but a doctrine of God as immanently triune that is derived by metaphysical deduction from the concept of First Cause, rather than solely by reflection on God's self-revelation in Scripture as Father, Son and Holy Spirit, is not Christian. For Pannenberg, Thomas's God, far from being "unitarily conceived," is internally triune—but none the better for that. (182)

Kerr is right to register Pannenberg's dissatisfaction. The psychological trinity of Platonism—thought eternally thinking and willing itself, and equally eternally, refracting into the great chain of being and thence returning to primal unity—is not the social Trinity of the evangelical narrative that makes creation history on the way to the Beloved Community. The two trinities move in opposing directions, the first to a return to origin, the second in an advance to new creation. There is a similarity. But it is the Christian who discovers it. As Pannenberg sees it, "With this account of the one being of God as this self-knowing and self-loving subsistent activity of existing, Thomas takes us, by conceptual analysis, to the brink of discovering the triune God. . . . Perhaps, even, it is not too audacious to suggest that, though Thomas reasons his way to the description of God as sheer act of existing, he presupposes all the time, consciously or otherwise, the Christian doctrine of creation" (194)—just as we have heard Burrell urge. After the event of divine self-revelation, Pannenberg continues, "the theologian's task is to show that what God is like is not completely unintelligible. Divine intervention is undeserved, unforced, and utterly free. . . . But that does not mean, on the other hand, at least when we reflect on it, that God's intervention is arbitrary, gratuitous and totally unintelligible" (194). Once again, however, we note that such an unveiled procedure gives us a Christian theology of nature, not a natural theology.

In Kerr's view, however, it is right that Thomas derives a good deal solely from meditation on the conditions attending a First Cause. The existence of this First Cause is not obvious, yet as it is per hypothesis the beginning and end of all things, neither is it solely a matter of faith. Both the claim to revelation and inferences from the nature of the world confirm the immanent activity of the One whom everyone calls "God." Of this One, we cannot know what he is—only what he is not.

> What is possible in this life, by reasoning, is that we may come to know of God *that* he exists, as well as *what must be appropriate* to God as "first cause of all things transcending all that he has caused" (cf. [*ST*] 1.12.12). That is to say, knowledge of God by using our heads comes from thinking about his relationship to creatures: thus God as First Cause, not any part of what he has caused; and, far from this being a defect on his part, it shows his transcendence. (185 [emphasis added])

Simplicity in that case would be no more than an apophatic cipher for transcendence. All it does, in Burrell's language, is articulate in a particular philosophical idiom "the difference" and to this extent account for it metaphysically.

The devil is in the details. To *what* extent? Despite the apparent minimalism of "knowing what God is not," as just claimed, Kerr cannot avoid going on, in that peculiar oscillation to which I have already pointed, to make kataphatic claims of an alleged metaphysical insight. Simplicity in Thomas, he argues, yields a doctrine of God as verb, not noun; not a thing but an event, an activity, *operatio*, the act of God's own being. The key passage is *ST* I.13.11: the most appropriate name for God is "He Who Is" because God's nature or essence and His existence "are identical"; God "is simply existing—*ipsum esse*," truly indicated, then, by the intensified infinitive of the verb "to be" (188). "Sheer existing" is "not such an inappropriate rendering, in less anthropomorphic language, of the God invoked in the liturgy, who responds to Job out of the whirlwind. . . . For Thomas, God is the activity of sheer being, whether or not that being is shared with us" (189). Accordingly, critiques of Thomas for turning God into an ice-cold block of substance are just wrongheaded; rather, "the risk for Thomas is not to reify God as a static and motionless entity, but rather, just the opposite, to make so much of the divine essence as activity" that Thomas in effect affirms the divine omnicausality (that Gunton feared) wherein "God becomes sheer process, *perpetuum mobile*" (190). Knowing what God is not, we know God as sheer process.

But, as Hegel asked, how is this different from nothing at all? Kerr acknowledges the power of the negative at work in this kataphatic "risk," this claim to metaphysical insight. "God, for Thomas, is not even an agent with capacities to know and love. God is nothing other than ceaseless and total actualizations of being, knowing, and loving—utter bliss" (192). Affirming God in this way as pure event, as *actus purus*, acting on others but in no way worked upon by anything or anyone else (*ST* I.25.1)—coming, then, very close to Spinoza's *natura naturans*—Thomas is said to have fended off the perpetual danger "that God is conceived as a being at our disposal, manipulable and controllable by creatures" (190). Of course, "something" that eludes all articulation can hardly be manipulated or controlled; to call it utter bliss or *actus purus* or pure event is only, in a kind of optical illusion, to speak the unspeakable and think the unthinkable. So again, how is this "something" different from nothing at all, from the reification of a No-Thing?

In sum, for Thomas divine simplicity is not only a cipher for apophatic transcendence, pointing to *some* God (claimant to deity) as the unique, the incomparable, hence the incomprehensible One; it is also a kataphatic account, albeit highly abstract, of *how* God is one as the timeless act of His own being. And the unity of these two functions of divine simplicity in Thomas is unstable, since the protological account of God's act of being is kataphatic—that is, comparable with creaturely being, and so in tension with apophatic transcendence, which admits of no comparison. Analogy collapses into equivocation. Being itself cannot be taken literally. So the criticism, then, will be that in this unstable tension the power of the negative always prevails, that the line that Thomas draws does not prevent Hegel but instead leads to Hegel. If that criticism may be sustained, the decisive question will not be whether Thomas presupposes in his natural theology knowledge of the Christian doctrine of the Trinity and accordingly of *creatio ex nihilo*, as surely he does, nor whether his metaphysical analysis of the divine simplicity in terms of the First Cause of all else that exists leads toward the revealed doctrine of creation out of nothing. Surely that is his (covert) intention. The question, rather, is whether in the process the psychological model of the trinity of mental operations from Neoplatonism, cosmologically derived from the metaphysical analysis of the First Cause, supplants the social model of the Trinity from the gospel narrative. Then, in the final analysis, under the relentless power of the negative the Father, Son, and Holy Spirit in their one life together—as also for us—evaporate into God beyond being and nonbeing, a *not nothing*—whatever that may be!

The instability in Thomas's synthesis may be viewed from yet another angle, already introduced. This "not nothing" is depicted, as if truthfully, as perfect Mind—a barely conscious anthropomorphism. Kerr cites Thomas Weinandy to this effect: "The persons are verbs, and the names designate the acts by which they are defined" (199–200). The explanation of the verbal action is psychological. Knowing always entails also loving, since we can never be indifferent to what is known, but knowledge requires us to love one way or another; on the other hand, nothing can be loved without the mind, since nothing can be loved willingly unless it is conceived by the mind (197; see also 201). Applied *ad intra* to God's self-knowledge, God taken as Mind is the sheer event of thought thinking and willing itself. Accordingly, Kerr expresses typically Western worries about tritheism wrapped up in the notion of person as something unique and incommunicable, shaped by memory and reflection, a center of consciousness and agency, and relationally subsisting. He acknowledges, "But this is another hermeneutical crux" (193), as indeed it is. For Thomas, he explains, there are, within the Godhead, "'processions,' first of intellection . . . and secondly of love" (194), and these, precisely stated, are what the trinitarian "persons" are: mental operations. The errors of modalism and subordinationism in that case are only that each in a different way takes the procession as movement toward something external to the divine Mind rather than as immanent to God's own consciousness (195) as an eternal event. All in all, then, we must hold to the model of the mind such that it controls the understanding of the social Three of the gospel narrative—even though, strictly speaking, all this is illicit anthropomorphism.

What would be the social trinitarian alternative? Kerr discusses Robert Jenson's proposal under six points. First, Jenson grants to Thomas that the distinction of nature/essence from existence/actuality restates the doctrine of creation—namely, that it parses on a metaphysical level according to a certain idiom the difference between Creator and creature. Second, "the contention that the essence or nature of God is 'an otherwise unqualified act of existing' is Thomas's 'decisive maxim'" (204). Thus far there is an agreement, expressed in Thomas's idiom. The problem, however, lies in what way the act of God's being is taken—that is, who the "subject" of the action is taken to be. The action of God's being may be taken as the eternal circulation of the persons—that is, beginning with the Father's begetting of the Son, on whom He breathes His Spirit, and circulating in the Son's return in the Spirit to the Father in the praise of His deity. Or the subject may be taken as the First Cause of the cosmos, as sheer activity, as Kerr puts it, *perpetuum mobile*. In that case, third, Jenson avers that it is a fatal error to think simply of God as the highest kind of causality (i.e., omnicausality) in the framework of cosmology and then ask how lesser kinds of things can relate to it. The Thomist would reply to Jenson, of course, that such is precisely what Thomas avoids in thinking the First Cause as not part of the nexus of causality (that as a being alongside other beings) but as the transcendent cause of causes. But for Jenson, it does not matter that the Christian intention of Thomas is to secure the transcendence and freedom of the First Cause (which, as per Burrell, is in fact an interjection into the metaphysical analysis). Here, ineluctably, the derivation of the subject in the act of God's being is still determined by its cosmological function, and as such it is attributed to the impersonal divine nature—not to the divine person who is the almighty Father but to a quasi-personified absolute power or capability of all-causation pictured as Mind. Moreover, even if God is seen as transcendent to the intramundane nexus of causality, God as First Cause is still bundled, so to say, with the cosmos into an eternal system. This entanglement, Jenson charges, cannot but obscure the biblical Creator/creature distinction that from the origin aims at the redemption and fulfillment of creation; it even tends to convert it back into the Neoplatonic chain of being. Hence it is God as Trinity—more precisely, as the gospel's social Trinity of persons—that blocks this retrogression into Platonism. Because the Father eternally begets His Son, on whom He spirates His Spirit, He is eternally His own world, with no ontological need of another, and, as such, freely becomes what He was not, the Creator of a world other than Himself. He is not the eternal, logically prior causality at work as the *archē* of the world system. (For just this reason, we may note, Jenson introduced in his *Systematic Theology*, in place of the topic *de Deo uno*, the topic "Patrology."[22] The act of God's eternal being, accordingly, is the Father's generation of the Son and breathing of the Spirit.)

Regarding the "simplicity" of this patrological conception of the act of God's being, Jenson offers a redescription of the convertibility of the so-called transcendentals: "God is being, and therefore he is truth *and* goodness and beauty; adjectivally, he is knowable and lovable and enjoyable. None of the three can be understood in isolation from the others."[23] Thomas would undoubtedly agree in the sense that all these differentiations reduce to one inconceivable identity; but Jenson's point seems to be rather that convertibility indicates a real exchange or circulation of distinct and abiding properties that characterizes truthfully the life of the Three as one life—simple, then,

---

22. Robert W. Jenson, *Systematic Theology* (Oxford: Oxford University Press, 1997), 1:115–24.
23. Ibid., 1:225.

in a complex way of perichoresis, concretely put, that harmonizes power and wisdom in love. The alternative of the social Trinity, then, leads Jenson to the reconceptualization of the act of God's being as the perichoresis of the persons, with their personal properties, as the event, exchange, circulation, conversation, harmonization—the "great fugue," as Kerr sees (204–5). In this case, simplicity does not tell us theoretically how God is one but rather describes God's oneness as the *eschatological* harmony of the Three, as the mutual qualifying of power, wisdom, and love in the account of God's being as the free act of creating a world *in order to* redeem and fulfill it.

I mentioned above Burrell's attempt to distinguish Thomas's transcendent First Cause from Heidegger's critique of ontotheology, even though it was Thomas, or a certain nineteenth-century reading of Thomas, that had filled Heidegger's crosshairs in that now commonplace attack on ontotheology. Jenson's critique of the fatal vulnerability in Thomas's treatment of divine nature, as presupposing the framework of the philosopher's quest for the *archē* or *principium* of the cosmological causal agent, however, dovetails in important respects with Kerr's account of Heidegger's critique of ontotheology: the God who is the cause of things is the god of "philosophy"—not, for Heidegger, a compliment! As Heidegger famously wrote, "Human beings can neither pray nor sacrifice to this god. Before the *causa sui*, human beings can neither fall to their knees in awe nor can they play music and dance before this god" (72).[24] Kerr observes how Heidegger traces the source of this ontotheological worldview to Aristotle's *Physics*: the "first mover, in the context of his picture of the world as *physis* and *kosmos*—as 'nature' always already exhibiting a 'beautiful order'. . . . Aristotle's 'world,' with its in-built origination and finality, was always already understood as 'made,' 'fabricated,' if you like 'created.' . . . It is taken for granted, however unwittingly, that there is a divine maker of the world—an origin that commands and a destiny that calls" (88).

If Kerr is right in this, Heidegger's critique of ontotheology is, from one angle, nothing but the articulation of his hard-earned atheism with respect to the first article of the primitive Christian baptismal creeds. From another angle, it is indeed at least a tacit critique of the confusion of the God of the gospel with the First Cause of the cosmos. As a result of these differing perspectives, Jenson and Heidegger quite diverge on what to make of ontotheology. For Jenson, the subtle supplanting of the eschatological God of the gospel by the protological First Cause evacuates history of promise

24. Cited from Martin Heidegger, *Identity and Difference*, trans. Joan Stambaugh (New York: Harper & Row, 1969).

and thus also the militant hope for the Beloved Community, and in its place introduces and reinforces a conservative cosmos-piety that resists divine pressures for just change. Heidegger, as Kerr sees more clearly than Burrell, seeks to liberate thinking from the very need to secure some rational foundation upon which the sum total of knowledge may be erected, and thus to liberate existential action from the teleology implied in having to conform one's life to the foundation so secured. "We should then begin at least—at last—to be cured of nostalgic desire for return to the source (*arche*, *principium*); we should be released from the obsession with achieving the ultimate end (*telos*, *finis*)" (88). This genuine atheism of Heidegger, in Kerr's reading, out-Kants Kant: "The human will to explain just does not reach the simpleness of the simple onefold of worlding" (89). What is intriguing in this rendering of Heidegger by Kerr is that we have as a result the radicalization and purification of divine *simplicitas* (89)—that is to say, a return back to its pre-Socratic sources, freed both from its cosmological functionalization in Aristotle and its Christian baptism in turn at the hands of Thomas.

"We have much to learn from Heidegger's anti-subjectivism," Kerr concludes—that is, against thinking "of ourselves as subjects, on this side of the world, as if the world stood over against us, on the other side of some gap" (90). The critique of the sovereign self of Cartesian-Kantian modernity as an agent over against the world, ghost in the machine though she be, is indeed valuable so far as it goes.[25] The difference between being a subject and being a person, however, is the difference that I introduced earlier with the term "patiency." A subject is an agent—since Descartes, a pure, sovereign self who by the act of thinking increasingly creates its own reality until it becomes idealism's, then existentialism's, self-positing self. A person is also an agent, though always and ever first of all as a patient of the range of communities in which it is embedded as embodied, as always already a being-there (*Dasein*), somewhere, in a physical environment and social world. Because Heidegger, a victim of neo-scholastic Thomism, does not know this theological distinction of person from agent or subject, he does not know that human agency is a function of human patiency, and human patiency a function of God's continuous creativity. Indeed, he cannot know it because he no longer wants to know the God whose creativity is continuous on the way to the coming of the Beloved Community. Heidegger's project, as Kerr judges, is "to relieve the world of being 'created'" even though it "depends on a radical misunderstanding of the Christian doctrine of creation ex nihilo as always already

25. Paul R. Hinlicky, *Beloved Community: Critical Dogmatics after Christendom* (Grand Rapids: Eerdmans, 2015), 97–105.

receiving the world as 'gift.' Where Heidegger sees the world explained in terms of an effect of some cause as demeaningly losing its incomparable mystery . . . Thomas celebrates the world as a miracle of divine grace" (93). Such receptivity is but another way of articulating patiency.

I have refined the question about Thomas's theology of nature now to the question of whether his Christianized doctrine of divine simplicity ultimately delivers us to silence before the unknown Beyond rather than to Jenson's "great fugue." It is a question that Kerr takes up: "The doctrine of divine simpleness seems to make God so utterly different from anything created— so 'totally otherwise'—that any claim to have knowledge of God would be ruled out on the grounds that that which is 'simple' could never be known by 'composites' such as we human beings are" (77). At this final juncture, Kerr points to 1 John 3:2, "We shall see him as he is," to exposit Thomas's apophaticism as eschatologically oriented: "If the created mind were never able to see the Godhead either we would never attain beatitude or our beatitude would consist in something other than God—which is contrary to faith (ST 1.12.1)" (78). Thus Thomas the Christian theologian wants to resist the ultimate implication of a purely negative theology, according to which *finiti ad infinitum non est proportio*: "The qualitative difference between finite and infinite seems so unbridgeable as to rule out any argument by analogy from the world to God" (60) or from above, from God to the world, namely, in the new Adam, Jesus Christ. Whether Thomas can succeed in this Christian resistance is a question best left at this juncture to Thomists.

The hermeneutical moral of the story for Kerr, in any case, is that any one-sided reading of Thomas leads to disaster. Kerr's hermeneutical point is that Thomas is always to be seen as battling on two fronts. He seeks the middle way based on Romans 1:20: "It is a matter of faith that God's existence can be discovered by reason" (60). The middle way, for him, is the analogy of being. "Any creature, insofar as it possess any perfection, represents God and is like God, for God, being simply and universally perfect, has pre-existing in himself the perfections of all his creatures" (*ST* I.13.2). Thus, when we predicate of God perfections we are familiar with in ourselves—"meaning them, however, 'in a higher way than we understand'" (186)—we are speaking reality. Thus the analogy of being is intended not just as a way of talking but is grounded "on the real relationship that creatures have toward God as source and cause of being" (186). So Kerr would conclude, accenting the kataphatic and indeed "ontotheological" function of the analogy of being.

This conclusion, however, is unstable, as argued. Just this properly Christian concern for securing the knowledge of God the almighty Father, Creator of heaven and earth who sent His Son in the power of the Spirit to save, founders on the cosmological framework assumed with its protological bias from which the doctrine of simplicity derives. If one can distinguish here between Thomas's concern and Thomas's idiom in which that concern is articulated, one will have to agree with Scotus that Thomas's doctrine of the analogy of being intends what it cannot finally deliver. It in fact oscillates unstably between univocity for the sake of a meaningful similitude and equivocation in a dialectic in which the power of the negative in the end prevails. Sheer pointing to a Beyond as the really Real of our reality that is on examination no more than a Not-Nothing is not, in any event, the Christian knowledge of God—not the God of the gospel, who comes to us in our weakness and for us in spite of our enmity to redeem His lost creation and bring it to fulfillment. I will return to the christological problem with the analogy of being in chapter 4. For the present, the task is to explicate the patrological account of the act of God's being as the alternative of trinitarian theology.

The Patrological Alternative

We have seen that within a certain philosophical idiom—Aristotle's cosmology as read by Avicenna's distinction between essence and existence and as (tacitly) Christianized by Thomas to envision the free act of creation befitting a wholly generous deity's "simple act of love"—Thomas succeeds in articulating the strong Creator/creature distinction that is one hallmark of genuine Christian theology. His achievement in this regard must be appreciated beyond its own context; it continues to make a claim on subsequent theology likewise to maintain in our own idioms this hierarchy of value such that in loving God above all, we love all creatures in and under God. Apart from this *ordo caritatis*—nothing other than Jesus's enunciation of the double love commandment (Mark 12:29–31), taken from Augustine onward as the doctrine of theological anthropology requiring pure and undivided desire for the one true God[26]—we have no theology of the Beloved Community. So much ought readily to be agreed upon.

Notwithstanding, by way of the considerable help of Fergus Kerr and assistance from David Burrell, we are now in a position to zero in precisely on the trinitarian problem even with Thomas's "baptized" metaphysics of protological simplicity—that is, why the notion must be clearly recast as Jenson's "maxim," in the present proposal, as a "rule" rather than taken as an independent and self-standing metaphysical axiom pretending to insight into

26. Augustine, *On Christian Teaching*, trans. R. P. H. Green (Oxford: Oxford University Press, 1999), 17–23, 34.

the how of God's unity as a timeless *actus purus*. As a rule, weak simplicity can show or refer to what it cannot declare or elucidate, since it holds, as a matter of truthful speech about God, that only the God of the gospel can bring about the state of affairs in which God and God's name are one. Just this trust in God to be God as promised is what faith lives by. Certainly Thomas denies that simplicity is a definition of God. He clearly denies that a definition of God is even possible. Rather, "to say that God's essence is to exist is a way, then, of saying that what he is cannot be defined."[27] As I have argued, however, so far as this denial is also an account of God's oneness, it is not less than an ontological description, even if not a formal definition: God is the One whose essence is to exist and whose existence is the fullness of His essence. As an account, it is doubly problematic for attempting to elucidate what God alone can demonstrate and for presuming to have solved the problem of the delay of the fulfillment with an insight that neutralizes the tension between the already and the not yet. A key term, however, in Kerr's statement is that it is "a way," one way among others, expressed, as we will see, problematically from trinitarian perspective in that the chosen philosophical idiom tends to disallow the notion of self-causation—or, better, self-determination—in God, which from the Christian perspective is essential for articulating the freedom of God and the gratuity of grace.

In place of this, Thomas, in affirming the timelessly simple identity of God's essence and existence, must exclude the motion, if you will, the cause and effect within God that is sung in the Nicene Creed, "of God from God, light from light, true God from true, begotten not made" and so also the movement *ad extra* of this same simply complex God from the origin to redeem and fulfill. Indeed, just as Thomas cannot affirm the truth of the creation of the world in time, so also must he take the trinitarian being of God in becoming as an unintelligible truth of supernatural revelation to be cut and pasted onto the intelligible substructure of protological simplicity. So granted, divine simplicity is for Thomas what we today would call an ontological *description*, by which the creature *recognizes* the eternal being of the Creator in qualitative distinction from its own temporal being, along the lines of Romans 1:20. God's oneness is ontologically described, just as is the creature's multiplicity. Yet, as indicated, this is tricky.

Recognition is a pragmatic matter of identification, so that creatures worship what is the Creator rather than other creatures. If we forget the practical location and purpose of such acknowledgment of God as Creator, we

27. John Marenbon, *Medieval Philosophy: An Historical and Philosophical Introduction* (London: Routledge, 2007), 240.

are tempted to transpose it into a speculative knowledge, as did Hegel with unprecedented rigor and radicalness in pointing out that to know what God is not is to know a great deal indeed about God. Then the slippage by which Thomas's purely apophatic "nothing that we can ever define" or dialectical affirmation of God as "not nothing" gets reified into the Something Beyond, the *perpetuum mobile* of sheer bliss, and so comes positively to determine the Christian discourse about God as a discourse of alienation and otherworldly flight. So on to Hegel: now in modern times, this very otherworldliness of the reified No-Thing is itself critiqued in order to embrace more consistently the real engine driving this machine—the dialectic of negativity—until it comes to rest in a kenotic deification of History. If that is at all right, just as Kerr averred at the outset, "We need to ask what it is, in Thomas's work, and in the uses to which it has been put by opponents as well as disciples, that makes certain misreadings attractive, and almost unavoidable" (16).

Clarification of the problem—the ambiguity or instability—of the doctrine of protological simplicity in this Christian synthesis leads to a choice. The kataphatic function of simplicity as an articulation of God's unity as the timeless identity of essence and existence must be abandoned for the sake of a more modest apophaticism. Simplicity should be affirmed, in the latter case, as a rule in Christian theology, respecting the incomprehensible unity of the Trinity, One of whom suffered at Another's will, as decreed by the Fifth Ecumenical Council. In that case, to be sure, the tacit notion of time in the metaphysical affirmation of God's timeless (and spaceless) self-identity will as well experience a corresponding revision. Our notion of God's eternity and immensity will not be the abstract negation of creation but instead will be constructed out of the time-like begetting and spirating and the space-like perichoresis of the Triune life. In this way, divine eternity and immensity will be understood as providing the divine capacity for the creature, so that fittingly but not necessarily God creates in order to redeem and fulfill in the coming of the Beloved Community. The Creator/creature distinction, more broadly speaking, is gained not by negating God's relation to the temporal world of becoming in a pseudo-insight but rather, positively, as Gunton required, by reflection on God's revealed acts to redeem and fulfill all that He has made. The logic of a positive derivation of the divine attributes by which God is ontologically described as Creator is that what God has in fact done and promises to do, God must be thought of as capable of doing; in short: God *is* the ineffable harmony of power, wisdom, and love in infinite circulation.

Then the sense of the maxim, or rule, would be this: so speak of the Father of the Son in the Holy Spirit as one God in the harmony of power, wisdom, and love that none can be who each one particularly is without the others—in eternity as in time—nor act in any one way of power, wisdom, or love that is not qualified by the others. In this section I am probing this alternative rendering of divine simplicity as a patrological qualification or rule of trinitarian harmony, not an insight into protological unicity, honoring Thomas's intention to secure the Creator/creature distinction ontologically but adopting neither his idiom nor his formulation of the doctrine.

In Kerr's discussion of Jenson, recall, we already heard an intimation of the problem and the alternative that is before us now. The act of God's being may be taken in one of two ways. One way—I will call it, after Jenson, the "patrological" account—is to take it as the eternal circulation of the persons—that is, beginning in the unbegotten Father's begetting of the Son, on whom He breathes His Spirit, so that in the Spirit the Son returns to the Father the praise of His deity, and so circulating ad infinitum. In that case, the *opera Dei ad extra* are innovations also for God by which this Triune God, whose being in eternally becoming acquires extrinsic properties in relation to the innovations that are His creatures supremely, henceforth, and forever in the christological union of the eternal Son with us as the man Jesus Christ. Creatures, in turn, are not mere replications of what God antecedently is, the refraction of the One into the Many by way of an emanation and/or analogical diffusion through the great chain of being. Rather, each creature is a genuine instance of created novelty (what Leibniz actually meant by monad as a principle of individuation) and thus a creative expression of difference for God its Creator as also, obviously, for creatures. Such creatures, made in the image of God for likeness to God, are accordingly summoned to love one another as different, not as the same, nor as analogically linked replications only idiosyncratically differing from the underlying sameness. Harmony comes not by awakening to an identity beneath the surface appearance but rather by the historical achievement of love, by God as also in and for creatures in a history constituted by encounter with real, not fictitious, others. Such is the "patrological" (Jenson) account of the act of God's being, whose ultimate mystery is the uncaused "cause" of the unbegotten Father, who begets and spirates.

On the other hand, as we have already heard at some length, by the way of metaphysical analysis of the First Cause of the cosmos, the eternal act of God's being may be taken as *sheer existence*, thought of as the necessary being, the perfect being. In that case, the "fatal error," as Jenson charged from the patrological perspective, is to think of God as the highest kind of thing and ask how to anchor lesser kinds of things in it as proper effects. This highest being, however, occupies an unstable place, oscillating between being beyond the world or grounding the world, transcendent or immanent, apophatic or kataphatic, depending upon the theological needs of the moment. But whichever of these two poles is emphasized, we are thinking here protologically of the Neoplatonic trinity of absolute God, mediating Logos, and animating Spirit, thought thinking and willing itself into the refracted materialization of the visible world of becoming within an eternal system. Here Romans 1:20 is taken to regard the cosmos as a theophany, revered in cosmos-piety with a corresponding ethic of duty. The critical charge against it from the patrological perspective is that it returns us to the great chain of being—that is to say, to the theology not of the God of the exodus but of Pharaoh, not of Easter but of Pontius Pilate.

Consider, for example, Zechariah 14:9: "And the LORD will become king over all the earth; on that day the LORD will be one and his name one." In Thomas's treatment of this text, the present "necessity of giving to God many names" is cosmological: finite and sense-bound creatures cannot know the First Cause essentially, but only by discursive extrapolation from His many diverse effects, and even then only by sheer pointing through these many names of many perfections to the *that* of God, who exists in the act of His own being, we know not what or how. The many names of polytheism are analogically harmonized to point to their one, albeit unknown, referent. "Were we able to understand the divine essence itself as it is and give to it the name that belongs to it," Thomas comments, "we would express it by only one name" (*SCG* I.31.4). Since we know that God is one in the sense of protological simplicity, if we knew what this ontological One was essentially, we could name it with one name adequate to its simple reality, as signed in the Tetragrammaton, taken as the best available name for God: THE ONE WHO IS. Thomas, as Kerr urged, does take this possibility of naming God as one "through His essence" as the eschatological promise of Zechariah in the sense of the beatific vision of the saints in heaven. This seeing of God essentially in God and by God eternally fills the creature's desire so that desire rests secure in the vision, *non posse peccare*, no longer able to defect and fall away.

Now consider, by contrast, Walter Brueggemann's treatment of texts like Zechariah 14:9. In his *Theology of the Old Testament* he devotes major attention to the "disjunctive rendering of Yahweh,"[28] depicted in wrenching anthropomorphism (e.g., Hosea 11:8–9, "declaring that an upheaval has occurred in Yahweh's life . . . [as] Yahweh redecides, in the midst of crises, how to be Yahweh [i.e., not like a jealous husband enraged at infidelity] and who to be as Yahweh [namely, as 'the holy One in your midst who will not come to destroy']").[29] For Brueggemann, then, the oneness of God's name will be sung

28. Walter Brueggemann, *Theology of the Old Testament: Testimony, Dispute, Advocacy* (Minneapolis: Fortress, 1997), 267–313.
29. Ibid., 302.

in the praises of the redeemed when the reign of God over all comes about. Then "the LORD will be one and his name one." This oneness will be at the same time, indeed, the result of the historically achieved unification of God with His people through the drama of His history with His creature, Israel, *pars pro toto*, humanity. It will be the oneness of God reconciling Himself by reconciling humanity lost to sin and so redeeming and fulfilling the lost promise of the creation. Brueggemann thus takes texts like Zechariah 14:9 as referring not only, as in Thomas, to the transformation of the saints at the beatific vision by their elevation to the heavenly presence of God, but also to the becoming of Yahweh as our God on the earth. "Yahweh becomes, by the reality of Israel's insistence, as Yahweh had not yet been"[30] even though, at the same time, "Yahweh's determination to be taken seriously on Yahweh's own terms . . . precludes any final equation of sovereignty with covenantal love or with pathos."[31] This final accent on Yahweh's freely chosen and persevering purpose in the election of the unworthy and unfaithful saves Brueggemann's account of holy passion from the bathos of the usual theologies of divine suffering today. The passion of Yahweh is holy and serves His sovereign purpose. It arises, indeed, from a sovereign self-determination, "I *am* the LORD *your* God," as Yahweh persists in this self-determination for Yahweh's own sake and the glory of His name. Yet passion it is, the "zeal" of the Lord of Hosts, the holy One in the midst of an unclean land of unclean people, Israel standing in here for us all.

When we reflect on this, we realize that creatures cannot even in sovereign and unilateral gestures of other-regarding love give themselves without giving themselves also into the use or abuse of the gifted, that we are thus affected in the very act of supreme agency that is giving ourselves to another. We acquire, as a result, properties that we had not previously had, as, for example, I once became and continued to become dear William's father; in the giving of ourselves to others, moreover, horizons emerge for our persistence in self-giving that we had not previously anticipated or imagined, as when Ellen and I, for instance, risked our children to go and teach in postcommunist Slovakia in the 1990s. Surely the holy passion of God (the "impassible passibility" of the fathers) in Christ—as Luke and John so emphasize—is to be thought along these lines; then we would say with Luther that the glory of our God is that in sovereign love He comes down into the depths. In the capacity for such love as is here perceived, received, and believed, God's oneness is revealed in Christ as His patrological self-determination from the origin to redeem and

30. Ibid., 279.
31. Ibid., 303.

fulfill the creation that we are. And this revealed oneness of God as the sole principle of origin both within God's eternal life and thus also in regard to creation will be fulfilled for us and thus manifest at the coming of His reign. In the interim, the eternal life that is capable of such persistent and faithful self-determination for others, in spite of unworthiness and in face of resistance, is taken as the holy and eternal passion of love that binds the Father and the Son in the Holy Spirit in an infinite and singular circulation that creatures may ever enjoy but never comprehend.

When Thomas, therefore, had to insist for the sake of protological simplicity that the external relations of God are only in creatures, not at all in God, we must ask biblically whether something has gone wrong at this precise point. Can God take on extrinsic and relational properties without change to His intrinsic and presumably nonrelational properties?[32] If we answer yes to that question, as seems evident that we should, we can next trace the error to a particularly interesting passage in *SCG* I.22, where Thomas denies that God is self-causing, *causa sui*. He sees chiefly two problems in this notion. First, there is the logical problem of the identity of the antecedent cause with the consequent effect. Who causes God to be God, if God is an effect that cannot and does not exist until being caused? To be before being is logically impossible,

---

32. But notice the nontrinitarian formulation of the question that forces a choice between relationship and immutability. God's intrinsic properties are relational if the subject of them is the Father, who begets the Son and breathes His Spirit on Him, so that divine power, wisdom, and love are always mutually qualified in God's eternal and immutable life, taken as this society. And if God's irreducible life is socially such, God can take on extrinsic properties in an amplification of His being by the incorporation of creatures such that the Father becomes Creator of a world of creatures, the Son becomes one of them, and the Spirit makes of them, united to the Son, God's temple, His habitation. Here God is God in voluntarily initiating and sustaining external relationships with creatures that in the event make God at God's own behest something that God was not. In that case, God is God for us not by timelessly preserving His eternal being against others but rather by temporally exercising His eternal being for others in freedom to love wisely. God's eternal being, we might say with Jonathan Edwards, is a "disposition" or "habit": "God's essence is a constantly exercised inclination to repeat his already perfect actuality through further exercises. God's actuality is already perfect because it is completely exercised in and through the inner-Trinitarian relationships. God's action in the world is therefore the spatio-temporal repetition of God's already-realized actuality" (Michael J. McClymond and Gerald R. McDermott, *The Theology of Jonathan Edwards* [New York: Oxford University Press, 2012], 529). McClymond and McDermott go on to comment that although "God does not add to his own actuality, God is continually involved in a process of self-extension by creating and then relating to other beings" (529). That God does not add to His actuality in extending Himself to others not God, as it seems to me, reflects the counterintuitive remnant, on the hypothesis of dispositional ontology, of classical simplicity; Edwards's breakthrough, paralleling his near-contemporary continental peer Leibniz, is to a dispositional divine ontology that, as Leibniz put it, "inclines God to create without necessitating creation." See chap. 3, "God against the Machine," in Robert W. Jenson, *America's Theologian: A Recommendation of Jonathan Edwards* (New York: Oxford University Press, 1986), 23–34.

a contradiction, the assertion of nonsense. Rather, we should understand that, as the *First* Cause, God is the Cause without cause, the One uncaused Cause—*Punkt*. Just this *Punkt*, moreover, is God's simplicity of being, the ultimate mystery of the cosmos that cannot be questioned further but only silently, speechlessly adored.

Second, then, self-causation would violate protological simplicity, since it would imply motion in God, which in Aristotelian idiom means moving from a state of potential to a state of actuality. But God, without beginning, is not in any sense an effect, not even a self-caused effect, not in motion whatsoever but wholly *actus purus*. Self-causation would combine essence with existence in some way, making God a composite with unrealized potential. We are speaking, Thomas clarifies in the middle of this analysis, of substantial not accidental change. A substance certainly can acquire accidental properties by its own actions, though in the unique case of God even this would be inappropriate, since then "God will suffer and receive the action of some cause" (*SCG* I.23.3) external to Himself, which contradicts God's reality as uncaused Cause. Thus Thomas denies to God not only involuntary suffering, which we might agree on, but also voluntary suffering, the suffering that is love willing to bear the burdens of others for the sake of those others, the holy passion and the zeal of the Lord of Hosts that takes the incarnate Son to Golgotha and through it to a glorious new creation.

Now, what further intrigues is that this rejection of God's self-causation comes from the passage in the *Summa contra Gentiles* where Thomas introduces the famous text from Exodus 3:13–14 about God's revealed name, HE WHO IS. Thomas teaches that this "name" (term) designates properly (but does not define) the essence of God that is His existence, and vice versa: "the divine being is God's essence or nature" (*SCG* I.22.10). It is a name that sheerly points to the sheer act of being that is divine. Thomas is very careful to clarify that this name describes and does not define, since we never can know what God is—that is, how our perfections, which have many names and which we ascribe to God in our praises, are real in God as one and the same, though manifestly these predications are not one to us but often are fraught with tension, as Brueggemann insisted. Thomas's way of articulating this unique case of HE WHO IS was to say, as we may recall, that God belongs to no genus; thus there can be no generic definition under which God is subsumed (*SCG* I.25), so that we can only point to God as the eminent reality. To call God "substance," thus, says nothing about what God is, only that God is ontologically as one. In the case of God, the term "substance" is "pure negation" (*SCG* I.25.10). All it indicates is the divine existence of perfect unity (*SCG* I.77), timeless self-identity. While this self-possession may be likened to the immaterial unity of mind, as known to creatures, this similarity is embedded in an even greater dissimilarity because there is no discursiveness to the divine Mind, which rather is to be thought of (as Kerr remarked) as spontaneously processing in the operations of knowing and willing *ad intra* (269), a perpetual-motion machine. As such, the divine Mind creatively intuits *ad extra* the creation as a refraction of its own ecstatic self-knowledge and self-love. As God is self-contemplative in this way ("thought thinking and willing itself"), participation in the blessedness of God's self-knowledge is the promised beatitude of rational creatures. God, then, is all cause and not at all effect.

Let us recall here again what we may agree upon. Given the Aristotelian idiom, the identity in God of essence and existence is a way of articulating the strong Creator/creature distinction; further, this articulation is an essential mark of the Christian doctrine of creation as the good work of God, destined by redemption for fulfillment. What is disputable, however, is a logical entanglement from the Aristotelian idiom that, as a minimum, disallows to God the acquisition of external properties, even when the sovereignty of God's will in the acquisition of those properties is affirmed. On Thomas's account of God's simplicity, God cannot properly say, "I *am* the Lord *your* God." Thus, protological simplicity obscures God's free self-determination in Christ, the plan hidden from the ages but now made known concerning the Lamb slain before the foundations of the world, namely, to redeem and fulfill the creation at the coming of the Beloved Community. How does Thomas's account stumble into these biblically unwelcome implications?

One could point to the role of causality in Thomas's thought. One could say that causality is an improper category for thinking the Creator/creature relation along the Heideggerian lines of the critique of ontotheology. But this objection is not illuminating and in fact leads us back into the unbaptized doctrine of simplicity, as we saw. As Kerr reminded us, to speak of a transcendent First Cause for Thomas is to intend omnicausality as the continuous presence in action of the Creator God enabling all creatures to do what they do (and suffer what they suffer). In light of this intention, it is a misunderstanding to object that causality in Thomas makes God an ontotheological god, a highest being alongside other beings in a destructive contest for agency. Thomas's idiom may fail him in delivering upon this intention, as I have argued that it in fact does in its unstable, if not unprincipled, oscillation between kataphatic and apophatic functions. But surely Thomas's formulations are to be read and understood in the light of his clearly announced purposes. Second, omnicausality, which is not asserting as in Zwingli or Spinoza the sole causality of God, is an inalienable feature of the Christian doctrine of creation that calls God the Father almighty, Creator of all that is not God. A God who is not ever-present to His creature, giving life, empowering its way, preserving it from harm, and bringing it to fulfillment is guilty of criminal abandonment and so ontologically self-destructs morally as well as metaphysically.

What, then, is the problem with causality? Only this: Thomas's determination of the idea of causality is protological and cosmological rather than theological and eschatological; that is to say, it is determined by a protological notion of God as *archē* and *principium* rather than by the eschatological promise, indeed from the origin, of God as the Father of the Son in the Spirit who as such is freely self-determined to redeem and fulfill His creation. In other words, the problem is the absence of trinitarian "patrology" and the filling of this void with "natural theology." I want now to connect this diagnosis to Thomas's denial of God's self-causality.

It is of course true, first of all, that if the only concepts we have to work with are those of divine nature, and if, moreover, we are thus treating nature as a quasi-agent rather than as a set of capabilities available to things or persons, then the first dilemma that Thomas laid against the patrological alternative of divine self-causality *ad intra* would hold. How can "God" (taken as nature) be (as cause) before being (as effect)? But matters appear quite differently if we are thinking in terms of divine persons, hence singing with the Nicene Creed of "God from God, light from light, true God from true God, begotten, not made," where "begotten, not made" draws a distinction between causality as we creatures know it ("making") and a causality in God the Father ("begetting") that is as ineffable as it is eternal. In this frame of reference, trinitarian patrology says nothing other than that "God causes God," specifically, that the Father "causes" the Son and the Spirit, if we must put it so abstractly. As Thomas Hopko rightly maintains from the perspective of Eastern trinitarianism, "There is the Trinity—because there is the one Father."[33] Hopko "dares to say" this because in the Bible "the term 'God' as a proper name [i.e., as a predicate, not as a personal name] belongs exclusively to him whose Son, Word, and Image Jesus Christ is, the One whose Spirit is the Spirit of God."[34] As a consequence, those who are "baptized 'in the name of the Father and of the Son and of the Holy Spirit' offer Eucharistic sacrifice of praise to the Father through the Son in the Spirit,"[35] having as their prayer the Our Father, to which the Son invites and the Spirit empowers. The circulation is manifest

---

33. Thomas Hopko, "The Trinity in the Cappadocians," in *Christian Spirituality: Origins to the Twelfth Century*, ed. Bernard McGinn, John Meyendorff, and Jean Leclerq, World Spirituality 16 (New York: Crossroad, 1989), 265.

34. Ibid.

35. Ibid.

but somehow is initiated with the Father, a way of divine being that is unlike anything that we can know or imagine but only describe and adore.

Hopko draws especially on Gregory Nazianzen's *Orations*, where the great theologian had written that when "we look at the Godhead, or the First Cause, or the Monarchia [i.e., the Father], that which we conceive is One"; this is the *person* of "the Father, who is 'greater' than his Son and Spirit as the 'sole cause of the Godhead,' and 'the cause of the cause of all things,' that is, the Son." In Basil of Caesarea's words, which Hopko also cites, the "one special mark of His own person [*hypostasis*], His being Father and His deriving His person from no cause," tells how He is individually known.[36] It is not, then, the notion of causality that is misleading; what is decisive is the frame of reference by which the causality is determined. It is theological in the case of the Cappadocian fathers, cosmological in the case of protological simplicity. The emanation scheme, according to the Cappadocians, is shattered by the monarchy of the Father, even as the holy Triad is eternally completed in the return of the Son in the Spirit giving the Father the praise of His deity. T. F. Torrance has correspondingly urged in commending the Eastern doctrine that the eternal Father of the eternal Son *becomes* the Creator of a world that is by nature other than their own eternal life.[37] Likewise, John Meyendorff explains that creation "is an act of the will of God, and will is ontologically distinct from nature. By nature, the Father generates the Son—and this generation is beyond time—but creation occurs through the will of God, which means that God remains absolutely free to create and not to create, and remains transcendent to the world after creating it. The absence of a distinction between the nature of God and the will of God was common to Origen and Arius. To establish this distinction constitutes the main argument of Athanasius,"[38] which was thus refined by the Cappadocians as the nature-person distinction. Thus we have a line of theological thought stretching from Athanasius through the Cappadocians that vindicates the freedom of God's self-determination in relation to creatures by anchoring it in the mystery of God's eternal being in becoming God from God in God for God. Or, what is the same, that act of God's being is the Father's generating of the Son and breathing of the Spirit, who returns the Son to the Father in the praise of His deity.

If this patrological account illuminates, must we not attribute the erroneous tendency that neglects the strong trinitarian distinction between nature and

36. Ibid.

37. T. F. Torrance, *The Trinitarian Faith: The Evangelical Theology of the Ancient Catholic Church* (Edinburgh: T&T Clark, 1993), 105–9.

38. John Meyendorff, *Byzantine Theology: Historical Trends and Doctrinal Themes* (New York: Fordham University Press, 1979), 130.

person and consequently treats nature as something real with a kind of agency (rather than as a mere set of characteristic possibilities by which we sort out entities) not only to Thomas but also to the entire Western tradition? Gunton called this predilection the "modalist tendency" of the Western tradition.[39] That searching question will take us back to Augustine in the next chapter.

The Trajectory of Protological Simplicity

For the remainder of this chapter, I wish to make two further points regarding the metaphysics of divine simplicity. The first is that the Christian revision of the doctrine as we have seen from Thomas is strained; considered on its own terms, the protological doctrine has an entelechy that moves in another direction entirely. This entelechy is, I submit, well captured in the contemporary case for *philosophia perennis* made by the Sufi Muslim thinker Seyyed Hossein Nasr. In tandem with this, the second point will be to challenge the increasingly widespread narrative of a "fall" from Thomas willy-nilly into contemporary nihilism, what Daniel Horan calls the "Scotus story."[40] I will argue to the contrary that the weaknesses linked above to Thomas's cosmological rather than patrological account of divine causality can be precisely identified and critiqued with the aid of the Subtle Doctor's so-called formal distinction. What motivates Scotus in positing the "formal distinction," as we will see, is something parallel to, if not inspired by, the trinitarian distinction of the persons that does not divide the essence. Moreover, Scotus saw in Thomas's cosmological account of the First Cause an inadvertent naturalism (the entelechy, I am saying, of protological simplicity) that compromised the biblical God's freedom. The introduction of the formal distinction enabled modal accounts to make intelligible God's free decision in creation. The nature-person distinction and the intelligibility of God's choice are matters that run in theological parallel, and just so serve to indicate the differing trajectories toward return to origin on the one side and advance to the eschaton on the other.

Bear in mind several qualifications, however, in what follows. First, this critique concerns not Thomas's entirely orthodox intention to articulate Burrell's "difference" but rather the adequacy of his conceptual articulation of this distinction to continue on, christologically, to the true union of the different

39. Colin Gunton, "Augustine, the Trinity and the Theological Crisis of the West," *Scottish Journal of Theology* 43, no. 1 (February 1990): 33–58.

40. Daniel P. Horan, *Postmodernity and Univocity: A Critical Account of Radical Orthodoxy and John Duns Scotus* (Minneapolis: Fortress, 2014).

natures. Second, the derivation of a *rule* of divine simplicity—that is, as a semantic qualification of the kataphatic language concerning the gospel's God, by the negative qualifier "infinite," as Scotus argues,[41] rather than the kataphatic claim to metaphysical insight, *actus purus*—is arguably more adequate to the proper apophatic concern of Thomas himself. That concern is to indicate the incomparability of God as the singularity, irreducible in being to all that He creates as other than Himself. God is this "one" as the qualitative infinite, "unbounded" in being, free in holiness to love wisely, the agency of the Father in the Son by the Spirit.

Yet there is a sense, let me note, in which the rule theory of simplicity in critical dogmatics for which this book argues, with occasional assistance from Scotus, does not have a dog in the fight between these rivals in natural theology. These medieval theologians are alike competing in the arena of "natural theology," where the prize is a rational foundation for supernatural theology, an endeavor that I decline in favor of a revealed theology at work interpreting "nature" as the creation of God destined in Christ for fulfillment in the Spirit. That said, it is nevertheless worth noting here that a path little taken in philosophical theology can be traced from Scotus to Leibniz, in which modal arguments usefully illuminate divine action. That is, if used by *revealed* theology, hence a posteriori, modal argument not only can avoid compromising the genuine transcendence of the one true God but also can exposit it as a capacity for His creation rather than as some ontological allergy to it.[42]

But we turn now to the entelechy of the classical metaphysics of divine simplicity. Historian Adam Drozdek, in a helpful study, *Greek Philosophers as Theologians: The Divine* Arche,[43] has traced the origins of the metaphysical doctrine of simplicity to the pre-Socratic philosophers Anaximander, Xenophon, and Parmenides (52), united in their quest for the *archē* or *principium* of the cosmic order. This quest is not idle curiosity. Nor is it pure science. It is motivated—theologically. It is a quest theologically to be delivered by rational insight from the poets with their unseemly myths of capricious and immoral gods. There is, moreover, a progression through these figures in the direction of Plato and his immaterial—that is to say, mental—conception of the divine as the Good and then on to Plotinus's conception of the One.

41. What is infinite cannot be exceeded; hence God is not composed of parts. See Richard Cross, *Duns Scotus on God*, Ashgate Studies in the History of Philosophical Theology (Burlington, VT: Ashgate, 2005), 99.

42. Paul R. Hinlicky, "Leibniz and the Theology of the Beloved Community," *Pro Ecclesia* 21, no. 1 (2012): 25–50.

43. Adam Drozdek, *Greek Philosophers as Theologians: The Divine* Arche (Burlington, VT: Ashgate, 2007). Henceforth, references to this work are followed by page numbers in parentheses in the main text.

The line begins with Anaximander's query into the attributes that make the divine divine, "extracting the essence of immortality [from the myths of the gods], which is infinity" (8). A "process of abstraction leads to the concept of infinity"—the *Apeiron*. The *Apeiron* is the *archē* of what exists, "its ground and substratum from which everything originates and into which everything returns," so that *Apeiron* is as readily translated as the Chaos as the Infinite. In any event, while everything else is generated and in time perishes, the *Apeiron* "always was and will be." *Der zeitliche Ursprung* of the cosmogonic myths becomes *der zeitlose Grund* in early philosophical theology. Divine because it is immortal and indestructible, the *Apeiron* is everlasting, ageless, and all-encompassing. It is the matrix of the universe (9). The "best description" of it "is in its privative name: something with no limit." But this description, "paradoxically," has the "advantage of predicating something positive of the *arche* without committing" to any particular view of its nature (11), as it is for us a chaos. That optical illusion of declaring the really real by a privative notion is precisely the virtue of protological simplicity.

Xenophanes is known for his "sharp criticism of the anthropomorphism of traditional religion" (15), though it would be erroneous to think that this criticism makes him a foe of the gods and their myths. Rather, what he sought was the separation of the domains of natural science and theology from their confused intermingling in the myths (17). Science studies the many of natural phenomena, theology the one unlike the many (17). There is "one God, greatest among gods and men, similar to mortals neither in form nor in thought," who "sees as a whole, thinks as a whole, and hears as whole, but without any effort he shakes everything with his mind" in an act of creative intuition anticipating later doctrines of God's eternal now; "he always remains in the same [place], not moving and it is unbecoming that he move to various [places] at various times" (17–18). Immovable, God moves all things as the cause of cosmic motion (19). Like Plato's Demiurge, the One of Xenophanes is a rational being who molds the world purposively by his creative intuition of things (20). As unmovable, the One is immutable. "God would not move since this would signify the presence of an imperfection in God; by changing place, God would move toward a place from which he is absent, and so he would satisfy the need of finding himself where he currently is not" (20). We cannot say who the one God is, since positive knowledge is of an empirical character and pertains to the many. We know that God is the unknown One by the path of negation (23), but this allows us to glimpse, as paradoxically as in Anaximander, the One God behind the gods. The thought here will become important shortly when we turn to Nasr, for in this thought of God beyond the gods Xenophanes "represents a vision which, in a more or less clear form, can be found in many ancient thinkers. . . . Considering the gods as manifestations of God, he does not completely reject traditional religion, but points to its incompleteness" (25).

The poverty of negative theology, however, leads Parmenides to the need for revelation. "By our own strength, we cannot see Being directly, we cannot tread the way of truth. It is a special privilege granted by the goddess to only a few" (43)—though Parmenides was willing to share his revelation with others. As in Xenophanes, the fact that all our knowledge is sensory and captive to the many phenomena implies that to think the One, to think Being itself and as such, we would have to rely purely on thought. But for mortal beings, that "is possible only through the divine and seldom bestowed illumination that can actualize it" (44). The two domains of scientific and theological inquiry in Xenophanes become in Parmenides the realms of appearance and Being, humanity being found in bondage to appearances. Nevertheless, the goddess's revelation of Being can tap into a latent capacity in humanity—*logos*. "*Logos* is the divine element in man because the goddess uses it to expound the way of truth," even though this divine element "is dormant in man, and it takes divine intervention to unearth it," captured as it is by the manifold of sensory phenomena; the mind is indeed "strangled" by its entanglement in the veil of appearances, but awakened by illumination, "man can stand face-to-face with Being, one, indivisible, and eternal" (46).

Following what preceded him in Anaximander and Xenophanes, Parmenides says about this Being that it is "whole, continuous, and unmoved, and thus immutable, . . . without beginning and without end, and yet neither was it nor will it be since it is now, all together" (48). An "extratemporal entity" that "exists in an eternal now," Being exists outside of time but—and this is crucial—within the "limits of its transcendent existence" (48), its perfection vis-à-vis the realm of appearances. So mutually delimited, the two domains together form a system, an eternal cosmos. The two are held apart in each one's own place of perfection or imperfection by *ananke* (necessity): "The hold of *Ananke* makes certain that whole, immutable, and continuous Being necessarily has to be within limits," and indeed, the establishment and sustenance of these limits *is* the cosmic order, the justice of things (49). Being itself is paradoxically the infinite that is limited by its necessary place in the cosmic system as the perfect and necessary being that substantiates the realm of appearances. This is "divinity in pure form, the essence of divinity abstracted from the world of the gods of mythology . . . for Parmenides, Being is God" (50), and the gods of the myths—paradigmatically, the goddess of his revelation—have been correspondingly demoted to angels, "ways of God's revealing himself to the mortals" (51). Yet there remains one anthropomorphic attribution in Parmenides's conception of Being: "Being itself must be intelligent and conscious" (51).

Drozdek concludes this discussion tracing the origin of the metaphysics of divine simplicity in a line that runs from Anaximander through Xenophanes to Parmenides by pointing forward through Anaxagoras's conception of Divine Mind and Plato's portrait in the *Timaeus* of the Demiurge onto its culmination in Plotinus, "in particular to his doctrine of the One 'which is not in place nor is it in time' (*Enneads* 6.9.3)" (52)—the timelessly self-identical One who is the *archē* and *telos* of the cosmos ordered as a great chain of being. If Drozdek thus provides the historical origin of the metaphysics of divine simplicity, the learned, elegant, and humane synthesis by Seyyed Hossein Nasr in his Gifford Lectures, published as *Knowledge and the Sacred*,[44] sets forth such a metaphysics of protological simplicity in a contemporary statement. His opening salvo, the "desacralization of knowledge," tells of the rise of Promethean humanity, especially in the modern West, where knowledge of the divine as *scientia sacra* has been radically severed from knowledge of the world and systematically devalued in the massive inversion of values that is contemporary secularism. The melancholy result is that the cosmos no longer hangs together as a theophany for modern people; it has become for them a treasure trove of disposable resources. This modern forgetfulness of Being cannot long endure; it defies perilously the way the cosmos really is. Yet, just because of the way the cosmos really is, according to *philosophia perennis*, rediscoveries of sacred tradition are inevitably occurring across the contemporary globe as humanity awakes to the horrors of the desacralization of the cosmos and the corresponding "deification of history" in the modern period.

By "tradition," Nasr means the traditions, all of them, from Hinduism and Shintoism through Buddhism on to the Abrahamic religions. All of these are the varied, culturally fitting manifestations of the primal revelation, carried on as *prisca theologia*. The primal revelation, passed on as particular theological traditions, serves to anchor the cosmic order in knowledge of the One, so that the multiplicity of appearances in the realm of becoming is known as a multiplicity of sacred forms, emanating from the divine source to compose the beautiful mosaic of cosmic order. As such, moreover, the varied traditions check and balance one another's naive claims to absoluteness and in their very diversity of ways to cultural synthesis are forced mutually to point away

44. Seyyed Hossein Nasr, *Knowledge and the Sacred* (Albany: State University of New York Press, 1989). I am grateful to theologian Larry Rinehart and to my former colleague Caner Dagli for calling the *philosophia perennis* to my attention. See Larry Rinehart, "Confessions of a Lutheran Perennialist," *Lutheran Forum* 45, no. 3 (2011): 58–61; Rinehart, *Esse & Evangel: Metaphysical Order in Evangelical Doctrine* (North Charleston, SC: CreateSpace, 2015).

from themselves to the One as to the common origin and goal of all. Such "principial" (= *principium, archē*) "knowledge" of the sacred is the "gnosis" that is salutary, that brings "deliverance." The following lengthy quotation brings Nasr's case for "sacred knowledge" together in a comparatively succinct statement.

> The Principle is Reality in contrast to all that appears as real but which is not reality in the ultimate sense. The Principle is the Absolute compared to which all is relative. It is Infinite while all else is finite. The Principle is One and Unique while manifestation is multiplicity. It is the Supreme Substance compared to which all else is accident. It is the Essence to which things are juxtaposed as form. It is at once Being and Beyond Being while the order of multiplicity is comprised of existents. It alone *is* while all else becomes, for it alone is eternal in the ultimate sense while all that is externalized partakes of change. It is the Origin but also the End, the alpha and the omega. It is emptiness if the world is envisaged as fullness and Fullness if the relative is perceived in the light of its ontological poverty and essential nothingness. These are all manners of speaking of the Ultimate Reality which can be known but not by man as such. It can only be known through the sun of the Divine Self residing at the center of the human soul. But all these ways . . . always terminate in the Ineffable and in that silence which is the "reflection" or "shadow" of the nonmanifested aspect of the Principle on the plane of manifestation.[45]

The passage barely calls for further comment. What was begun in the pre-Socratics finds here a fresh, contemporary statement. It is the protological metaphysics of divine simplicity speaking in its own voice for our times.

In the light of all that has preceded in this chapter, I want now only briefly to explicate two, as it seems to me, problematic implications of Nasr's case. One is the analysis Nasr makes of the West's idolatrous deification of history as the peculiar product of the desacralization of knowledge, in the background of which stands the peculiarly Christian doctrine of the incarnation—a doctrine suspect, to begin with, in the perspective of the protological metaphysics of divine simplicity. "The deification of the historical process in secular terms," Nasr writes, "has taken place in the modern world not only because the metaphysical teachings concerning time and [timeless] eternity have been forgotten as a result of the desacralization of both knowledge and the world but also . . . as a result of the particular emphasis of Christianity upon history which is not to be found in other traditions."[46] There is a large element of truth in this charge; Marxism above all is *the* Christian heresy of modernity,

---

45. Nasr, *Knowledge and the Sacred*, 133–34.
46. Ibid., 233.

with liberalism's "manifest destiny" not far behind.[47] And yet equally there is a failure here to contend with the fact that the incarnation—central, not peripheral, to Christianity—simply does militate against the protological metaphysics of divine simplicity in just the ways that Nasr laments. And to the extent that this is true, Christianity is not one of the traditions of timelessly primal revelation and cosmos-piety. It is instead from the origin (Gen. 12:1–3) an evangelical mission bringing blessing to the nations. It originates in a historically particular revelation that brings an eschatological piety and a corresponding ethic of discipleship.

It is not an accident, in this connection, that in keeping with Neoplatonic emanationism, Nasr singles out the correlative doctrine of *creatio ex nihilo* as demonstrating the "inadequacy of the theological formulations [of the Abrahamic religions] in themselves and without the aid of the sapiential doctrines"[48]—that is, without the sacred "gnosis" of the primal revelation of the One that deabsolutizes the naive claims of the varied traditions to truth in history. For primal revelation, the "eternal now," apprehended in the gift of illumination, tells not of a creation in time or the creation of time but rather of a timeless creation-and-revelation of the One in the many. Thomas, as we recall, resisted the emanationism implicit in his sources because of his dogmatic commitment to the Catholic faith, with its strong distinction of Creator and creature, even though, as Nasr sees, the emanationist scheme is the natural entelechy of the protological metaphysics of divine simplicity. According to *scientia sacra*, Nasr writes, "*ex nihilo* does not mean literally from nothing but rather from 'possibilities' in the principial order which, to quote Ibn 'Arabi, have not yet 'smelled the perfume of existence' and which are existentiated and externalized upon the terrestrial plane from a preexistent state or even states. Creation in this sense is always a descent"[49]—the key word here being "always."

Yet to this "always" of eternal creation as emanation, Thomas's Catholic faith opposed the *epaphax*: "In the beginning, God created"; "In the fullness of time, God sent forth His Son"; "And He who sits upon the throne declared, Behold! I make all things new!" Thus Nasr's lamentable "deification of history" is christologically promised in the sense that the really distinct Creator and creature become united socially in a communion of love that is the eschaton of history taken as *creatio continua*. The *epaphax* redeems time, not *from* time; it goes forward to a *novum*, not backward to an origin. The

47. Hinlicky, *Luther and the Beloved Community*, 301–57.
48. Nasr, *Knowledge and the Sacred*, 232.
49. Ibid.

truth of this promised "deification" of the creature is the fulfillment that is the coming of the Beloved Community, God's future, to the earth upon which the cross of Jesus stood.

Likewise in keeping with Neoplatonic emanationism is the argument that Nasr brings to bear against the modern theory of the evolution of natural forms and the corresponding "Darwinization of theology." "The power of creation," Nasr writes, "belongs to the creating Principle alone which is pure actuality itself. What evolution does is to deify the historical process not only by considering it as the ultimately real but also by transferring the power of *creatio ex nihilo* from the transcendent Divinity to it."[50] Given his critique of *creatio ex nihilo*, as we just witnessed, it is hard on the face of it to know what to make of this criticism of evolutionary theory in the name of *creatio ex nihilo*. Natural selection, in any case, cannot and does not claim the power of *creatio ex nihilo* but only accounts for the immanent transformation of life forms on the materialist principle *ex nihilo nihil fit*. What Nasr really has in mind, then, surfaces in the following statement: "Also, from the metaphysical and cosmological points of view, form is the imprint of an archetype and divine possibility and not an accident of a material congregate. . . . Forms of living beings have a qualitative reality which cannot evolve from any other form unless that form were also present 'somewhere,'"[51] namely, in the divine Mind from which the archetype emanates to "existentiate." The immanent mutation of forms posited in evolutionary theory, then, obscures perception of the theophanous reality of the cosmos, the transparency of living forms to ideas emanating from the mind of God to form the formless matter into the beautiful mosaic of cosmic order. The material mutation of forms according to evolution, then, undermines in principle the claim of a perennial cosmic order, though per hypothesis it can do this only as illusion and error that cannot be sustained in the teeth of reality. In the interim, however, this Darwinian error of modern secularism makes something beautiful into what is ugly, red in tooth and claw; it makes something that is transparent to beauty dark and ugly, the lawless law of the jungle.

To be sure, it is still somewhat unusual to find dogmatically Christian theologians critically embracing natural evolution as the *fit* mechanism of God's *creatio continua*,[52] but natural evolution can be theologically interpreted,

50. Ibid., 236.
51. Ibid.
52. George L. Murphy, *The Cosmos in the Light of the Cross* (Harrisburg, PA: Trinity Press International, 2003). Contemporary biology is indeed incompatible with an immanent or natural teleology, and indeed progressed by overcoming Aristotle on just this point. But overcoming Aristotle and defeating the biblical doctrine of creation are not the same thing, especially when

as it seems to me, by the christological "deification" of history on the way to the coming of the Beloved Community. Be that as it may, we are given by this *Auseinandersetzung* with Nasr over evolution a neat segue to the final consideration of this chapter. For even our reliable guide into Thomisms past and present, Fergus Kerr, voices the current myth of a fall from the protological metaphysical tradition in Thomas's doctrine of simplicity, when Cajetan, contaminated by Scotism, "focused on the forms and essences of beings only, and not on the existence of all things as participation in the pure actuality which is God" (83). That is to allege that Scotus reverted to emanationism and substituted a Platonic ontology of essences for the existential act of being. According to his narrative, Scotus reverts from Thomas to Avicenna, making the divine into a quality that can be participated in with varying degrees of intensity rather than a pure act that created existences resemble in various concrete ways. But we have seen in Nasr how the actual entelechy of the protological doctrine of divine simplicity is emanationism. Thomas may have blocked this, or thought he had blocked it, by finding a place, indeed a priority, for existence over essence. Just this union of heterogeneous components, this composition, is what makes his synthesis unstable. The "Scotus story," accordingly, does not correspond to reality.

It may be that it also gets Thomas wrong. It is a much discussed question in contemporary studies whether and to what extent Neoplatonic forms of thought, including emanationism, survive in Thomas's vast and synthetic thought. Certainly the "analogy of being" (a doctrine of Thomism, not Thomas as such, as we will see) intends to state "the difference" between Creator and creature by regarding creatures not as semidivine ideas of God actualized in matter but rather as finite substances analogous to God in the mere act of their creaturely being. But the criticism that Scotus reverts to Platonism appears, once again, to find fault with an alleged "implication" of Scotus's thought that is actually created by superimposing on Scotus the metaphysical commitments of his accusers. Taken on his own terms, Scotus's reprioritization of possibility over actuality by deriving simplicity from divine infinity aims to explicate the freedom of God's decision in creation against what he regards as Thomas's thinly veiled ambiguity on the eternity of the world that would be a natural, if not necessary, implication of the timelessly eternal act of God's being. Scotus can hardly be faulted to the extent that Thomas's account, despite reiterated Christian intentions, seems (recall Gunton's "misreading" on omnicausality) to

---

we take creation as eschatological from the origin. In that case, the theology of creation is an interpretation of natural evolution, which in its insight into emergent properties is as such open to a variety of metaphysical or theological interpretations. Interpretation is also cognition. See Hinlicky, *Beloved Community*, 31–34, 61–72.

necessitate thinking an eternal act of creation by a timelessly generative divine nature! Between Thomas and Scotus, dare I venture, the medieval tradition of natural theology comes upon the horns of a dilemma under the *shared* axiom of protological simplicity. If infinite, the One's freedom is unbounded, a *deus exlex*. If pure actuality, the One's will is necessary, *natura naturans*. Far be it from me—anti-Kantian extraordinaire—to call this standoff "an antinomy of pure reason"!

There are exceedingly difficult questions involved here that Richard Cross and, more recently, Daniel Horan have sorted out, though consideration of them in detail would draw us far too deeply into the intricacies of medieval philosophy than is needed for the present purpose of distinguishing the natural trajectory of protological simplicity from a rule version for Christian theological discourse in its eschatological comportment. Suffice it to say in summary of Cross and Horan that, in the first place, Scotus intends his doctrine of univocity as a logical and semantical, not ontological, explication.[53] It is simply the requirement that we use concepts uniformly, in the same sense, also when classifying very different things. Moreover, conceptual distinctions as such are nothing real in extramental reality but rather are inventions constructed for human convenience to relate things or persons from a specific perspective and interest for a specific purpose or audience. Real distinctions in extramental reality, moreover, can be discovered and learned only by the univocal application of concepts. Such real difference is obscured by a priori ontological analogicity that focuses always on similarity; but real difference is noticed and clarified by the consistent, nonequivocating application of concepts. When read through Thomist analogical eyes, then, Scotus's claim that concepts—including the "vicious abstraction" that is the concept of being—are commonly applicable to realities as really different as humanity and God seems to make the ontological claim that both creature and Creator

---

53. See further the "Symposium on Freedom and Creation," featuring a sharp exchange between David Burrell and Richard Cross, in *Faith and Philosophy* 25, no. 2 (April 2008): 177–212. Burrell argues here that univocity "cannot but elide the axial 'distinction' of creator from creatures" (183). To this Cross replies that semantic univocity does not entail univocity of being, since concepts are indeed abstractions (191); Burrell's Thomist fear of ontotheological idolatry in Scotus is predicated on a conceptual realism that Scotus does not share (192). According to the present proposal, I need not take sides in this medieval debate, since I am arguing that natural theology is contextually impossible in the ways that either Thomas or Scotus imagined, with the result that we today see that the unity of God's being is the object of revealed faith, not its philosophical presupposition. Moreover, the nominalism that I am articulating in denying that the essences are anything real except as concepts useful to humans for navigation in the flux of becoming is, I am claiming, theologically warranted by strong trinitarian personalism, where the one divine essence is nothing other than the ways in which the Father, the Son, and the Holy Spirit are, as persons in community, the one true God.

are instances of something really real—Being as such, as though Being as such were for Scotus not only extramental reality but the really real as such rather than a vicious abstraction. Scotus, Cross and Horan insist, makes no such ontological claim. He claims only that creature and Creator can logically fall under the same concept, though undoubtedly in dramatically different ways that become luminous just because the same concept is univocally applied. There is thus a certain imperialism in this Thomist accusation, as if the idiom of Thomism were not just "one way" among others to articulate Christian claims to truth, as if this "one way" did not also face aporias, conundrums, and vulnerabilities of its own.

In the second place, as already intimated, Scotus finds inadequate the inherited logical distinction between distinctions in extramental reality and conceptual distinctions made in the mind only. It is inadequate for a specifically Christian theological reason: it fails to articulate theologically the difference *and relation* between Creator and creature and thus cannot make lucid creation *as* the free decision of God to be for His creature who is infinitely other than God. Here I will employ a few pertinent theological illustrations of Scotus's invention of yet a third logical way of making distinctions. A real distinction in extramental reality is the difference between the creature, whose existence is given, and the Creator, whose existence is infinitely giving—*esse Deum dare.* We discover this difference and thus distinguish God and humanity in extramental reality just because we employ the concept of existence, meaning "being there," univocally. God the Giver is there for creatures infinitely, omnitemporal and omnipresent, and so unilaterally. Creatures, by contrast, are somewhere finitely as localized recipients of God the Giver's *creatio continua.* What it would mean ontologically to explicate these different ways of being is a question of another order, but that explication cannot even get off the ground until the difference is noticed and clarified. It is noticed and clarified by univocity.

Let us take another example. The difference between the Lord's Supper as eucharistic offering of praise and as testament for us of Christ's self-donation is a conceptual distinction; it is made in our minds to clarify the senses in which the Lord's Supper is unification with Christ's praise of the Father in the Spirit and unification by the Spirit with Christ's offering for us. But in extramental reality the Lord's Supper is one and the same *koinōnia* in the body and blood of the Lord. We cannot in reality separate these two senses of one and the same thing. If we forget that this is a conceptual distinction, however, we must separate the two senses and turn them against each other, as if only one or the other sense is true to the extramental reality or as if the extramental thing were one of these two but not the other. But what if there is something in the extramental reality of the Lord's Supper itself that justifies a conceptual distinction, yet not an existential separation? That possibility of interpretation could be explicated by Scotus's formal distinction—that is, a merely conceptual distinction that has some basis in extramental reality. Again, *what* this basis would be is a question of another order. But the question cannot launch inquiry until it is rightly framed.

Neither the way of real distinction nor of conceptual distinction seems sufficient for articulating the simplicity of God, if that is taken according to the eschatological reading of Zechariah 14:9 as His free self-determination from the origin to redeem and fulfill His creation, the mystery hidden from the ages but now made known in Christ (Rom. 16:25–27; Eph. 1:4–5). Certainly the real distinction separates the giving being of God and the given being of creation into two natures; but just so, it does not *eo ipso* unify them again christologically. Just as certainly, a conceptual distinction connects the notion "creature" to the really different notion "Creator" by an analogy of imperfect to perfect being. But is such a conceptual connection by way of natural similitude adequate to articulate the God of the gospel, who is really present effecting all things in the divine freedom that loves wisely in the folly of Christ crucified—from the day of the origin on to the day of the resurrection?

A third kind of distinction, the formal distinction, holds that there is an inseparable relation in extramental reality between conceptually distinct things. And this serves to make intelligible Christian claims about the unification of the Creator and creature, the christological deification of history, and the prospect in the Spirit of holy secularity on the way to the coming of the Beloved Community. The distinction between nature and person in the Trinity, between the humanity and deity of the incarnate Son, between the bread and wine and the body and blood of the crucified and risen Lord in His Supper may all be grasped by Scotus's "formal distinction"—that is, a distinction that does not separate in reality but conceptually clarifies ontologically internal relations. When we apply this idea of a formal distinction, furthermore, to the question on which theistic attempts to domesticate protological simplicity founder—Spinoza's taunt concerning what imperfection could have moved the perfect being to commence creating, the alternative being the eternal creation of the *natura naturans*—we gain illumination regarding the freedom of God's choice of this world from its origin as site of a coming redemption and fulfillment. We can, in other words, distinguish conceptually this world from all other possible worlds in order to understand this one, on which the cross of Jesus stood, as the one for which God freely and at great cost determined Himself in an eternity that is capable of time. In that case, the rule of divine simplicity is the instruction: so speak of the Father and the Son and the Holy

Spirit as this One and Only who is freely self-determined to redeem and fulfill this creation, in which I write and you read these words.

EXCURSUS: TRUE GNOSIS
IN CLEMENT OF ALEXANDRIA

Seyyed Hossein Nasr lifted up Clement of Alexandria, who flourished as the leader of the catechetical school in Alexandria at the turn of the third century, for seeing "Christianity as a way to wisdom." Indeed, in the Christian tradition "none is more important" than Clement in this connection. In particular what attracts Nasr to Clement is that he fought gnosticism, that "knowledge, falsely so-called" that had been battled by Irenaeus before him, on behalf of a true gnosis, Nasr's *scientia sacra*, the *philosophia perennis*. Clement's gnosis was an "esoteric knowledge" abiding "in the spirits of men" and "handed down to them orally and secretly from the apostles and ultimately from Christ himself"; it was a gnosis "that implied knowledge of God and the angelic world, science of the spiritual significance of sacred Scripture, and the attainment of total certitude."[54] It is significant, Nasr urges, "as far as the later history of the Christian tradition and the place of gnosis in it is concerned that he was not canonized as a saint and that the regularity of transmission of sacred knowledge did not continue for long."[55] The oral chain of *prisca theologia*, holy tradition of primal revelation, as we have seen previously, is the hermeneutical key to the reading of sacred Scripture; Clement, so Nasr claims, knew and practiced this, but after him it was largely lost. In this excursus I take up Nasr's claim about Clement in order sharply to dispute it. The kind of gnosis that Clement advocates, as we will see in chapter 3, is profoundly shaped instead by Paul's battle in 1 Corinthians against the "gnosticism" that Nasr commends.

It is a question of what it really means to know that "God is one" (1 Cor. 8:4) in the light of the gospel, the foolish announcement of the Messiah's cross (1 Cor. 1:18) that promises His resurrection (1 Cor. 15:12–19) to others who entrust themselves to Him as a gift. If God is one as Father in, through, and with the "one Lord Jesus Christ," then God is known in loving God (1 Cor. 8:3) in the love with which God has loved the world in Christ, not counting their trespasses. Divine simplicity, then, may not be confused with the insight of the "natural" mind's ascent to the timelessly ineffable and

54. Nasr, *Knowledge and the Sacred*, 17.
55. Ibid.

indivisible (1 Cor. 2:14–16). Rather, divine simplicity must be thought as the love that "never ends" (1 Cor. 13:8), having begun in the origin, reached into the fallen creation at the cross, and now awaiting resurrection to life eternal. In Clement we have an instance of such Pauline knowledge of God that I call not *philosophia perennis* or *scientia sacra* but rather "critical dogmatics."[56] What we learn from Clement is not the esoteric mystery of primal revelation but rather the exoteric mystery (1 Cor. 4:1) of divine love for humanity, even in its sinful corruption and decay. And in the divine love for humanity we will find that better doctrine of divine simplicity, which requires us to see the Father's appeal through the Son in the Spirit as the one true self-expression of the eternal God, who is antecedently the Beloved Community and thus does and can promise Himself to us all (1 Cor. 15:28).

Sitz im Leben

It is indeed the case that we meet a different kind of orthodox Christian response to the challenge of gnosticism than what may be seen in Irenaeus.[57] Much of Clement's writing is devoted to the refutation of the teachings of Marcion, Basilides, and Valentinus. The latter two were the philosophical leaders of the most important, mature gnostic systems. They had acquired a degree of philosophical respectability by assimilating elements of Platonism. We can well imagine that in the cosmopolitan climate of Alexandria, where a large Hellenistic Jewish community had long existed and where Philo's pioneering attempt to reconcile Athens and Jerusalem had been made a century and a half before, gnosticism of various sorts flourished. Perhaps it even predominated over orthodox, catholic Christianity of the kind represented by Irenaeus. In this context, the status of being a "gnostic"—one who truly knows—might be something regarded as highly desirable. Hans Lietzmann's characterization is worth citing in full:

> By [Clement's] time, the great Gnostics had already passed away, but their schools remained, and influenced both Christians and pagans. Those who pursued philosophical inquiries held Plato to be the most important force. . . . Clement felt himself at home in a world of this kind; he wrote for it, and enjoyed a wide public, because he was already one of themselves, and had no need to struggle for recognition as was the case, e.g., with Justin and his fellow apologists. In Alexandria, mental life and culture had developed more rapidly than elsewhere,

56. Hinlicky, *Beloved Community*, 3–55.
57. Hinlicky, *Divine Complexity*, 137–58.

a fact which signified a better pathway for Christianity. Clement was a philosopher and a Gnostic, a philosopher at the beginning, a Gnostic at the end, but both as a Christian: and he tried to prove to the world that it was in this very combination that the solution of its problems was to be found; at the same time it afforded complete insight into the apparently simple and broadly outlined doctrines of the church catholic. He expressed these opinions to his reader in a vocabulary and a style expected of a writer of *belles-lettres*. . . . [Clement] was the first Christian writer whom the literary world was compelled to recognize.[58]

As was the case with Irenaeus, Clement's chief opponents were in fact those whom we today call "gnostics." Unlike Irenaeus, however, Clement himself is not dominated by his conflict with gnosticism. He is rather to be understood chiefly as an evangelist to the Greek intelligentsia. In good Pauline fashion, Clement was willing to become a "gnostic to the gnostics" in order to win them for Christ.

Rather than simply contradict and oppose the gnostics, as did Irenaeus, with the clear and categorical alternative of the biblical history of salvation, Clement took over their own ideal image and spoke of the catholic Christian as the "true gnostic." This is a strategy of immanent argumentation or, perhaps, co-optation. One tries to convince the opponent that she misunderstands her own ideal, and that the truth of that ideal is rather to be found in one's own position. In the process, of course, the very ideal of knowledge, "gnosis," is transformed. Clement, in fact, pioneered the understanding of Christian theology as "faith seeking understanding," of theology as faith's knowledge of God. When he speaks of the true gnostic, he means the "true intellectual," not the mystagogue who possesses esoteric or occult knowledge. He is talking about theological existence, the life of the mind captivated by the gospel of Christ, trained by the Logos, intellectually contemplating the God who had revealed Himself in Christ. As Lietzmann put it, "As far as content goes, gnosis is nothing else than knowledge of God and, in Clement, has nothing to do with the fantastic speculations of curiosity trying to find out details about all the secrets of the macrocosm or the microcosm."[59]

Despite Clement's rhetoric, there can be no doubt that Clement really did oppose gnosticism substantively and theologically. Clement sharply "attacked the essential [gnostic] distinction between psychics who are only acquainted with faith, and pneumatics who possess knowledge. All baptized Christians possess the Holy Spirit."[60] Likewise, Clement speaks lovingly of the visible,

---

58. Hans Lietzmann, *A History of the Early Church*, trans. Bertram Lee Woolf (New York: World Publishing, 1961), 2:292.

59. Ibid.

60. Ibid., 2:291. See Clement, *Stromata* 1.6, drawing on Paul's doctrine of justification by faith.

sacramental church as the "mother" of believers,[61] where we find the Word of God (*Paed.* 1.6 [220]). She is the bride of Christ and the "Helper of our salvation . . . because she alone remains to all generations, rejoicing ever, subsisting as she does by the endurance of us believers, who are the members of Christ" (*Paed.* 1.6 [214]). Similarly, Clement upheld the "divine Scriptures" (*Protr.* 8 [194]). On all these decisive questions, Clement clearly sides with orthodox, catholic Christianity. What concretely, then, did Clement have in mind with this new ideal of the true Christian gnostic?

The True Gnostic

In antithesis to the determinism of the gnostic sects, Clement insisted that the human creature can, and indeed must, really change. Human "nature" is taken as the history of the human being with God, the concrete way of being human that each one becomes as person; the human being is a person before God and in relation to other persons concretely, in and through the communities in which his or her life is lived (1 Cor. 6:15–20; 15:33). It is not the case that some are by nature spirit and others are flesh—a gnostic version of double predestination in which the human being can only unfold or realize a predetermined nature. Rather, all of the biblical history of salvation bears witness to mutability, to the possibility, and indeed the saving necessity, of change (1 Cor. 15:51). Just as by Adam's sin the "truly noble freedom of those who lived as free citizens under heaven" was subjected to bondage, so also "if one of those serpents [i.e., the "brood of vipers" whom John denounced] even is willing to repent, and follows the Word, he becomes a man of God" (*Protr.* 1 [172]). To be a Christian is to have been thus changed: "We, too, are first-born sons, who are reared by God, who are the genuine friends of the First-born, who first of all other men attained to the knowledge of God, who first were wrenched away from our sins, first severed from the devil" (*Protr.* 9 [195]).

Clement at times makes the standard Platonic interpretation of the image of God to account for this possibility of human change, based on intellectual affinity to God. The human person can change because, in truth, the human mind is the created image of God, which was created in order to be made like God. "For the image of God is His Word, the genuine Son of Mind,

61. Citations of Clement are from Alexander Roberts and James Donaldson, eds., *The Ante-Nicene Fathers*, vol. 2, *Fathers of the Second Century: Hermas, Tatian, Athenagoras, Theophilus, and Clement of Alexandria* (repr., Peabody, MA: Hendrickson, 2004). I use the following abbreviations: Strom. (*Stromata = Miscellanies*); Protr. (*Protrepticus = Exhortation to the Heathen*); Paed. (*Paedagogus = Christ the Instructor*). The book and chapter citation will be followed by the page number in *ANF 2*.

the Divine Word, the archetypal light of light; and the image of the Word is the true man, the mind which is in man, who is therefore said to have been made 'in the image and likeness of God,' assimilated to the Divine Word" (*Protr.* 10 [199]). This intellectualist tendency in anthropology, inherited from Platonism, appears with greater or lesser force regularly in Greek Christian theology. But we must not be misled by the mere appearance of ideas that most educated people of this period in any case regarded as self-evident (compare Cicero's discussion of the image of God).[62] In any event, it is indeed the case that knowledge is a causal power; the event of information causes changes in the knower by its incorporation, as it were, into the mind's apparatus. That insight into insight as the vehicle of human change, and the importance of education (in Christian context, catechesis) is not somehow tainted philosophy; it was Clement's vocation as leader in Alexandria of a catechetical school.

In truth, the chief reason Clement provides for the possibility and necessity of human change is not the intellectual nature of humanity but rather God's philanthropy, God's special love for humanity manifest in the Logos. What does the Logos, the Creator's "instrument," desire? "To open the eyes of the blind, and unstop the ears of the deaf, and to lead the lame or the erring to righteousness, to exhibit God to the foolish, to put a stop to corruption, to conquer death, to reconcile disobedient children to their father. The instrument of God [= the Logos] loves mankind. . . . And the only advantage He reaps is, that we are saved" (*Protr.* 1 [172–73]). Thinking of the tender love of the Logos, Clement exclaims, "O surpassing love for man! Not as a teacher speaking to his pupils, not as a master to his domestics [servants], nor as God to men [!], but as a father, does the Lord gently admonish his children" (*Protr.* 9 [195]). Not as "God to men, but as a father"—not, that is, as divine nature to human nature, but as the Father of the Logos to the humanity being changed into children of God. Unchanged humanity is indeed in desperate need of this Logos of God, in whom the divine love is intelligibly communicated. "Sick, we truly stand in need of the Savior; having wandered, of one to guide us; blind, of one to lead us to the light; thirsty, 'of the fountain of life, of which whosoever partakes, shall no longer thirst'; dead, we need life; sheep, we need a shepherd; we who are children need a tutor, while universal humanity stands in need of Jesus" (*Paed.* 1.9 [230]).

With such doxological outbursts, Clement frequently breaks into song about this divine love for humanity, made manifest supremely in the incarnation of

---

62. Cicero, *The Nature of the Gods*, trans. Horace C. P. McGregor (Harmondsworth, UK: Penguin, 1972).

the Logos. Citing Philippians 2, Clement wonders at the Logos, "the merciful God, exerting Himself to save man" (*Protr.* 1 [174]), and bows before His cross: "Generous, therefore, is He who gives for us the greatest of all gifts, His own life; and beneficent exceedingly, and loving to men, in that, when He might have been Lord, He wished to be a brother to man; and so good was He that He died for us" (*Paed.* 1.9 [231]). On the basis of this redeeming love of God in the Logos incarnate for His own alienated and disgraced creature, Clement draws the same anti-gnostic theological conclusion as had Irenaeus about the goodness of all created being: "Nothing exists, the cause of whose existence is not supplied by God. Nothing, then, is hated by God, nor yet by the Word. For both are one—that is, God" (*Paed.* 1.8 [225]). Humanity can and must change because God in Christ changes not the nature, which is good albeit subject to corruption, but the mutable person who has fallen under the power of sin: "The Lord ministers all good and all help, both as man and as God: as God, forgiving our sins; and as man, training us not to sin. Man is therefore justly dear to God, since he is His workmanship. The other works of creation He made by the word of command alone, but man He framed by Himself, by His own hand, and breathed into him what was peculiar to Himself" (*Paed.* 1.3 [210]). Human beings can change because they are the unfinished work and creatures of God, the special objects of redeeming love.

So, second, when Clement speaks of the Christian as the "true gnostic," he simply points to the human being who was created in order to know God, to come to the knowledge of God. "Love for God expresses itself also in the effort to know him more and more fully. The knowledge of God is an end in itself not a mere means to a farther end."[63] "There was," Clement writes, "an innate original communion between men and heaven, obscured through ignorance" caused by sin, the demons, and idolatry; these powers "have turned man, a creature of heavenly origin, away from the heavenly life" (*Protr.* 2 [178]) to worshiping the forces of nature or, more philosophically, to deifying ideals abstracted from nature, or the mythical accounts of nature. But in reality, humankind has been so "constituted by nature, so as to have fellowship with God": "Placing our finger on what is man's peculiar and distinguishing characteristic above other creatures, we invite him—born, as he is, for the contemplation of heaven, and being, as he is, a truly heavenly plant—to the knowledge of God" (*Protr.* 10 [200]). It is the knowledge of God that makes true humanity.

Precisely for that reason, "sin is eternal death." But dying sinners are delivered from sin and death because they know God in Christ, as true gnostics,

---

63. Arthur Cushman McGiffert, *A History of Christian Thought*, vol. 1, *Early and Eastern, from Jesus to John of Damascus* (New York: Scribner, 1954), 190.

especially now that we have come to know the most precious and venerable name of the good Father, who to a pious and good child gives gentle counsels, and commands what is salutary for His child. He who obeys Him has the advantage in all things, follows God, obeys the Father, knows Him through wandering, loves God, loves his neighbor, fulfills the commandment, seeks the prize, claims the promise. But it has been God's fixed and constant purpose to save the flock of men: for this end the good God sent the good Shepherd. (*Protr.* 11 [204])

This is a typical passage from Clement, emphasizing God's philanthropy, saving purpose, and wonderful plan realized and made known in Christ. Thus we can see that despite the difference in rhetoric and strategy from Irenaeus, substantively it comes to the same thing over against the gnostic theosophy: the knowledge of God is the knowledge of God's saving plan, the Logos, incarnate in Christ's cross and resurrection, which manifests the universal divine philanthropy and always finds the way to make good out of evil.

The philanthropy of the Logos incarnate, redeeming the Father's creation, leads Clement to a generous Christian humanism, which is expressed in mottos such as "God hates nothing that exists," "All truth is God's," and "Truth is one, just as there is only one God." This humanism leads Clement, as it did Justin Martyr before him and Thomas Aquinas after him, to appropriate aspects of Greek philosophy in service of the gospel that he is proclaiming to people of Hellenistic culture. Thus Clement also takes up the Platonic-philosophical ideal of knowledge as the assimilation of like to like and argues that the philosophical quest for true knowledge of the Good is fulfilled in Christian theology, as we will shortly see. Nevertheless, we note that this is really a *Christian* humanism, grounded as it is not in the naturally known natural capacities of humanity but in the surprise of the gospel narrative of the Logos activating divine philanthropy. An interesting indication of this new Christian humanism, not especially well attested in Hellenistic humanism, is Clement's feminism.

The Greek philosophical tradition, going back to Socrates's less-than-flattering portrait of Xanthippe, is deeply stamped with misogyny and associated with anthropological dualism, which equates reason and affinity to the divine with the male mind and passion and closeness to rude matter with the female body. Likewise, the gnostic rejection of sexuality and the bodily life dominated in the minds of many in the Alexandria of Clement's time. It is quite striking then, when Clement defends marriage and repeatedly argues, in light of the Christian experience of faith, that "the virtue of man and woman is the same":

For if the God of both is one, the master of both is also one; one church, one temperance, one modesty; their food is common, marriage an equal yoke; respiration, sight, hearing, knowledge, hope, obedience, love all alike. And those whose life is common, have common graces and a common salvation; common to them are love and training. "For in this world," he says, "they marry, and are given in marriage," in which alone the female is distinguished from the male; "but in that [future] world it is so no more." There the [heavenly] rewards of this [earthly] social and holy life, which is based on conjugal union, are laid up, not for male and female, but for man, the sexual desire which divides humanity being removed. Common therefore, too, to men and women, is the name of man. (*Paed.* 1.4 [211])

Clement is a true intellectual. But as a Christian humanist, he disdains elitism and instead boasts, "The individual whose life is framed as ours is, may philosophize without Learning, whether barbarian, whether Greek, whether slave—whether an old man, or a boy, or a woman" (*Strom.* 4.8 [419]). The difference between the sexes is purely sexual: "Pregnancy and parturition, accordingly, we say belong to woman, as she is woman, and not as she is a human being," and it is this "peculiar construction of the body," Clement notes as a child of his day and age (indeed, of all ages prior to modern technologies of birth control), destines woman "for child-bearing and housekeeping" (*Strom.* 4.8 [420]). But Clement insists that this economic difference, rooted in procreative function, does not touch upon woman's intellectual or spiritual abilities. "Women are therefore to philosophize equally with men," and Christian women, defying tyrannical or unbelieving husbands, "will philosophize" (*Strom.* 4.8 [420]). Clement's humanism is a Christian humanism that still grasps the revolutionary import of Galatians 3:27–28. All people—male and female, slave and free, young and old—can be changed by baptismal union with the Logos of God in Jesus Christ. All these become true gnostics, lovers of the divine wisdom incarnate in Jesus Christ.

So the human being can change because she is the creature of God created for fellowship with God and because the Logos of God appears in Christ, who dies for them that they may now live to God, calling and empowering this lost creature to fellowship with God. Similarly then with Irenaeus, salvation is *theosis*, assimilation to God.[64] Theosis is not a human work of ascent, as Platonism thinks on the basis of the kinship of the rational human soul to the divine, but rather a divine work in us. Only God can deify: "Godliness, that makes man as far as can be like God, designates God as our suitable teacher, who alone can worthily assimilate man to God." The "Lord himself, the lover of man" speaks and teaches such salvation, "for this, and nothing but this, is His only work—the salvation of man" (*Protr.* 9 [196]). Christ has bestowed "on us the truly great, divine, and inalienable inheritance of the

---

64. *Pace* McGiffert, *History of Christian Thought*, 186, 200.

Father, deifying man by heavenly teaching, putting His laws into our minds, and writing them on our hearts. What laws does He inscribe? 'That all shall know God' . . . [And how will God be known?] 'I will be merciful to them,' says God, 'and will not remember their sins'" (*Protr.* 11 [203–4]). Christians are taught to know God in His loving fatherly mercy by the Logos incarnate: "One alone, true, good, just, in the image and likeness of the Father, His Son Jesus, the Word of God, is our Instructor" (*Paed.* 1.11 [234]).

This change in humankind to knowledge of God is above all evident, according to Clement, in theology—that is, in the new discipline of "philosophizing" about the Word of God. All believers "philosophize," Clement says, because thoughtful reflection on the love of God in Christ is the very meaning of human existence as the actualization in them of God's salvation. It is in this sense that Clement maintains that "without philosophy a man may be a believer, but he cannot comprehend the things of faith."[65] For Clement, the Christian theologian's life, the theological existence of the "shepherds" who "preside over the Churches" after the "image of the good Shepherd," is the true fulfillment of what gnostics and Platonists had erroneously sought in their own works, speculations, and mystical ascents. Here is true meat for the soul (*Paed.* 1.6 [219]). Clement accordingly defends the simple faith of believers against the criticisms both of gnostics, who regard faith as the false consciousness of those who are not truly spiritual, and of Platonists, who regard faith as mere subjective opinion taken on authority.

But for Clement, following Hebrews 11:1, faith is really the foundation of all knowledge, by way of which we adopt indemonstrable first principles and on this basis proceed to the procurement of sure knowledge. But in Clement a historical and social a priori, namely, gospel and church, replaces the putatively rational a priori knowledge, whether it be the divine spark of the gnostics or the recollection of the soul according to the Platonists. Thus faith is the act and decision of obedience to Jesus Christ as the incarnate Logos of God, who in coming to believers opens up the entire world to understanding in the light of divine philanthropy. Clement by the same token insists that faith inwardly and of necessity matures to knowledge. Theological knowledge is understanding what the faith in Jesus really means, how it reveals the philanthropy of God and the destiny of creation in theosis and the corresponding way of new and holy living in the Spirit. Thus "knowledge is characterized by faith; and faith, by a kind of divine mutual and reciprocal correspondence, becomes characterized by knowledge." Theology is the knowledge of faith, the learning and aptitude of the Christian thinker, the "true gnostic"

65. Ibid., 184.

(*Strom.* 2.4–6 [350–54]), who knows God who knows humanity in the Logos incarnate. This "produces intelligent faith by the adducing and opening up of the Scriptures to the souls of those who desire to learn; the result of which is knowledge (*gnosis*)" (*Strom.* 2.11 [358–59]). This is not only intellectual or doctrinal knowledge; it is knowledge of a new existence in Christ, what we today might call "existential knowledge." It claims the whole life of the believer. If Christ is the "truth, and wisdom, and power of God, as in truth He is, it is shown that the real Gnostic is he that knows Him, and His Father by Him" (*Strom.* 2.11 [359]). This citation of 1 Corinthians 1:24b should be borne in mind when we turn to chapter 3 below.

The Defense of Philosophy as Handmaiden to Theology

Clement regarded philosophy as "in a sense a work of Divine Providence" (*Strom.* 1.1 [303]), doing for the Greeks what the law of Moses had done for the Jews, namely, preparing the way for the gospel. God "is the cause of all good things" (*Strom.* 1.5 [305]), and "philosophy came into existence, not on its own account, but for the advantages reaped by us from knowledge, we receiving a firm persuasion of true perception, through the knowledge of things comprehended by the mind" (*Strom.* 1.2 [304]). Therefore, we should, Clement argues, regard philosophy as "a schoolmaster to bring 'the Hellenic mind,' as the law [did for the], the Hebrews, 'to Christ'" (*Strom.* 1.5 [305]). Thus at the very beginning of his vast, sprawling work *Miscellanies* (*Stromata*), Clement announces, "Our book will not shrink from making use of what is best in philosophy and other preparatory instruction" (*Strom.* 1.1 [302–3]). He acknowledges the criticisms of conservative fellow Christians who oppose his use of philosophy:

> I am not oblivious of what is babbled by some, who in their ignorance are frightened at every noise, and say that we ought to occupy ourselves with what is most necessary, and which contains the faith; and that we should pass over what is beyond and superfluous, which wears out and detains us to no purpose, in things which conduce nothing to the great end. Others think that philosophy was introduced into life by an evil influence, for the ruin of men, by an evil inventor. (*Strom.* 1.1 [303])

To these and similar arguments by those "who demand bare faith alone"— that is, acceptance of dogmas strictly on ecclesiastical authority without the human dignity of understanding why the dogmas, said to be revealed by God, are true—Clement replies, "How necessary is it for him who desires to be partaker of the power of God, to treat of intellectual subjects by philosophising! And how serviceable it is to distinguish expressions which are ambiguous, and which in the Testaments are used synonymously! . . . [Scripture] demands skillful modes of teaching in order to [provide] clear exposition" (*Strom.* 1.9 [310]). Faith in authority is not Christian faith in the philanthropy of God revealed in the Scriptures.

For Clement, "philosophy" is not some particular dogma of this or that school; rather, it is the art of logical analysis and the skill of expositing texts wisely.[66] "Philosophizing" means discoursing rationally about the texts that discovers the meaning in the words. It does not mean subscribing uncritically to the worldviews of a certain school of thinking or submitting revelation to the straightjacket of human reason. Rather, the theologian—that is, the Christian philosopher—engages critically with the various philosophical doctrines to discern

the philosophy which is in accordance with divine tradition [that] establishes and confirms providence, which, being done away with, the economy of the Savior appears a myth. . . . For the teaching which is agreeable to Christ deifies the Creator, and traces providence in particular events, and knows the nature of the elements to be capable of change and production, and teaches that we ought to aim at rising up to the power which assimilates to God, and to prefer the dispensation [*oikonomia*, i.e., the gospel] as holding the first rank. (*Strom.* 1.11 [312])

Surely this is Clement's most powerful argument for theology as knowledge of God as an evangelical mandate, which Wolfhart Pannenberg renewed at the beginning of his illustrious theological career.[67] If "fundamentalist" Christians do not think that somehow the God of the Bible is the one true God, hence the universal God of all—whose providence holds sway over all, who prepares all to hear the gospel of Christ, thus concretely the God whose Logos somehow is also manifest, preparing the way in the universally admired philosophical progress of Greek civilization—then the claim that God acted in Christ itself appears as unfounded and ungrounded—that is, as a mythical bolt from the blue, the mirror image of the gnostic redeemer who visits his chosen few in the name of the unknown Father far above. Unwittingly, conservative Christians, who are unwilling to find correlations between the Logos active in all nations and the God revealed in Christ, make the incarnation appear like a

66. Ibid.

67. Wolfhart Pannenberg, *Basic Questions in Theology: Collected Essays*, trans. George H. Kehm (Philadelphia: Fortress, 1972), 2:119–83.

secret mission from an unknown God rather than the redeeming mission of the universal Creator God, whom all nations in some measure apprehend.[68]

Hans Lietzmann describes the historical context of Clement's pioneering advocacy for theology as the discipleship of the mind: "In all the greater towns at the end of the second century, Christianity had penetrated into the upper classes; in Alexandria, this fact necessitated formulating a theology to deal with the question of the relationship between culture and Christianity."[69] W. H. C. Frend further explicates the resulting tensions that Clement experienced in his historical context with more conservative fellow Christians:

> He was confronted in Alexandria by considerable numbers of Christians who wanted nothing to do with philosophy or philosophical Christians. Clement came to dislike and despise these people and their claims to orthodoxy. "The so-called orthodox," he declared, "are like beasts that work out of fear. They do good works without knowing what they are doing." Such people "are scared of Greek philosophy as they are of [actors'] masks, fearing it would lead them astray." The "orthodoxists" were "dumb animals that have to be driven by fear."[70]

The perception of fear underlying the anxious self-identification as "the orthodox" from this Catholic Christian who loves the church, as we have seen, is penetrating and spot-on. Orthodoxy is an intention in theology and the Spirit's work in progress. To claim it already as one's own possession in order to evade difficulties is also to avoid learning better the gospel of God. So this indictment of fundamentalist fear is not mere invective on Clement's part. Clement means that by avoiding rational reflection on the meaning of the Christian faith, whether out of fear or sloth, such so-called orthodoxy in fact fundamentally turns gospel into law, knowledge of God into ignorance of God, faith into a work, and mercy into the strange merit of those who boast not in the cross of Christ but of their own blind and willful beliefs. This defensive and fear-induced stance never penetrates to clear understanding of the philanthropy that moves the God of the gospel in all His works and ways, including His work in preparing the Greeks to receive the gospel by philosophy. Trying to defend the authentic biblical tradition, conservatism

---

68. In contemporary evangelical theology, my former colleague Gerald R. McDermott has made this case for Clement in his sketches resourcing a Christian theology of the world religions. See *God's Rivals: Why Has God Allowed Different Religions? Insights from the Bible and the Early Church* (Downers Grove, IL: IVP Academic, 2007), 85–97; Gerald R. McDermott and Harold Netland, *A Trinitarian Theology of Religions: An Evangelical Proposal* (Oxford: Oxford University Press, 2014), 14–15, 60, 81–82, 117–19.

69. Lietzmann, *History of the Early Church*, 2:286.

70. W. H. C. Frend, *The Rise of Christianity* (Philadelphia: Fortress, 1984), 288.

in fact transforms the tradition into a self-righteous human religious work. This kind of obscurantism is disastrous in the evangelistic situation of cosmopolitan, pluralistic Alexandria. Frend continues, "It was hopeless to tell the educated catechumen that the Greek poets were inspired by the Devil. 'The earth is the Lord's and the fullness thereof, and anyone who seeks to help catechumens, especially if they are Greeks, must not shrink from scholarly study.' For these, the new religion could be presented as a natural progression from their past and its claims supported by reference to current philosophical speculation."[71]

It may be too strong to speak of "natural progression" here. Indeed, in the name of the Logos revealed in Christ, who becomes the instructor of disciples in the new way of life, Clement virtually prosecutes the "customs" of Greek civilization, which entrench error and throw up roadblocks to the coming of the Logos's reign. The appropriation of Greek culture by Clement is in fact critical and selective, and to the extent that philosophy, going back to the pre-Socratics, was already the indigenous critique of the poets and the myths of the gods, it may be said that there is a "natural progression" from Greek to Christian philosophizing. Since "truth is one," writes Clement, "the barbarian and Hellenic philosophy has torn off a fragment of eternal truth not from the mythology of Dionysius, but from the theology of the ever-living Word"; and now the Christian "philosopher," who knows the Word and Wisdom of God incarnate in Christ, "brings together again the separate fragments, and makes them one" (*Strom.* 1.13 [313]).

Emphasizing the logical, analytical side of Clement's appeal to Greek wisdom, Lietzmann describes Clement's

> defense of philosophy . . . as [a] rational means to attain knowledge of the content of faith. Philosophy does not make Christian truth more true, but reveals the lack of content of the attacks directed against it on the part of sophists [= gnostics]; it erects a protective wall for the vineyard of the Lord. . . . Its clarity helps in passing on the truth, its dialectic is a protection against heretical invasions. . . . The practical goal becomes quite plain [in the *Miscellanies*], viz. to repulse heretics, understood essentially as Gnostics.[72]

According to Lietzmann's interpretation, Clement primarily deploys logical techniques of analysis, learned from the philosophers, to clarify the orthodox faith and distinguish it from gnosticism. Clement says expressly, "I do not think that philosophy directly declares the Word, although in many instances

71. Ibid.
72. Lietzmann, *History of the Early Church*, 2:289–90.

philosophy attempts and persuasively teaches us probable arguments" (*Strom.* 1.19 [322]). Philosophy is not

> the cause of comprehension, but a cause along with other things, and co-operator. . . . While truth is one, many things contribute to its investigation. But its discovery is by the Son. . . . Perspicuity accordingly aids in the communication of truth, and logic in preventing us from falling under the heresies by which we are assailed. But the teaching, which is according to the Savior, is complete in itself. (*Strom.* 1.20 [323])

Drawing on such statements by Clement, Lietzmann sets himself against the influential, though complex and probably incoherent, view of Adolph von Harnack regarding the intellectual "Hellenization of the gospel." On the one hand, Harnack praised the antifundamentalist Clement for his intellectual freedom and independence vis-à-vis church authority: "In the Christian faith as he understood it and as amalgamated by him with Greek culture, Clement found intellectual freedom and independence, deliverance from all external authority,"[73] which elevated faith "out of the province of authority and obedience into that of clear knowledge and inward, intellectual assent emanating from love to God."[74] So, according to Harnack, "gnosis" represents for Clement not only "a means of refuting heathenism and heresy" but also a way of identifying the essence of Christianity, "ascertaining and setting forth what is highest and inmost in Christianity."[75] On the basis of critical, scientific research, Harnack states, Clement wanted to give Christianity "a philosophical form and bring it into harmony with the spirit of the times."[76]

This could be done, however, only with some violence to the ecclesiastical tradition. Harnack asserts that "apart from evangelical sayings, the Church tradition, both collectively and in its details,[77] is something foreign to him; he has subjected himself to its authority, but he can only make it intellectually his own after subjecting it to a scientific and philosophic treatment."[78] As a result, in Clement's hands Christianity is violently transformed to become "the doctrine of the creation, training and redemption of mankind by the Logos,

---

73. Adolph von Harnack, *History of Dogma*, trans. Neil Buchanan (New York: Dover, 1961), 2:329.

74. Ibid., 2:325.

75. Ibid., 2:324.

76. Ibid., 2:321.

77. That is, "Clement did not possess the Church tradition in its fixed Catholic forms as Origen did" (ibid., 2:331).

78. Ibid., 2:324.

whose work culminates in the perfect Gnostics."[79] Thus "the goodness of God and the responsibility of man," monotheism and morality, become the "central ideas"; at his hands "Church tradition was here completely transformed into a Greek philosophy of religion on a historical basis."[80]

This devastating judgment, first pronounced against Irenaeus, who, according to Harnack, unconsciously Hellenized the gospel, also applies to Clement, who consciously did so. "When the Christian religion was represented as the belief in the incarnation of God and as the sure hope of the deification of man, a speculation that had originally never got beyond the fringe of religious knowledge was made the central point of the system and the simple content of the Gospel was obscured."[81] The notion of redemptive incarnation and saving theosis—as in the motto taken over by the Alexandrians from Irenaeus, "God became human in order that humans become divine"—is, according to Harnack, a foreign imposition from Platonism that obscures the gospel. This is Harnack's severe indictment of the entire development—be it in the dogmatic form adopted by Irenaeus or the apologetic form adopted by Clement—which was leading to the trinitarian theology of the Nicene Creed.

Christian Platonism

It is important to recall, then, that philosophy, even Greek philosophy, is not some monolith. Platonism was but one school alongside others for most of its history, and in the course of its history it also grew and developed (in its later stages, under direct pressure from the growing Christian movement). We have already seen how Clement critically engaged the various philosophical options in the name of the gospel, criticizing materialistic or atomistic doctrines that denied providence. Clement also criticized the merely rationalistic critique of polytheism by

> philosophy itself, through its conceit making an idol of matter. . . . [These pre-Socratics] did not indeed pay religious honor to stocks and stones, but deified earth, the mother of these,—who did not make an image of Poseidon, but revered water itself. . . . However much they think to keep clear of error in one form, they slide into it in another. . . . They have learned the impious doctrine of regarding as divine certain first principles, being ignorant of the great First Cause, the Maker of all things, and Creator of those very first principles, the unbeginning God. (*Protr.* 5 [190])

79. Ibid., 2:326.
80. Ibid., 2:330.
81. Ibid., 2:318.

Bearing in mind the contested, pluralistic context of philosophical views and counterviews that early Christian thinkers like Clement engaged, how can we understand the affinity that those like Clement and, before him, Justin Martyr[82] found in Platonism? Clement advocates for "the distinction":

> It is the Lord of the spirits, the Lord of the fire, the Maker of the universe, Him who lighted up the sun, that I long for. I seek after God, not the works of God. Whom shall I take as a helper in my inquiry? We do not, if you have no objection, wholly disown Plato. How, then, is God to be searched out, O Plato? [Clement quotes from the *Timaeus*:] "For both to find the Father and Maker of this universe is a work of difficulty; and having found Him, to declare Him fully, is impossible." Why so? . . . For He can by no means be expressed. Well done, Plato! Thou hast touched on the truth. . . . God is one, indestructible, unbegotten, and . . . somewhere above in the tracts of heaven, in His own peculiar appropriate eminence, whence He surveys all things, He has an existence true and eternal. (*Protr.* 6 [191])

This idea of the transcendent being of the Creator God, which is qualitatively other than the finite being of created things, seems to form the point of contact between biblical faith and Platonism.

An ontological line of division separates the creature, whose being is always derivative, from the Creator, who has life in and of Himself. God is one, indestructible and unbegotten. The creature is many, mutable and generated. We can note here, however, that in the future just this characterization of the difference in being between God and the creature that is christologically expressed in the doctrine of the two natures will unavoidably cast doubt on the true, natural deity of the Son, whose personal distinction from God the Father lies precisely in the fact that He is the begotten God, that his divine being is derived from or generated by the Father. Arthur McGiffert comments, "A God who is at once the absolute, out of all relations, beyond space and time, unapproachable, incommunicable, unknowable, and at the same time a personal father, the creator and providential ruler of the universe and a loving and gracious being who cares for men and saves them—it is no wonder that Clement found difficulty in combining these two."[83] Clement senses the problem, but resolution of it is beyond his historical horizon. For him the terms *ousia* and *hypostasis* are still synonyms. The conceptual, or rather (to borrow from Scotus) the formal, distinction between nature and person is not yet accomplished; the gospel has not yet worked this metaphysical revolution on its tactical ally, Platonism. Clement is content to assert without further

82. Hinlicky, *Divine Complexity*, 128–37.
83. McGiffert, *History of Christian Thought*, 205.

argumentation the full deity of the Logos over against the subordinationist tendencies in earlier apologists.[84]

A further affinity with Platonism, in Clement's eyes, is an ethical interpretation of discipleship, drawn from philosophizing about the Logos in the disciplined speculation of theology, namely, that the human vocation is to become like God. Again, in Clement's words:

> He is the Gnostic, who is after the image and likeness of God, who imitates God as far as possible, . . . practicing self-restraint and endurance, living righteously, reigning over the passions, bestowing of what he has as far as possible, and doing good both by word and deed. . . . Now Plato the philosopher, defining the end of happiness, says that it is likeness to God as far as possible. . . . For the law says, "Walk after the Lord your God, and keep my commandments." For the law calls assimilation following; and such a following to the utmost of its power assimilates. "Be," says the Lord, "merciful and pitiful, as your heavenly Father is pitiful." (*Strom.* 2.19 [369])

Thus, in parallel to Plato's charge, Clement understands salvation as the ethical following of Jesus through the purification of cross-bearing discipleship, works of mercy, and self-denial up to and including martyrdom if need be. All this is the ethical way to the deification of eternal life. Christians follow Jesus in order to go where he is (heaven) and to become like him (heavenly). The theology of the martyrs, which Clement earnestly defends against the ridicule of gnostic rivals, is expanded and generalized by Clement into a universal summons of all Christians to discipleship.

One certainly may detect influences of asceticism and elements of Stoic ethics here, but the fundamental motif is taken from the Gospels and the statement of the Epistle to the Hebrews that Jesus is the author and pioneer of faith, who blazed the trail for His disciples to follow. Platonism but provides a conceptual apparatus for thinking this out. The terms *sophrosyne* and *apatheia* enter into theological vocabulary as a result, the first meaning "self-restraint" and the second "serenity, impassibility." As an ethical ideal, these mean "to live superior to the ordinary interests and vicissitudes of life, entirely free from the desires and ambitions that sway the mass of men."[85] Drawn from Stoicism, in Clement's hands the negative ideal of self-forgetfulness becomes but the presupposition of self-donating and active love for God and all others. McGiffert observes,

> Love is the supreme motive in all well doing. The ordinary Christian is moved by the fear of punishment and the hope of the reward [thus, lives under the law].

84. See ibid., 204–6.
85. Ibid., 186.

But the Gnostic is moved solely by love—love for God and for the good—and in his love goes beyond the righteousness of the law . . . [it is] a life of freedom from the law. The goodness of the Gnostic is not legal goodness; it is the spontaneous expression of love for God.[86]

Only a person who has acquired freedom from passion is capable of such self-giving love, the holy passion of the Lord, just as God, who is supremely "apathetic," gives His own Son in love for His alienated creature.

The Difficulty of Evaluating Clement

Not surprisingly, modern evaluations of Clement's "Christian Platonism" are quite diverse and mutually incompatible. We have already heard Harnack's sharp but baffling evaluation of Clement, whom he seemingly praises and attacks for one and the same thing. We can also surmise the more favorable judgment by Lietzmann, who stresses the doxological accent: "Superior conviction and calm assurance help Clement to express his ideas in poetic language, and produce a hymn of triumph to Christ as the herald of the final and eternal truth."[87] Frend rightly notes, "Basically, nothing could be more opposed than the Jewish and Greek views of God, of creation, of time and history, and of the role of humanity in the universe." Yet Frend incomprehensibly suggests that the Logos theology of Hellenistic Judaism, as initially developed by Philo and now taken up anew with vigor by Clement, his heir in Alexandria, "would prove the most hopeful means of establishing common ground between Greek and biblical ideas of the universe."[88] This supposition that the Logos could function as a bridge concept is fundamentally mistaken; it worked and continues to work the confusion of the psychological model of the Neoplatonic trinity, where the second hypostasis is a mental operation, with the social model of the gospel narrative, where the second hypostasis is the creature Jesus, the Son of God. The confusion of the Son of the eternal Father with the mediating agent of Middle Platonism is rather the very problem that Nicene theology will have to overcome. (Frend himself draws attention to the inevitably "embarrassing concessions to polytheism" that uncritical accommodation of the Logos as Platonism's "second God" had to cause in Christian theology.)[89]

In this regard, Aloys Grillmeier is much more correct to say that in comparison with Justin and the apologists, the tendency in Clement's theology

86. Ibid., 191.
87. Lietzmann, *History of the Early Church*, 2:280.
88. Frend, *Rise of Christianity*, 368–69.
89. Ibid., 283.

is not to depict the Logos as a "second God," who can by virtue of his lesser being represent the transcendent and real God to lower creatures in the cosmic hierarchy of being and vice versa represent the creatures to the absolute God. Clement's Logos retains his transcendence even in the incarnation. In Christ, for Clement, we really meet God, not his angel, extrinsic image, or created replica. Moreover, this Logos is fully identified with the historical person of Jesus, which unmistakably qualifies Clement's doctrine of the Logos as substantively non-Platonic. The real problem in Clement, according to Grillmeier, is the typical one in "Logos-Sarx" type Christologies that prevailed in Alexandria—namely, that the Logos seems to displace the rational human soul of Christ, a tendency indicated by some quasi-docetist christological statements that Clement made on occasion.[90] This christological difficulty leads McGiffert to this perhaps overly sharp but telling criticism: "Christ's incarnation and work therefore had no such value to Clement as to Irenaeus. It was the eternal Logos he chiefly thought of; the incarnation was only an incident. On earth the Logos simply continued the work he had always been doing, the work of a teacher and revealer."[91] The potential for such a quasi-docetist Christology certainly is present in Clement, as would later appear in Apollinarius.

Clement of Alexandria's contribution was to show that Platonism and Scripture could be allied at least tactically against the radical dualism of the gnostics and so in defense of the suffering creation as the good work of God, the object of redemption and of a promised fulfillment. The idea of the incomparable, inexpressible transcendent being of the Creator, and of His abundant goodness toward His creation, much more than the doctrine of the Logos as mediating being between absolute and relative existence, reflects a real convergence in world affirmation that in fact united Platonism and biblical faith in God against gnostic despair of the world. Though converging from different angles of approach that eventually had to diverge again, prophetic faith and Platonism, moreover, shared in the criticism of idolatry, which worshiped the creature in place of the Creator, the copy instead of the original. Recognition of such convergences does not mean, in and of itself, accommodation, let alone a capitulation to Hellenism.

Jaroslav Pelikan's evaluation of Clement is the most nuanced. He urges, against Harnack, that "it is misleading to speak of Hellenization. For, as Henry Chadwick has stated the paradox, 'Clement is hellenized to the core of his being, yet unreserved in his adhesion to the Church.' What else could a

90. Aloys Grillmeier, *Christ in Christian Tradition*, vol. 1, *From the Apostolic Age to Chalcedon (451)*, trans. John Bowden, 2nd rev. ed. (Atlanta: John Knox, 1975), 135–36.
91. McGiffert, *History of Christian Thought*, 201.

Greek Christian be than a Greek, especially one like Clement who understands himself as an evangelist to the Greeks?" Pelikan continues,

> Although theologians quoted Scripture in support of ideas originally derived from philosophy, they often modified these ideas on the basis of Scripture. . . . [This complex interaction means that] at most, it would appear valid to distinguish between the apologetic and the kerygmatic tasks performed by the same theologians, and in such a distinction to keep the entire picture in view, with all its tensions.
>
> It is even more of a distortion when the dogma formulated by the catholic tradition is described as "in its conception and development a work of the Greek spirit on the soil of the gospel." Indeed, in some ways it is more accurate to speak of dogma as the "dehellenization" of the [Platonic, philosophical] theology that had preceded it. . . . [The] chief place to look for hellenization is in the speculations and heresies against which the dogma of the creeds and councils was directed.[92]

If we keep Pelikan's counsel in mind, we get a very different picture of Clement of Alexandria than that of a Hellenizer. We get instead the picture of an evangelist of the Greeks.[93] Even though Clement stands in the tradition of the second-century apologists, he is much more a preacher and evangelist than an apologist, a pioneer who left an unfinished work rather than a speculative philosophy. Clement's lengthy *Miscellanies* (*Stromata*), which, as the title indicates, is a smorgasbord of unfinished essays and undigested thoughts, has dominated the interpretation of this theologian's legacy at the expense of the shorter but much more coherent and finished works *Exhortation to the Heathen* (*Protrepticus*) and *Christ the Instructor* (*Paedagogus*), Clement's "gospel" and "ethics," respectively. Clement probably conceived the three writings as a trilogy, which would first convert the unbeliever to the Christian faith, then instruct the new Christian in discipleship, and finally open the mind of the neophyte Christian to theological reflection. In any case, if we base our sketch on these two first, finished works, we get a much more coherent and impressive understanding of Clement's contribution on the road to the doctrine of the Trinity's "dehellenization of philosophical theology."

Evangelization of Hellenism

Whatever his dependence on the Logos scheme of Middle Platonism, in Clement the figure of the Logos has been thoroughly biblicized. For Clement,

92. Jaroslav Pelikan, *The Christian Tradition: A History of the Development of Doctrine*, vol. 1, *The Emergence of the Catholic Tradition (100–600)* (Chicago: University of Chicago Press, 1971), 55.
93. See McGiffert, *History of Christian Thought*, 179.

the Logos is first of all the ceaselessly exhorting, terrifying, urging, rousing, admonishing, and awakening voice of the living God (*Protr.* 9):

> Our loving Father—the true Father—ceases not to exhort, admonish, train, love us. For He ceases not to save, and advises the best course: "Become righteous," says the Lord. Ye that thirst, come to the water; and ye that have no money, come, and buy and drink without money. He invites to the laver, to salvation, to illumination, all but crying out and saying, The land I give thee, and the sea, my child, and heaven too; and all the living creatures in them I freely bestow upon thee. Only, O child, thirst for thy Father. (*Protr.* 10 [198])

The Logos of the loving Father is "good news," a "divine promise of grace," which commands, "Believe Him who is man and God; believe, O man. Believe, O man, the living God, who suffered and is adored. Believe, ye slaves, Him who died; believe, all ye of human kind, Him who alone is God of all men" (*Protr.* 10 [201]). The "trumpet of Christ is His Gospel," and through it,

> the heavenly and truly divine love comes to men. . . . [And it is this] exhortation to the truth alone, like the most faithful of our friends, [which] abides with us till our last breath. . . . What, then, is the exhortation which I give you? I urge you to be saved. This Christ desires. In one word, He freely bestows life on you. And who is He? Briefly learn. The Word of truth, the Word of incorruption, that regenerates man by bringing him back to the truth. (*Protr.* 11 [204])

Such is the Logos: "The Instructor of humanity, the Divine Word, using all the resources of wisdom, devotes himself to the saving of the children, admonishing, upbraiding, blaming, chiding, reproving, threatening, healing, promising, favoring" (*Paed.* 1.9 [228]). This Logos of God truly expresses and communicates God's own love, God's philanthropy. "You have, then, God's promise; you have His love: become partaker of His grace" (*Protr.* 1 [173]). The Logos expresses and actualizes God's love, and thus Clement can say, like Irenaeus, "The greatest and most regal work of God is the salvation of humanity" (*Paed.* 1.12 [235]).

This articulation of God as love for humanity in the incarnation of the Logos has far-reaching implications for the doctrine of God. The true God is the living, loving, saving God, whose providence is exercised all about us. Like Irenaeus, Clement perceives that the trinitarian relation of the Father and the Son is the basis for God's free and loving act of creating a world other than Himself. God's justice, he writes, "is shown to us by His own Word from there from above, whence the Father was. For before He became Creator He was God; He was good. And therefore He wished to be Creator and Father.

And the nature of all that love was the source of righteousness—the cause, too, of His lighting up His sun, and sending down His own Son" (*Paed.* 1.9 [232]). Here we have the Christian perception of God as transcendent in his being, as God to God for God antecedent to the free act of creation, thus qualitatively different from all things created and yet at the same time infinitely near in loving power that gives life and light to all things.

This perception led Clement to introduce a distinction, which became important in Byzantine theology, between the essence and energy of God for articulating the "formal distinction" (Scotus again!) between God's transcendent being and immanent operation. As Plato had said, Clement writes, God is

a Being difficult to grasp and apprehend, ever receding and withdrawing from him who pursues. But he who is far off has—oh ineffable marvel!—come very near: "I am a God that draws near," says the Lord. He is in essence remote; "for how is it that what is begotten can have approached the Unbegotten?" But He is very near in virtue of that power which holds all things in its embrace. "Shall one do aught in secret, and I see him not?" For the power of God is always present, in contact with us, in the exercise of inspection, of beneficence, of instruction. (*Strom.* 2.2 [348])

This distinction between the essence and energies of God has important implications for theological language. Because God in essence is utterly ineffable, in principle any kind of metaphor can be taken up as a vehicle of the Word of God: "spiritual" things are not closer to God than "material" things, but any created reality, visible or invisible, intellectual or not, is equally distant from God in essence and equally present to God in action. The validity of the metaphor theologically will then be determined by its utility in articulating the truth of the gospel. By the same token, all anthropomorphism in language about God is and must be deliteralized and decoded.

Clement quite freely employs, for example, feminine metaphors for God to express the loving energy radiating from God's ineffable essence to creation: "God, of His great love to man, comes to the help of man, as the mother-bird flies to one of her young that has fallen out of the nest" (*Protr.* 10 [197]); and, "To those babes that seek the Word, the Father's breasts of love supply milk" (*Paed.* 1.6 [221]). Notwithstanding the foregoing apophaticism (negative theology) inherited from the Platonic philosophical tradition with respect to God's essence, for Clement it is Jesus who identifies God to God and so also to us. Thus (to anticipate later terminology) while God qua essence remains infinitely beyond our comprehension, we truly know this very mysterious, incomprehensible God personally in Jesus, His Father, and their Spirit, who are personally the operators of the divine operation of the divine essence in eternity and in time. Christians thus know how to distinguish without separating the mysterious essence of God and His loving energies, which give and uphold all creation. They know how to make this distinction just because they "have as [their] teacher Him that filled the universe with His holy energies in creation, salvation, beneficence, legislation, prophecy, teaching, . . . the Teacher from whom all instruction comes; and the whole world, with Athens and Greece, has already become the domain of the Word" (*Protr.* 11 [203]).

The Logos is Jesus Christ, who "though despised as to appearance, was in reality adored, the expiator of sin, the Savior, the clement, the Divine Word, He that is truly most manifest Deity, He that is made equal to the Lord of the universe; because He was His Son, . . . not . . . altogether unknown when, assuming the character of man, and fashioning Himself in flesh, He enacted the drama of human salvation" (*Protr.* 10 [202]). This "Jesus, who is eternal, . . . prays for and exhorts men. . . . 'Come to me. . . . For I want, I want to impart to you . . . the Word and the knowledge of God, My complete self. This am I, this God wills, *this is symphony, this the harmony* of the Father, this is the Son, this is Christ, this the Word of God, the arm of the Lord, the power of the universe, the will of the Father'" (*Protr.* 12 [205], emphasis added). Our "Instructor is the holy God Jesus, the Word, who is the guide of all humanity. The loving God Himself is our Instructor" (*Paed.* 1.7 [223]), "like His Father God, whose son He is, sinless, blameless, and with a soul devoid of passion; God in the form of man" (*Paed.* 1.2 [209–10]). Whatever Christians know of God they know from God, who reveals himself in His Word incarnate, the man Jesus as symphony, harmony, and perichoresis of love. This knowledge of God is the gift and goal of their existence. The Christian who knows the Logos as Jesus is the "true Gnostic."

The study of Clement in this lengthy excursus illustrates the contrast and sometimes tension between the dogmatic function of theology, which is to teach the Christian faithful and ward off gospel-threatening error, and the apologetic function of theology, which is to evangelize the common mind by uncovering the universal reach of the gospel. We are wise to follow Pelikan's counsel and not set these two functions into principled opposition to each other. A critical dogmatic understanding of the discipline of theology freely borrows the tools of philosophy out of fidelity to the confession of faith for the sake of the clarity of its content, for pertinent example, as we will shortly see, in 1 Corinthians 8:6. A know-nothing biblicism, by contrast, does not even succeed in knowing the Bible. It would be all the more erroneous to blame Christian Platonists for somehow corrupting a pure biblical theology of the Word. Precisely by attempting to relate the biblical theology of the Word to the best philosophy of their day, the Christian Platonists were protagonists in the ever-new conflict of the gospel of the incarnate Logos with the powers and principalities of a world that has closed itself off to the coming of God's reign by closing the minds of its denizens. The disciplined logical-analytical work of Christian Platonists like Clement brought the confrontation of biblical and philosophical monotheism into the clear light of reason for believer and unbeliever to apprehend. It thus made the gospel itself unmistakably clear *as* the trinitarian distinction between nature and person. As a result, the simplicity of the God of the gospel is newly understood as the love of the Father and the Son in the Holy Spirit. In the wisdom that is folly to the world seeking God by its own wisdom, this complex simplicity or simple complexity is there for us in the word of the Messiah crucified. As we have seen in Clement, this divine love, for all its mystery and offense, is *known* in faith, where faith is itself union with the Son in the power of the Spirit to the praise of the Father, now and to the ages of ages.

3

Muddle, Not Mystery

Clarity on a Collapsing Synthesis

The reason that the inherited doctrine of simplicity is ambiguous, at root, is that the statement that it tries theologically to interpret, "God is one," is ambiguous. It is ambiguous in our reality because in the world that we inhabit, God appears not as one but as one of many so-called gods and lords. The affirmation that God is one is, then, a statement of faith against appearances, just like all the other basic claims to knowledge of God in Christianity: the world is creation; Hebrew slaves are Yahweh's chosen; the one suffering for others is the Servant of the Lord—that is, the crucified man Jesus is the Son of God; the loaf and cup are His body and blood; the sinner is righteous; the assembly is holy; these ashes and dust will be raised to new life; and so on. These statements contradict our present perception in order to point ahead. Just like any of these statements alleging to know God in Christian faith, however, the statement that God is one can be taken, not in faith as a sign that contradicts (Luke 2:34–35) to promise the new creation aborning, as per the preceding chapter's reading of Zechariah 14:9, but rather as a static religious representation awaiting liberating philosophical comprehension.

As we have seen, going back to the pre-Socratics, divine oneness is understood to de-divinize the phenomena of nature for scientific investigation and explanation and to expose the capriciousness and injustice of the gods in the myths of the poets for the sake of political sovereignty. Oneness is comprehended as the highly abstract *nature* of timeless self-identity and lifted up as the worthy conception of divinity, as it backs an ordered world, a cosmos. Or, taking the world as history coming to self-consciousness, as did Hegel in the modernization of this philosophical trajectory, oneness is interpreted as the self-diremption and self-recovery of abstract, timeless, otherworldly self-identity through a process of becoming that is not other than the world's history. Yet theologically, either way is sleight of hand. The cosmogonic myths are in this way transposed into abstraction and universalized rather than simply discarded for the sake of scientific progress and rational political life. The nature of being indivisible is found serviceable as providing the stable ground of the world of multiplicity and change, the unknowable One that funds the Many. The Logos or rationality of the process of becoming is the true, timelessly abiding element through all change, if the real is rational and the rational is real, as in Hegel. We have exchanged Heraclitus for Parmenides here, but the inversion is only another transposition if the timeless One backing the cosmos has become the timeless Logic backing the progression of change.[1]

On the other hand, the statement "God is one" can be taken as the exclusive deliverance spoken by the God of exodus and Easter, to which deliverance this same God pledges His fidelity in time through eternity. The exclusiveness is theological, as Gerd Theissen explains: "The one and only God of the Bible is a God of those who have escaped, of fugitives and exiles, the deported and prisoners of war. This God may not be detached from the stories about him: the stories of the homeless Abraham, the fugitive Jacob, the enslaved Israelites in Egypt, the oppressed tribes in the period of the judges. . . . If we detach him from this history, he soon becomes the God of the rulers."[2] In this drama of liberation God's unity is manifest as unity through time, keeping faith with His Word from the beginning and requiring a corresponding fidelity of the delivered, whom He addresses as those redeemed from bondage and set free for fulfillment as His creatures.

Unity here is the essential *property* of this character, the liberating God, in pledging and requiring fidelity, who is one and the same God in making and keeping promises. Here the oneness of God is taken not as a suppositing substance but rather as the free and committed subject or, better, the self-determining person, in Eberhard Jüngel's catchphrase, a who, who is *more than* (not less than) *necessary*—that is, more than a substance, whether as the

1. I am grateful to theologian Larry Rinehart for this insight into Heraclitus.
2. Gerd Theissen, *Biblical Faith: An Evolutionary Approach* (Philadelphia: Fortress, 1985), 71.

necessary first being or cosmological cause or perfection of being. Here too the myth (narrative, if you prefer) of exodus and Easter is not merely discarded for a more enlightened insight but rather is hermeneutically understood (not comprehended theoretically) in the commandments that correspond to and qualify His self-identification as the Lord, our God, who brings out of bondage: to have no other gods, to make no images for Him of our own, not to abuse His name for purposes of our own, but rather to honor the Sabbath when the saving narrative of His deliverance is called again to mind and heart. This agent does not become known as the act of His own eternal being (though, on reflection, He too cannot be thought of as less than that). Rather, He makes Himself known as the One who comes on the human scene with His Word promising to make all things new, faithfully innovating along the way as need be, already now in requiring and bestowing a corresponding fidelity on adherents by the breath of His own Spirit.

To be sure, the two doctrines of divine unity can dovetail and their claims overlap. They can and have allied against gnosticism, which is a consistent doctrine of despair of this world as substantially a misbegotten prison house rather than a good, divine creation fallen under the captivity of a usurper. In contests with the magicians of Pharaoh or the Baalim of Canaan, Yahweh had to demonstrate that the natural world too is a history over which He is the liberating Lord, thus also the Lord of the origin, the free Creator of all things. In capturing human desire by the worship it inspires, the philosophical One must also be mediated to the lower world of matter in the great chain of being by a cascade of descending ideas represented in the polyphony of cults speaking the babel of their many names for God.[3] Both claims, be it noted, are today under suspicion. The suspicion is not, as is superficially thought in the train of Feuerbach and Durkheim going back to Kant, about transcendental illusions now exposed by the rise of natural science. The genuine alternatives are not naturalism or idealism, resolving scientific knowledge into its object or its subject respectively. Christian theology of nature is more than a viable way through our new state of knowledge.[4]

The deep suspicion arises rather from the ever-mushrooming gnosticism of Euro-American civilization;[5] the new gnosticism arises as a desperate strategy of psychic survival under an imperium of political sovereignty that has lost the canonical story that once constrained its worst excesses and sometimes

3. Arthur O. Lovejoy, *The Great Chain of Being: A Study of the History of an Idea* (Cambridge, MA: Harvard University Press, 1964).

4. Alister E. McGrath, *A Fine-Tuned Universe: The Quest for God in Science and Theology* (Louisville: Westminster John Knox, 2009).

5. Philip J. Lee, *Against the Protestant Gnostics* (New York: Oxford University Press, 1987).

guided it in more humane directions.[6] We call it "postmodernity," and it means the collapse of the metanarrative of Christendom with the decay of the classical Western synthesis of Christian Platonism into the pluralist cacophony of contending interests that cannot discover a common good in a demystified and pointless cosmos of matter in motion. This new doctrine of despair ironically funds with apathetic nonresistance (i.e., the "whatever" response) the juggernaut of the biopolitical regime, first manifest in National Socialism,[7] but now recurring by the Satan who disguises itself as an angel of light (2 Cor. 11:14). In face of this monster with a charming face, liberal calls for secular unity or conservative calls for the restoration of Christendom are alike idle chatter. What is needed is the one Lord, Jesus Christ, who breaks into the strong man's house and binds him (Mark 3:27). The deep battle for the future of humanity on this globe is one being fought along these lines within the hapless churches, ostensibly the representatives of the reign of God, though more often than not little more than funeral societies. Our situation is dire (Mark 4:9), and so the disputation undertaken in this book is a matter of some urgency.

The metaphysics of divine simplicity thus seems to many whose primary adherence is to canonical Scripture as the matrix of Christian theology the reification of a vicious abstraction; its restoration would mean, so far as we are thinking clearly, a return to the polyphony of the many cults all equally close to and equally distant from the One, with Christians and other gnostics claiming the superiority of knowing this. The liberating command of the God of exodus, "I am the LORD your God," seems in turn to those whose loyalty is to "God beyond the gods" a biblicistic and literalistic credulity that remains on the level of myth until ontologically clarified. Both versions of simplicity today still have their advantages. If one is looking for a harmonization that defangs the religions under the benign imperium of political sovereignty, protological simplicity appeals. If one is looking for the destabilization that defangs political sovereignty by the subversive penetration of the alternative order of the Beloved Community, eschatological simplicity attracts. As mentioned, these rival versions of simplicity can even temporarily converge in practical alliances. What neither can suffer in principle any longer is their synthesis, for, as the Spokesperson of the biblical version put it, "No one can serve two masters." One version or the other will in fact prevail as the driving motor, as they are notions that exhibit diverging trajectories. But if Christendom was

6. Robert W. Jenson, "How the World Lost Its Story," *First Things* 36 (1993): 19–24; online: http://www.firstthings.com/article/2010/03/how-the-world-lost-its-story.

7. Paul R. Hinlicky, *Before Auschwitz: What Christian Theology Must Learn from the Rise of Nazism* (Eugene, OR: Cascade, 2013).

the attempted synthesis of the two doctrines of simplicity in what can broadly be called Christian Platonism, there is no going back. There is no going back because the synthesis has proved to be untenable. In such a world the church will have to learn to stand again on its own two feet—that is, the gospel and its Scriptures, provided these are taken with metaphysical seriousness.

The evidence for this claim is indeed canonical. In Corinth the "strong" party of Christians was thinking of the *ecclesia* as one cult among others, indeed a highly enlightened one that knows that all others, deep down, are thinking, or ought to be thinking, as they do; under the surface differences, others are just the same, who would be "strong" like them if only they could. The overlap appears when Paul concedes the truth, in the abstract, of the statement "God is one" to the party in Corinth that understood itself as stronger and more gifted in gnosis than the weak, who were literalists and fundamentalists, not yet enlightened. Yet what "the strong" have forgotten, as Paul elaborates, is that their epistemic access as erstwhile idolaters to the truth "God is one" has come about through the one Son of the one God and Father. In Paul's word concerning this Son, they have met in Him the liberating event on the earth of the love of God for them, "not many wise, not many powerful, not many well born." Though this apostolic word seems "folly" to the sapient (those "in the know"), it is indeed a paradoxical announcement regarding bizarrely "good" news of a crucified victor (1 Cor. 1:17–31). And further, Paul teaches, this access of faith by the folly of preaching news that is bizarrely called "good" is itself a manifestation and demonstration of the oneness of the one God and Father through the one Lord Jesus Christ *in His Spirit* (1 Cor. 2:1–3:16), the *Holy* Spirit, who unifies the "natural man" (1 Cor. 2:14) with the crucified Christ in death in order to bring forth from that grave "Spirited" children who now live to the God and Father.

This is gnosis. This is what is necessary to know. This is the real Christian gnosis, as we saw in Clement, since "in this present evil age" both strong and weak are still demonically assailed under the masks of "so-called gods and lords" who would seduce them from this newly "Spirited" way in the world. Because the strong have forgotten about this persisting battle, in which the new and saving Lord Jesus had first won them, and have come in their forgetfulness to think they have already prevailed as resurrected and now supernatural beings, they know the truth "God is one" in a false way. It is for them but a liberating ideology that frees them ("All things are lawful" [1 Cor. 10:23]) from the scruples of the weak;[8] it is not a conscience-binding claim that forms them

8. Hans Conzelmann, *1 Corinthians: A Commentary on the First Epistle of the Corinthians*, trans. James W. Leitch, Hermeneia (Philadelphia: Fortress, 1975), 139–45.

together also with the weak, the literalist, the fundamentalist as one *koinōnia* in the body and blood of the Lord (1 Cor. 10:14–22; 11:17–32), through whom they have been accessed—that is, bought with a price that they may glorify God in their bodies together (1 Cor. 6:20).

So Paul regrounds the falsely thinking party of the strong in Corinth with the prototrinitarian confession of faith, that "for us there is one God, the Father, from whom are all things and for whom we exist, and one Lord, Jesus Christ, through whom are all things and through whom we exist" (1 Cor. 8:6). In this way of the redemption and fulfillment of His creation by the missions of His Son and Spirit, God is one "for us." As Luther might have put it, then, "It is one thing that God in heaven is one and quite another that God is one for us, that God's will is done on earth as in heaven." The latter is not a simple, let alone timeless, manifestation of the former, however, but rather a complex enactment of divine sovereignty coterminous with natural and human history—the coming of the reign of God to the very earth on which stood the cross of Jesus. Its claim to truth depends on its actual fulfillment, as if to say, "If Christ has not been raised, your faith is futile and you are still [dead] in your sins" (1 Cor. 15:17), or, what is the same, if God does not become "all in all" (1 Cor. 15:28), then this God of the gospel never was the one true God, also of the origin.

Under such epistemic conditions of access, then, it is self-deception to abstract from this God for us to a heavenly being beyond the fray that secures adherents from the risk and the hope of faith for this very earth as the site of fulfillment and object of redemption for the coming Beloved Community. If that is right, Paul, then, would likely be amazed to learn how so astute a pupil of his, as Augustine of Hippo proved to be centuries later, could have stumbled over his manifesto to the Corinthians that "Christ is the power and wisdom of God."

How Augustine Stumbled (cf. 1 Cor. 1:23) over the Folly of God

This stumbling occurred in the sixth and seventh books of Augustine's massive treatise *De Trinitate*; there Augustine, after faithfully and indeed insightfully reporting through the first four books on the Eastern doctrine of the Trinity that had been ratified in the course of the first two ecumenical councils, articulated a certain prima facie objection to it. Commenting on 1 Corinthians 1:24, he wrote, "Equality seems to be lacking here, since the Father is not himself, according to this text, power and wisdom, but the begetter of power and wisdom."[9] Augustine's objection about the apparent lack of

9. Augustine, *On the Trinity*, trans. Edmund Hill (New York: New City Press, 1991), 205.

equality seems, then, to be concerned with ontological inequality among the Three, usually taken as a subordinationism of the second and third persons, though in this case it seems that it is the Father's deity that is diminished, if He is wise and powerful not in Himself but in Christ His Son. Like Marcella of Ancyra a generation earlier in the East, Augustine seems to be concerned for the equality in divine nature of the Father and Son. But in fact his concern is with protological simplicity.

He went on to argue that if Christ were the wisdom or power by which the Father is wise or powerful, then the Father has power or wisdom not of His own, but by another, His Son. If that is so, then the one God's nature is separated into parts, some lacking to the Father but belonging to the Son. Of course, theoretically, such parceling of parts could be balanced among the Three to equalize them each in contributing something essential, however unseemly it would be to think of the one God as a composite in three parts dissimilar in content but equal in value. Just so, the concern is not really equality. Rather, it is the thought of a composite deity. Yet this concern about composition too conceals a presupposition, namely, that "nature" is a some-thing, reality, substantial. If, by contrast, we took "nature" semantically as a conceptual class specifying the perfections that befit the divine and, further, construed befitting attributes of divinity according to what properties or capacities must be at the disposal of the God who as personal subject freely creates everything other than God for the good of the Beloved Community—as we learn the deity of God from the gospel—then we could see that individual divine persons utilize and so manifest particular properties from that class of divine perfections according to their personal distinctions and corresponding economic roles, even as these personal identities and economic roles are indi-visible in the sense of mutually entailing one another. And in fact, Christian worship performs just this distribution in the doxological attribution of all power to the Creator Father, all wisdom to the Logos incarnate, and all good-ness to the hallowing Spirit.

Thus, if Augustine had not been assuming the substantiality of con-cepts, and instead actually understood (he acknowledges that he does not) the nature-person distinction from Eastern trinitarianism (obscured by the Latin rendering of *ousia* as *substantia*, seemingly synonymous then with the Greek *hypostasis*, translated into Latin as *persona*, as I will discuss below), he would have seen the fittingness of the incarnation of the Son—*only* the Son; that is, he would have seen the "subordination" of the incarnate Son in the economy corresponding to the immanent derivation of the Son from the Father and return in the Spirit to the Father in eternity. And he would have seen that such an economic "subordination," based upon an immanent "derivation" and "return," is nonetheless saving (i.e., the Pauline "He who was rich for our sakes became poor"). It is saving just because of the Son's equality to the Father with respect to access as a subject to the same divine properties or capabilities as the Father (*homoousios*), although He has them and uses them concretely in the personal way of being Son of the Father and thus according to His economic role as the incarnate Word and Wisdom of God "for us and for our salvation."

The problem that Augustine has is not really subordinationism, then, but rather the apparent violation of divine simplicity expressed in Paul's celebration of Christ the power and wisdom of God. No matter that the persons are *essentially* linked, the apparent separation of essential attributes of deity as such in 1 Corinthians 1:24 violates protological unity and makes of divine nature a composite (if, that is, we are thinking of divine nature as something substantial). What is composed can also decompose; what is put together can also fall apart. In the case of God, that is unthinkable (but how thinkable is the cross of the Son of God, which, according to 1 Cor. 1:18–25, is the stumbling block of God's folly, wiser than human wisdom?). The divine bearer of perfections, like wisdom or power, must instead be thought as the one, indivisible divine *nature* that Father and Son each wholly and equally (but somehow differently) *simply* are. The one divine substance is thus thought wholly and equally to supposit or underlie—*sub-stantia*—the three divine persons. This is what is really real in God, taken absolutely.

Augustine came to this deleterious conclusion by lamenting "our desire to express the inexpressible."[10] This speculative desire, he claims, has forced us into an unsolvable conundrum of how three can be one and one can be three, with the result that "we just have to admit that these various usages were developed by the sheer necessity of saying something, when the fullest possible argument was called for against the traps and errors of the heretics."[11] Just so, however, a muddle is now sanctified as a mystery. The Trinity of God has been turned into an unintelligible datum, a mathematical conundrum, a supernatural truth "transcending reason" that can only be revealed as a dogma to be believed and taken as such on faith in the authority of the revelation, which is in reality the authority of a self-proclaimed ecclesiastical orthodoxy against those arbitrarily designated, but no longer understood, as deviants. That is to say, the Trinity of God has ceased to be thought of as God in His truthful self-revelation for us and our salvation, evoking faith; instead, an ideology about God that professedly makes no sense has been substituted

10. Augustine, *On the Trinity*, 218.
11. Augustine, *On the Trinity*, 227.

for God revealing God by His Word and Spirit. And this sanctified ideology is now required to be held on pain of eternal loss.

The problem with Augustine's subtle refashioning of the doctrine of the Trinity is the same problem presented by the zealously pro-Nicene Easterner Marcellus, who so championed the equality of Son with Father in divinity that he erased the personal distinction between them.[12] It was precisely Athanasius's realization (with the aid of the Cappadocians) of the problem with Marcellus's modalist erasure of the personal distinctions that paved the way for the revolutionary distinction between *ousia* and *hypostasis* that is executed in the mature doctrine of the Trinity from the council in Constantinople in 381. Augustine is saved from being Marcellus *redivivus* only by his express agnosticism—that is, his ultimate apophaticism that conveniently anoints as a mystery the contradiction that he has forced between trinitarian personalism and protological simplicity. In the end, it is all a "mystery" about which we say something that makes professedly no sense rather than say nothing at all; we speak merely to contradict the "heretics" but cannot now show the error for what it is by accounting for the gospel's trinitarian discourse.

In fact, the muddle conceals tendencies dangerous to the theological understanding of the gospel, beginning with the substitution of ecclesiastical authority for theological understanding (for which cause Athanasius seven times endured exile); the muddle demands implicit faith in the church rather than shows forth the church's explicit faith in the God of the gospel. The absolute-relative distinction in language for God that Augustine devises to parse substantial and personal attributions of God respectively inevitably suggests that God is God for God absolutely, indivisibly, but God for us appears as the Three, relatively. That precisely would be modalism, in which God in His essential reality is something infinitely other than God in His historical self-revelation as the Three of the gospel narrative. The one divine nature thus reified, it is now inevitably thought of as a foundational fourth, the One, over against the Three, and so we come to the de facto quaternity of Western modalism. In the process, the intelligibility of seeing the one God of the gospel as the dramatic story of Jesus, His Father, and their Spirit for us and our salvation is squandered, swallowed up in a pseudoapophatic fog of putative ineffability that is in fact ecclesiastical mystery-mongering.

The error in Augustine's doctrine of simplicity that so leads him astray is the major topic considered in this chapter. "What it comes to is this," Augustine

---

12. Jaroslav Pelikan, *The Christian Tradition: A History of the Development of Doctrine*, vol. 1, *The Emergence of the Catholic Tradition (100–600)* (Chicago: University of Chicago Press, 1971), 207–8.

concluded, "every being that is called something by way of relationship is also something besides the relationship."[13] This statement against relational ontology resources the modalist tendency of Western theology to separate ontologically the absolute and the relative God, on the basis of what Augustine first devised as a semantical strategy. It came to be articulated as a strong distinction between an immanent or ontological Trinity and an economic Trinity, which scheme lends an antimodalist veneer to what remains essentially a modalist way of thinking. But even the original semantical strategy of distinguishing absolute and relative attributions was forced upon Augustine by his failure to understand person as the patient-agent constituted essentially in community by the circulation of life in love, in the admittedly unique case where what is real is the Beloved Community of the patient-agents, the Father of the Son in the Holy Spirit, as the one, holy, and eternal God. But it is Augustine's uncomprehending reduction of person to the bare relations (or mental operations, under the psychological model with which he so much experimented) by which they are distinguished that forces in turn the reification of divine nature in their place. The result is that the really real divine substance of timeless self-identity along the lines of the protological metaphysics of simplicity is treated as a quasi-agent, fully actual and incapable of patiency. But by patiency the Son and the Spirit divinely receive their being from the Father, even as the Father divinely receives his personal identification as the Father in the eternal return of the Son in the Spirit to the praise of His deity.

The path before us for the remainder of this chapter is as follows. We will next consider a helpful recent historical resourcing of the contemporary debate on simplicity from the pen of Gavin Ortlund, a supporter of protological simplicity, which requires us to recognize the factual variety of divine simplicities that have appeared in the history of doctrine and, furthermore, provides us with a very helpful distinction between strong and weak versions of the doctrine of divine simplicity. This will lead us directly into a succinct consideration of Lewis Ayres's powerful case for Augustine and the Western tradition's strong doctrine of protological simplicity. Ayres makes the best case I know of against the critique of it being prosecuted in this book. Ayres defends, if I may recast his position in my own terms, the very ambiguity of the received doctrine of simplicity in the West that I am attacking as a muddle, not a proper mystery, and so trying to resolve in this book. This *Auseinandersetzung* with Ayres will prepare the way for debate with the main interlocutor of this chapter, Maarten Wisse. Wisse has written an insightful, if one-sided, book on Augustine from a classical Reformed perspective that

---

13. Augustine, *On the Trinity*, 219.

takes no prisoners, left or right. His work complicates matters in a helpful way by opposing certain truisms in Radical Orthodoxy's claim to Augustine via Thomas, just as it serves in a dialectical way to confirm the Régnon thesis that Ayres is concerned to undermine. After a brief retrospect on the Cappadocian campaign against the "strong" simplicity of the later hyper-Arians for the sake of the nature-person distinction entailing a "weak" version of simplicity, I will conclude this chapter with consideration of the Norwegian Lutheran Knut Alfsvåg's innovative case for christological apophaticism to properly understand the Pauline "Christ the power and wisdom of God."

The movement of the argument of this chapter, then, toward the christological problem will lead into the final chapter. In the process I will show that simplicity is best taken as an apophatic qualification of the primary kataphatic self-presentation of the God of the gospel. It is to be taken, then, as a rule—in fact, as nothing other than the first table of the Decalogue. In so doing, we will have discovered the christological problem that must accompany the protological metaphysics of divine simplicity: the tendency toward modalism in Western theology correlates with a Nestorian tendency in Western Christology. Moreover, this separation of Jesus Christ the Son of God into two sons, one of Mary and another of God, albeit in analogy to each other, is concealed in doctrines that privilege similitude over paradox as key to the gospel's theological language. But it is paradox, according to 1 Corinthians 2:2, that is the gateway to the similitude of the newborn children of God, members of Christ, the new Adam.

The Diversity of Simplicities

According to a recent study by Gavin Ortlund,[14] a variety of doctrines of simplicity have appeared and contended in the history of Christian theology, and it is helpful to sort out these diversities of simplicity, so to say, into strong and weak versions. What all have in common, he contends, is the conviction that God has no parts, that God is in no way a spatial or temporal composite, but, as the unbounded or infinite divine life must be thought of, God is without beginning or end and without boundaries, eternal and immeasurable. God to God for God is thus ontologically a spatial and temporal infinity, capable, then, of being omnipresent and omnitemporal should God in fact create a world of time and space other than God for creatures to inhabit. That being said, the major sorting of doctrines of simplicity that he provides puts the

14. Gavin Ortlund, "Divine Simplicity in Historical Perspective: Resourcing a Contemporary Discussion," *Modern Theology* 16, no. 4 (October 2014): 436–52.

doctrines of simplicity, holding to these convictions about deity, into baskets of "strong" and "weak" versions.

Thomas Aquinas's version is the classical representative of the strong version of simplicity in that it maintains, as we have seen, a thesis of timeless self-identity. According to this, God is fully and timelessly identical to His attributes in one fully actual existence, so that all predications made about God from the side of creatures in their multiplicity tell us about these creatures in relation to God rather than anything specific about God, taken absolutely. The weak version of simplicity has a variety of forms but always allows that God is not *substantially* identical to attributions that we make of Him, yet may truly be said to participate in these attributions in the manner (1) of instantiating properties as a subject, as it were, "accidentally," or (2) of acquisitions derived from extrinsic relations. (For the sake of clarity, let me note here that the tacit adoption of a substance/accidents scheme by Ortlund will remain problematic for the weak version of simplicity that I will incorporate in the course of this section for the rule version of simplicity, since personal subjects are substantially, not accidentally, formed in their histories by their relations. The difference between the tri-personal life of the eternal and immeasurable God and that of a rational creature is that God from God forms God in God, while the creature is formed by this same tri-personal God for a share in eternal life by union with the Son.)

The substantial nonidentity with divine properties in weak simplicity, which provides for God's free self-determination and protects God's irreducibility *as a subject or person* to freely undertake relations with creatures, may be understood to reflect a nominalism that is neither Platonic nor Aristotelian; that is, it reflects a metaphysics that does not regard "nature" as anything real but instead takes "nature" as a conceptual classification of capabilities (properties that may be accessed, as in, "It is proper to God to give life") by which we creatures efficiently sort things and persons for the processing of information in the tasks of life. So if I, the creature, say that God is all-powerful, what I mean is that some particular God, as subject, has access to all possibilities. Yet, at the same time, I am saying that as subject, God may or may not choose to exercise, or to instantiate all the possibilities that are available to Him. God is freely self-determining in a uniquely unlimited way and thus also to creatures when He relates to them.[15] He may or may not

15. "God is He for Whose will no cause or ground [*ratio*] may be laid down as its rule or standard; for nothing is on a level with it or above it, but it is itself the rule for all things. . . . Causes and grounds may be laid down for the will of the creature, but not for the will of the Creator—unless you set another Creator over him!" (Martin Luther, *The Bondage of the Will*, trans. J. I. Packer and O. R. Johnston [Old Tappan, NJ: Revell, 1957], 209). It is

create a world. He may or may not create this particular world. While His choices can and should be seen in retrospect to be fitting expressions of His deity as the harmony of power and wisdom and love, they are never necessitated by His nature, which would be the case if divine nature were what is really real in God. Consequently, we cannot know in advance what God must be; we must look and see how God actually operates and learn what God is from who God is, as revealed in God's operations, as per Paul's scripturally definitive statement, "Christ is the power and wisdom of God."

Moreover, according to weak simplicity taken in this nominalist way against a realist conceptualism, God may acquire extrinsic or accidental properties and in this way—without prejudice to divine irreducibility to relations with creatures—become something that God had not been. God can *become* Creator, incarnate, the temple of redeemed humanity, and so forth, and these extrinsic and acquired properties truly become His own and thus proper to Him. Moreover, this decided God does and therefore can suffer—to be sure, not in the pathetic fashion of creatures but precisely as the freely self-determined God. God preeminently does and can suffer wills contradicting His own, as in God's long-suffering patience with sinful humanity. That is to say, God may forgo possibilities at His disposal, as the Noah saga finally teaches (Gen. 8:21), for the sake of actualizing new and redemptive ones (Gen. 12:1–3). Indeed, it would seem that the ability to affirm such choices of God and intend such affirmations truthfully is crucially important, indeed essential, to Christian theology, as we may recall from R. T. Mullins's argument in chapter 1. But then this God cannot be tucked neatly into a metaphysical straightjacket in which it is a disqualifying imperfection to have as one's disposition unactualized possibilities, internally or externally. Rather, as in Mark 10:27 and 14:36, the perfection of God will be understood in God's having all possibilities but using them (instantiating or actualizing them) only in perfect harmony with wisdom and love and according to God's own tri-personal way of being.

With this basic sorting, we can appreciate the diversity of ways that notions of the divine simplicity have functioned in the history of Christian doctrine. The Cappadocian fathers, according to Ortlund, rejected the strong doctrine of simplicity in their battle with Eunomius and his hyper-Arian followers (the position later advocated, as Ortlund notes, by Maimonides and Avicenna), while for Augustine and Thomas the point of the strong version was not to reconcile God's threeness with monotheism but rather to ground God's

---

interesting to note here in passing that the power to freely or spontaneously initiate something new within the causal nexus that Luther here ascribes solely to God becomes in Kant the noumenal freedom ascribed to the practical subject as the basis for his ethics of duty and morality of merit.

threeness in a natural unity over against Jewish, Islamic, and philosophical accusations of polytheism. The Eastern tradition, codified in John of Damascus,
however, sought with its essence-energy distinction (already visible in Clement
of Alexandria, as we have seen in the excursus to chap. 2) to safeguard God's
unfathomable essence even from the kataphatic identification of it as Being
Itself in strong simplicity, as we find (although ambiguously and unstably) in
Thomas. The essence-energy distinction of Byzantine theology warned that
God is essentially beyond being and nonbeing, simply unfathomable, the
Not-a-Nothing said nevertheless to be truly present as such and knowable
in His operations where this essence presents as the Three. But this recollection of the kataphatic God of the gospel can be nothing but a bald assertion,
according to this scheme, since it is impossible to know how a known and
an unknown are one and the same. In the end, any such identification of the
essence and the energies is a leap in the dark, even when we assert a truth of
revelation. In the West, by contrast with Byzantine theology, Anselm followed
the lead of Augustine and prepared the way for Thomas by the kataphatic
analysis in the *Proslogion* of the notion of perfect being as thought thinking
and willing itself, yielding the psychological trinity—that is, the act of being
perfectly that is God depicted as Mind without body. Perfect-being theism
seems the natural outcome of this kataphatic line of thought, though again,
this similarity must always be asserted within an ever-greater dissimilarity,
which will finally undermine it too. The power of the negative, once admitted, devours all.

The simplicity doctrine of Pseudo-Dionysius, according to Ortlund, represents something of a middle way between East and West, since he, like Plotinus,
thinks of God as essentially beyond the distinction of being and nonbeing,
just so as the "cause of all unity and distinction which itself transcends the
very categories of unity and distinction."[16] Connections, then, may be made
in Pseudo-Dionysius both to the East's derivation of divine simplicity from
the infinity of the unknowable divine essence and to the West's articulation
of the essence as a thinkable Being Itself, the perfect union of essence and
existence in the simple act of perfect being. Yet the coherence of such a synthesis in Pseudo-Dionysius's thought may be doubted. Pseudo-Dionysius
"uses divine simplicity and Trinity to explain unity and diversity in creation;
he apparently does not consider that they need explanation themselves,"[17] let
alone explanation of how the two motifs hang together. Be that as it may, in
the West the Dionysian view served, as Ortlund especially notes, the rejection

16. Ortlund, "Divine Simplicity," 444.
17. Ibid., 445.

of "a univocal Creator-creation relation" in that God transcends "the very categories of being and distinction."[18] This rejection of univocity by negative theology, then, becomes axiomatic in Thomas, for whom creatures may be likened to God in some ways, but God is like them in no ways. This in time produces the famous analogy of being (as I will discuss in detail in chap. 4), a similarity asserted in the notion of existence within an ever-greater dissimilarity. Ultimately, then, even when we say kataphatically that God is Being Itself, it cannot be taken as a literal statement, but only as a statement that God is the somehow perfect in relation to us imperfect beings. To us, God is Being Itself, hence the notion is not properly ascribed to God as if we had any idea what Being Itself is for itself. Rather, God as Being Itself points beyond its literal formulation to "God above God" (Paul Tillich came to a similar realization)[19] and so ends ultimately in the silence of apophaticism (or rather, befuddlement).

Thus we strike again upon the peculiar oscillation (having one's cake and eating it too!) that attends the strong doctrine of simplicity: in a seemingly unprincipled way it either deploys as if a kataphatic insight into divine nature as the timeless self-identity of *esse ipsum subsistens* that grounds all multiplicity and change or, if pressed, retracts apophatically as if to deny that this grounding is a cause in any way that we can apprehend or even imagine. Thomas, following Augustine, reconciled strong simplicity with trinitarianism by a semantical strategy according to which God is predicated absolutely with respect to His simple essence but relatively with respect to His tri-personhood. Given this parsing, attributions do not properly befall God but rather the creatures who make them (e.g., I say that God is just when God is just to me, wrathful when God is wrathful to me, Jesus when God is Jesus to me). Applied to God, attributions must be assigned substantially to the divine essence. However, their diversity on the lips of creatures retracts into the ineffable and timeless self-identity of God, in whom all perfections are simply one and the same indifferently. Then all statements by creatures about God are equally true and equally false.

We creatures may perceive differences, say, between power and wisdom and love, between Jesus and, say, Stalin as putative icons of God, and we may even think that these diverse attributions are important for saying in what way(s) God is divine—namely, as Creator of all that is not God for the sake of the Beloved Community (if we are Christians), or in some other way (if we are not Christians). For example, we might want to privilege power and

18. Ibid.
19. Paul Tillich, *Systematic Theology* (Chicago: University of Chicago Press, 1967), 2:5–12.

say that God can be whatever God wills, a theology of divine voluntarism; or wisdom, and say that God is the intelligence that unifies the cosmos as a coherent system, a theology of intelligent design; or love, and say with Plato that God is only responsible for the good and cannot be faulted for the rude material with which He must work. We might in just these ways play the attributes against one another or, conversely, try to harmonize them, as Leibniz did in his *Theodicy*. All this talk about God, however, is really talk about ourselves, since in God these and any other perfections that we might imagine are simply, timelessly one and the same being in its eternal perfect and indifferent actuality.

Ortlund himself seems persuaded to the path taken by Augustine and Thomas. How else is God's unity to be secured and made irreducible to creatures than to make creaturely attribution fall short of its object? Ortlund concludes that the new debate about simplicity is evidence that perichoresis "alone" does not suffice. "Why should the interpenetration of the three persons yield one undivided unity, and not some complex aggregate?"[20] Thus, some version of simplicity is required because it "is able to bind the three persons, not merely *into each other*, but into the one divine essence."[21] Simplicity is a "mechanism by which to unite the divine persons as *one*"[22]—that is, as more than a numerical one, as substantial reality or ontological unity.

Ortlund's objection overlooks the fact that perichoresis is not an independent metaphysical postulate (as critics, perhaps not altogether unjustly, take Zizioulas's "being as communion")[23] supposedly put to work to render the same service as protological simplicity. Relational ontology is an invention of Christian thought, a revision of classical metaphysics by the eschatology of the gospel. It comes to pristine expression in the Johannine exegesis of the event of Jesus Christ in the high priestly prayer (John 17). Perichoresis here is not "alone," nor are the distinct persons "alone," since they exist as persons only in essential communion with one other, this harmony of love being what God is for God in God and thus also for creatures in the history that this same God initiates with them. This Father cannot be the Father that He is apart from the Son on whom He breathes His Spirit, and so on through the Son and the Spirit. However, a weak doctrine of simplicity does the work here of qualifying this perichoresis as that of the One who is Creator of all that He is not. This "weak" way has the advantage that it does not absorb the God

20. Ortlund, "Divine Simplicity," 452.
21. Ibid.
22. Ibid.
23. John D. Zizioulas, *Being as Communion: Studies in Personhood and the Church* (Crestwood, NY: St. Vladimir's Seminary Press, 1993).

appearing in the gospel as the Three into heavenly mists, but instead specifies God's oneness in relation to creatures as that of the Beloved Community. Thus, it also allows the divine acquisition of properties new to God as also to creatures in His history with them that is the creation destined for redemption and fulfillment by the missions of the Son and the Spirit. Weak simplicity can do this because it is not burdened with the metaphysical straightjacket of Aristotelian naturalism, according to which "nature" or "essence" must be potential if not actualized, so that, as a consequence, possibilities must be forbidden to the One who purely is He Who Is. This naturalism comes at too high a price for Christian theology, since it makes God the prisoner of His supposedly perfect actuality.

Could such a deity have truthfully said on that same occasion of the revelation of the divine Name, "I have observed the misery of my people who are in Egypt; I have heard their cry on account of their taskmasters. Indeed, I know their sufferings, and I have come down to deliver them" (Exod. 3:7–8a)? Weak simplicity does allow this statement as a truthful word from God about God. It works semantically to allow the trinitarian revolution's reinterpretation of nature as but clarifying concepts classifying sets of possibilities, where the determination of one such set as divine cannot be adduced a priori but instead must be gained from the claims of a claimant to the title—that is, from a person. Ontologically, nothing here is accorded reality status but things or persons appearing in history, which are not natures but rather have natures as things or subjects or persons. So also a putative God who does not appear in history is a No-Thing—at least nothing to us who are creatures inhabiting history. For the same reason, cooking up schemes of self-transcendence to get out of history is but the factory of idols, our reifications of No-Thing rather than our reception of the God who gives, *esse Deum dare*.

One would have to canonize the metaphysics of Aristotle in order to avoid this acute rejoinder to the objection to consistent perichoresis according to a weak account of divine simplicity. Ortlund acknowledges this alternative possibility in a footnote given to Nicholas Wolterstorff, though he does not attend much to it. It is the claim that the ancients tended to work with a "constituent ontology," according to which an entity relates to its nature and properties as constituent components, while contemporaries tend to think in terms of a "relation ontology," according to which entities relate to their natures by exemplifying them.[24] The point of a "relation ontology" theologically is that the trinitarian persons are free subjects of the divine nature, that divine nature is instantiated in what these persons do in their history with one another and

24. Ortlund, "Divine Simplicity," 444n50.

with us, and that the circle here is a virtuous one that enables knowledge of God in the missions of His Son and Spirit to redeem and fulfill the creation. This God is precisely not prisoner to a divine nature that is a metaphysical dream in any case. The God of the gospel is not the One who can only time-lessly and identically exemplify an empty tautology (yet supposedly, in Christian adaptation, exemplify it differently according to a revealed distinction of persons that no longer makes any sense and can do no theological work). In any event, Ortlund has helpfully resourced this contemporary debate by showing that the history of divine simplicity is not simple, that no single version of it may claim to be the settled *consensus fidelium*.

In Defense of Augustine

Lewis Ayres's *Nicaea and Its Legacy* is, in my view, the best contemporary case from the patristic sources opposing the modern nominalism in ontology just referenced.[25] I wish to indicate from the outset of this engagement, however, that I concur with Ayres's call "to resist the modes of narration common in modern systematics" insofar as the contemporary academic requirements of systematicity overwhelm the textual sources of Christian theology (indeed, the very same accusation was made by the Reformation against "scholastic theology").[26] I further concur with his corresponding summons "for developing new skills of attention to particular creedal texts and authoritative theologians as a foundation for reading the plain sense of the Scripture," although I prefer to express this point by speaking of canon, creed, and confession as together forming a hermeneutical whole.[27] In any case, let this agreement be kept in mind in what follows, for I will not agree with Ayres, in Wolterstorff's terminology, that a "constituent ontology" is better suited than a "relation ontology" for the theological exposition of the unity of the Triune God. "Modernity" and its predecessors, including medieval theology, are not such gross, monolithic, and undifferentiated magnitudes as his opposition to "seeing modernity as providing a necessary reorientation of Christian doctrine" would suggest.[28] The danger of nostalgia is equally pertinent.

25. Lewis Ayres, *Nicaea and Its Legacy: An Approach to Fourth-Century Trinitarian Theology* (Oxford: Oxford University Press, 2006).

26. Paul R. Hinlicky, *Beloved Community: Critical Dogmatics after Christendom* (Grand Rapids: Eerdmans, 2015), 47–48.

27. Paul R. Hinlicky, "Luther's Anti-Docetism in the Disputatio de divinitate et humanitate Christi (1540)," in *Creator Est Creatura: Luthers Christologie als Lehre von der Idiomenkommunikation*, ed. Oswald Bayer and Benjamin Gleede (Berlin: de Gruyter, 2007), 147–66.

28. Ayres, *Nicaea and Its Legacy*, 422.

In this connection, Ayres humorously titles a late chapter in his book "In Spite of Hegel, Fire, and Sword," naming the enemy who is modernity. But, in reality, Hegel can hardly be accused of holding to the "weak" doctrine of simplicity articulated above and recast as rule, as advocated in this book; this polemic against Hegel (descended, as we will see in the next chapter, from Przywara) amounts to something of a distraction, if not a red herring. To be sure, Hegel can be read in a "left-wing," atheistic way as philosophizing the death of the abstract otherworldly god and its rebirth as the world coming to self-consciousness. Hegel, ever the dodge, can also be read in a "right-wing" fashion, as I think Jenson is at times guilty of.[29] And this right-wing reading would revert to a kind of Origenism in which God must be taken as essentially creative and thus incomplete without a creation by which to actualize Himself. Despite the historical Origen's undoubted orthodox intention, and indeed his significant contribution to the development of the doctrine of the Trinity with the notion of eternal generation (a not unimportant point in the case that Ayres makes for simplicity), Origenism, as it later developed, had to be rejected as a deviation. On the other hand, given the moribund state of the Western doctrine of the Trinity in the early nineteenth century, even this much of an advance from frigid deism and complacent theism to living and breathing Origenism in Hegel was a contribution to the doctrine's renewal through the course of the twentieth century.

For Nicene trinitarianism, in contrast to Origenism old and new, God's eternal existence *is* the Father birthing the Son, on whom He breathes the Spirit, so that in the Spirit the Son returns to the Father the praise of His deity in an infinite circulation of life. As such, this perfect act of eternal becoming, which I denominate the "Beloved Community," can and does turn outward; its circle spirals out of its own infinite abundance to give, redeem, and fulfill the life of creatures. Out of love the Father of the Son in the Spirit chooses to be unblessed with us rather than blessed without us. Within its own life as also without, *esse Deum dare*. Yet a genuine gift can never be forced or necessitated. It reflects the power to initiate spontaneously. God, who is by nature the Father giving His being to the Son and the Spirit, *becomes* by a free act of will the Creator of a creation other than God—not out of a need, even need of creative self-expression, but out of surplus in what is known from the origin to be a costly act of love for others, inferior in being and morally derelict as we have become.

Along these lines, Ayres has to acknowledge and does acknowledge, especially in the case of Gregory of Nazianzus, just this way of articulating the

---

29. See, for example, Hinlicky, *Beloved Community*, 339–40.

unity of the divine Trinity as a circle of eternal becoming. "For Gregory, the generative nature of God eternally produces the triunity as the perfection of divine existence."[30] He cites from Gregory's *Oration* 29.2: "The one eternally changes to two and stops at three—meaning the Father, the Son, and the Holy Spirit. In a serene and non-temporal, incorporeal way, the Father is parent of the 'offspring' and originator of the 'emanation' . . . [though] we ought never to introduce the notion of involuntary generation." Involuntary generation would once again privilege some antecedent concept of divine nature over person; but the Father's act of being is the personal self-surpassing that results in the communion with the Son in the Spirit. The eternal event of God's life as His personal act of being is qualified in the way of weak simplicity by Gregory as "serene," "non-temporal," and "incorporeal." Indeed, Gregory maintains that "we must define a Trinity for the sake of perfection," not the other way around—that is, define perfect being for the sake of unifying the Three, as happens in Augustine, as we have seen. Ayres acknowledges that Gregory's teaching here is the development "of an important strain of earlier pro-Nicene thought," though in the same breath he softly faults Gregory for regarding "triunity as the perfection of divine existence" and as such the "point of departure" for theological thought rather than as a position to be argued. As a result, he says, "Once fully pro-Nicene theologies emerged in which all three persons were described as irreducible, then the pressure grew to show not only how this three-in-oneness did not contradict the divine simplicity, but also how this three-in-oneness was an expression of what it meant to be God."[31]

In a similar way, after a discussion of Gregory of Nyssa, Ayres acknowledges that Nyssa's (weak doctrine of) simplicity merely disallows the implication of ontological subordination in the teaching on the monarchy of the Father. Yet, this concession does not suffice, as Ayres continues, to overcome subordinationism, since "the priority of the Father as cause—even if it is the priority of one who eternally gives rise to a mutuality of loving exchange—is in some sense still a priority."[32] To which Nyssa might be imagined to reply, "Precisely. What is your point?" To which Ayres would, with Augustine, respond, "At the same time Scripture demands that we speak of a unitary divine power and nature,"[33] while cause, and being caused, hardly seem to be unitary in power and nature. The Augustinian reduces the tri-personal operation of God revealed in Scripture to the simple nature of the One as its expression

30. Ayres, *Nicaea and Its Legacy*, 244–45.
31. Ibid., 245.
32. Ibid., 363.
33. Ibid.

in time, the One appearing as Many in relation to the many (not, then, with the indivisibility of the Father of the Son in the Spirit who as such becomes freely self-determined to redeem and fulfill His creation through the missions of His Son and Spirit, as the principle *opera Dei ad extra indivisa sunt* should be understood).

Instead, then, of inviting us to understand theologically the God of the gospel "according to the revelation of the mystery that was kept secret for long ages but is now disclosed" (Rom. 16:25b–26a), Ayres summons us to the analogy of being, as if it were axiomatic that we take God's action as the (mere) repetition in time of what God is timelessly and self-identically rather than a repetition by which the God of the gospel acquires lost humanity as His own—that is, acquires an extrinsic property as properly now His own. Ayres thus impugns the Régnon thesis as a distortion produced by modernity: "For those modern commentators who accept the account of east and west as differentiated by a preference for social or mental analogies, failure to deploy some sort of social analogy of necessity implies a failure to distinguish the three persons appropriately."[34] Of course, the reader recognizes that I have been (more than!) "implying" a Western tendency to modalism on account of Augustine's (and Anselm's and Thomas's and even in some moods Luther's)[35] filtering of the teaching on the Three of the gospel narrative through the Neoplatonic model of divine simplicity as mind perfectly thinking and willing itself and parsing God by the distinction of absolute and relative predications. Ayres then concludes, "However, such an equation is not a necessary one and its deployment reveals a lack of understanding of the peculiarly modern preoccupations that make it seem plausible."[36]

34. Ibid.

35. See Luther's "Promotionsdisputation of Erasmus Alberus" (1543), in which Augustine's absolute-relative scheme is defended and Scotus's formal distinction is repudiated, in Dennis Bielfeldt, Mickey L. Mattox, and Paul R. Hinlicky, *The Substance of the Faith: Luther's Doctrinal Theology for Today* (Minneapolis: Fortress, 2008), 191–97. This stance of the later Luther may be compared to the gloss that the earlier Luther made on Lombard's *Sentences*:

I, unless blessed Augustine would say otherwise, but I would say, that the Father is not the Father except from the Son or by filiation. Thus neither by Himself is He wise, but through the Son who is His wisdom by which He is wise. Neither by Himself is He good, but through the Holy Spirit who is His goodness. Thus it is that whenever He is called powerful, wise, good, always at the same time all three persons are named. The reason is because "father" is relative. And, as Ambrose puts these things: He is not able to be named or called Father, unless the Son is also co-named. Thus being wise and wisdom are relative. And He is not able to be named such, unless the Son also is co-named. ("Marginal Notes of Martin Luther to the *Sentences* of Peter Lombard," in *D. Martin Luthers Werke: Kritische Gesamtausgabe* [Weimar: Hermann Böhlau, 1883–2007], 1:38 [my translation])

36. Ayres, *Nicaea and Its Legacy*, 363.

This latter judgment is, I fear, sophisticated nostalgia. It not only imagines that a millennium of East-West separation over trinitarian theology was much ado about nothing (i.e., the *filioque* violates the monarchy of the Father in Eastern perspective, and it does so for the sake of Augustine's modalistic equalization of the Father and the Son, thus transformed into the psychological model of the willing of itself in the divine Mind that proceeds from the thinking of itself and the thought of itself); it also fails to see the Cappadocians' strong distinction of nature and person as the metaphysical revolution of trinitarianism (and its echo later in the West in Scotus's prioritization of possibility over actuality in the life of historical subjects and the corresponding doctrine of the formal distinction in order to assert the freedom of the biblical God as a subject from the necessitarian implications of Aristotelian naturalism). This is a revolution that has also worked itself out, incognito, in "modern preoccupations" with the irreducibility of persons to natures—that is, for the inalienable human dignity of the individual against "essentialism" in the sense that a supposed nature imposes a normative teleology over the actualization of the person in its existence. Moreover, all modern progress of Catholic theology in this regard has to be discredited by Ayres as a fall from Thomist heights. In the chapter assigning all error to modern thought, exemplified in Hegelianism (though with no appreciation for how Hegelianism completes scholastic theology as begun under Anselm's *fides quaerens intellectum*, or how it undoes Scotus by absorbing Christian freedom back into the necessitarianism of the dialectic of history—an updated victory for Aristotle over the gospel), this discrediting of modern Catholic progress in theology takes the form of an imperceptive critique of Karl Rahner's recognition of the serious problems in the strong doctrine of simplicity.

Ayres writes, "Although Rahner did not directly deny the Thomist principle that God's relationship with the world is not 'real' in God (that is, that this relationship does not affect God's being), he pushes the doctrine of God's immutability as far as he can."[37] In a footnote he cites Rahner's consideration of the very christological issue to which we are drawing near, the canonical statement *kai ho logos sarx egeneto* (n.b., *egeneto*):

> If we do call [the Incarnation] a change, then, since God is unchangeable, we must say that God who is unchangeable in himself can change in another (can in fact become man). But this "changing *in* another" must neither be taken as denying the immutability of God in himself nor simply be reduced to a changement [*sic*] of the other. . . . We must maintain methodologically the

37. Ibid., 410.

immutability of God, and yet it would be basically a denial of the incarnation if we used it alone to determine what this mystery could be. . . . This we can and must affirm, without being Hegelians. And it would be a pity if Hegel had to teach Christians such things.[38]

This statement cited from Rahner cautiously formulates a christological challenge to Thomism's strong simplicity that prima facie has considerable force; Rahner then merely offers up some guidelines for meeting the challenge. Ayres's comment, then, is revealing indeed: "One might have hoped that a Catholic theologian would maintain such a doctrine a little more than 'methodologically.'"[39]

But "methodologically" is precisely right, if we today wish to honor the concern that Thomas expresses in his entangled formulation of divine immutability, so that we can proceed in continuity with Thomas at his best without being bound to his formulations, let alone metaphysics. Otherwise, we equate Catholicism with thirteenth-century Thomism and add to the canon of Holy Scripture Aristotle's *Metaphysics*. Not only would this require us to attribute immutability to a divine nature rather than to the Father—who begets the Son, on whom He breathes His Spirit, who thus fittingly but freely creates a world of creatures and in the fullness of time becomes incarnate as one of them, in order faithfully to make all of them a living temple for His indwelling—but it also would force us to deny that these canonical relationships with creatures are real for God, as in Ayres's remark made in passing rightly notes that strong simplicity denies that God's relations to creatures are, or rather become, real in God in the way of acquired properties. At a minimum, charity requires that the uncomfortable fact of Christian theological history must be insisted on here: the manifest variety of doctrines of simplicity indicates that orthodoxy in this connection is still a work in progress.

The Radicality of Protological Simplicity

Engaging now with Maarten Wisse's *Trinitarian Theology beyond Participation: Augustine's "De Trinitate" and Contemporary Theology,*[40] I will argue in this section for Mullins's thesis that the true radicality of protological simplicity goes unrecognized by its Christian advocates. Wisse's defense of

38. Ibid., 410–11n52, quoting Rahner, *Theological Investigations*, vol. 4, trans. Kevin Smyth (Baltimore: Helicon, 1966), 113–14n3.

39. Ayres, *Nicaea and Its Legacy*, 411n52.

40. Maarten Wisse, *Trinitarian Theology beyond Participation: Augustine's "De Trinitate" and Contemporary Theology* (London and New York: T&T Clark, 2013).

Augustine's "stumbling" over 1 Corinthians 1, as I put it, indeed represents a more radical and thus more clarifying defense of the claim of Augustine's strong doctrine of simplicity on contemporary theology. In a summary statement of his interpretation Wisse suggests how Augustine's radical doctrine undermines even the later accounts in Anselm and Aquinas of divine intellection:

> This Trinitarian understanding of God is different from the Trinitarian structure of the human person [for Augustine]. The Trinitarian understanding of God is inconceivable and unique, so that no copy and paste is possible between God and the structure of human beings. Exactly this unique character of God is then the foundation of the Trinitarian character of the human person because this unique character of God constitutes a unique relationship between God and human beings that is not mediated by an innerworldly relationship.[41]

For Wisse, the ascending analogies from human mind to divine Mind always and radically break down because in truth God's inconceivable uniqueness is expressed but not understood, let alone comprehended in the unintelligible ascription of threeness to oneness and oneness to threeness, as is required by the strong doctrine of simplicity. God confronts us as the nonsense of an ultimate and irresolvable contradiction: the Three are the One and vice versa. *Punkt.*

There is a sense in which the present proposal for a rule version of simplicity, with ontologically weaker claims, comports with Wisse's insistence in the name of Augustine that the Triune God's being is inconceivable and unique; this convergence appears when the position for which I am arguing maintains that the doctrine of the Trinity gives us neither a theory, nor an explanation, nor a definition of God but rather a description of the being of God at work in the world that suffices cognitively for the identification of the God of the gospel in time and His adoration to all eternity. Let that agreement be noted from the outset. The question is whether we impose simplicity on the Triune God from outside, with a notion that we will have come to on other grounds, or whether we discover a specific simplicity in the claim of the gospel's God to be, and to prove to be, the one true God, a notion that qualifies as consistent and eternal the unfathomable, unique, and incomparable perichoretic life of the Father, who begets the Son, on whom He breathes His Spirit as an eternal circulation of love.

Because Wisse's defense of strong simplicity in the name of Augustine is radical, he in effect undoes the synthesis that Ayres attempts and thus, from the opposite direction of my overarching argument, confirms the Régnon thesis. That is clarifying indeed, even if in the contemporary polemic (against

---

41. Ibid., 223.

Radical Orthodoxy and kindred forms of neomedievalism) his case is codeter-
mined by some unfortunate false antitheses and beset with not a few aporias
("rough edges" he calls them)[42] of its own, as we will see. It is in any case
an indication of the plasticity of Augustine's legacy, which can be oriented
to his philosophical conversion from gnosticism to Neoplatonism or to his
later biblical and especially Pauline maturation, that Wisse's no-holds-barred
retrieval of Augustinian simplicity speaks against the gravamen of Ayres's
claim for the harmony of Eastern and Western trinitarianisms.

If Ayres represents a reading of Augustine as the precursor of Thomas and
of Thomas as the theologian who delivers Augustine into the arms of Aristotelian existentialism from the clutches of Platonic essentialism, and in the
process blockades the Hegelianization of modern theology, we have in Wisse
a Calvinist Augustine *contra mundum*. The great virtue of the metaphysical
doctrine of simplicity as deployed by Augustine is that, so Wisse argues, it
"defunctionalizes" the Trinity, making the Trinity opaque, "irrational," not in
any way continuous with the cosmos, unserviceable for any scheme of participation.[43] As such, far from Platonizing God, the inconceivably simple Trinity,
depicted categorically as unlike any life we know, is *the* antidote to Platonic
schemes of continuity in the great chain of being.[44] "A strongly ontological
form of participation of all that is in God," by contrast, "turns Christianity
and the Church into a mere illustration of an ontological fact that is the case
even when we do not live up to it."[45] Wisse's Augustine thus parts ways with
Thomists on the analogicity of being; all the analogues explored in the latter
books of *De Trinitate* prove unhelpful to Augustine, according to Wisse's
reading. The continuity of nature, so important for Thomism, is ruptured
by the ultimate surd of God's unfathomable triunity that does not comport
with any being that we know or even imagine.

It is helpful to note how Wisse praises Ayres for "refuting the charge [against
Augustine that was just prosecuted in the previous section] of a divine essence
that would be prior to the persons in relation" and doing so with the help of
the simplicity axiom; he says further that, on the basis of clear passages in
Augustine cited by Ayres, he "accept[s] Ayres' argument against the idea that
the essence is something prior to the persons."[46] In such passages Augustine is

42. Ibid., 297–300. For example, a concluding salute to Vladimir Lossky (302–9), who more
than anyone established for contemporary theology the nature-person distinction of Eastern
trinitarianism!

43. Ibid., 52, 61, 68–69, 90, 288.

44. Ibid., 235, 250.

45. Ibid., 309.

46. Ibid., 80.

repeating the doctrine of the Trinity that he has learned from the East, even if he has not understood it. By the same token, if Wisse had really understood this argument of Ayres for the harmony of East and West that he claims here to accept, he would see that priority of the persons to the essence entails some other, hypostatic or personal, account of the origin in God—that is, a patrology, the monarchy of the Father. Ayres at least understands this much of the challenge and tries to reconcile it with Augustine's manifest preference for making the unity of persons something natural rather than patrological. So it is not surprising to read immediately following upon Wisse's praise of Ayres how Wisse hastens to express a "worry" that just this conciliation of essence and person makes Augustine too "coherent." In fact, Augustine prefers to speak of "three somethings (*tria quaedam*) [only] in order to say something rather than nothing."[47] This is to have one's cake and eat it too.

The tension here between advocates of strong simplicity is intriguing. Ayres, according to Wisse, makes the argument that "the triune communion is a consubstantial and eternal unity; but there is nothing but the persons" by way of a grammatical (i.e., semantical) approach: because the persons are each God in essence, not by relationship, and yet because the essence is simple, we can say that the Father, Son, and Holy Spirit are each God and are the numerically one God. Whatever the divine ontology actually is, this is how we can talk about it, namely, as one absolutely and as three relatively. Rules for speaking about God need not comport with God, since we cannot know God, but only know correct speech about God according to a particular tradition of theological discourse. *Satis est*. So Wisse, in any case, reconciles himself to Ayres's attempt to reconcile East and West.

This "grammatical approach" (be it noted here until I take the matter up again in the conclusion) is akin to what I am calling for in a rule version of simplicity, though I hold that a rule version implies an ontology and is and must be grounded in a cognitive claim, and that that ontology will be a weaker view of simplicity than that of Ayres or Augustine, not to mention Wisse. But Wisse, as we will see, otherwise embraces an emphatically stronger and decisively ontological version of protological simplicity as signifying numerically a single substance (hypostasis?) that is incomprehensibly also three somethings. As a result, he only flirts with Ayres's grammatical approach. Indeed, he faults Ayres (and Joseph Ratzinger!) for failing to see that such strong simplicity implies not relations to others (the "Triune communion") but rather the persons' self-relation to, or timeless self-identity with, the numerically single divine substance. Ayres (like Ratzinger), in his desire to preserve the communion

47. Ibid., 81.

of the Three under strong simplicity, evades this implication, Wisse argues, when in fact "Augustine's theology does not take the Threeness in God as the real clue to the understanding of God."[48] The problem with Ayres (and Ratzinger) is they in fact want to have their cake and eat it too: they want the advantages of strong simplicity and of relational ontology without the cost of deciding between the two (of course, one might say the same of Rahner, whom Ayres so sharply criticized).

In the present argument I take Wisse to be right about Augustine's not taking "the Threeness in God as the real clue to the understanding of God," although, as is evident, I also take both Wisse and Augustine to be wrong about strong simplicity in trinitarian doctrine. Just that critique is, in a manner of speaking, the Régnon thesis. And that is clarifying, as we will see, against confusing attempts of contemporary Catholic theology (Ratzinger is the chief object of Wisse's critique,[49] but Rowan Williams[50] and John Milbank,[51] not to forget Lewis Ayres, among others are criticized) for harmonizing a strong Augustinian doctrine of simplicity with relational features from the Eastern doctrine of being in communion.

My disagreement with Wisse is not a matter, as his polemics would have it, of rationalizing into transparency the ultimately mysterious being of the Triune God in order to interpret the world as His creation freely destined for redemption and fulfillment. For Wisse, as is by now evident, theology should be far more a matter of engaging God with love than perspicuous understanding of God in truth;[52] as for the present proposal, the mystery of God's unity *as* the perichoretic Three requires a doctrine of simplicity, albeit a weaker one that works as a maxim or rule of faith, not as an a priori insight into the nature of absoluteness as the reified alpha privative of indivisibility. The "distinction" of the strong Creator/creature relation, christologically of the "two natures" doctrine, is in any case axiomatic for a Christian theology that intends orthodoxy.

Yet this distinction is not in the possession of any particular metaphysical articulation of it, as Wisse tends to claim on behalf of his Augustine *contra mundum*. In Wisse's words, "The ontological 'gap' that a Christian understanding of creation causes precludes the possibility of thinking the whole of

---

48. Ibid.
49. Ibid., 93–107.
50. Ibid., 79–82.
51. Ibid., 147–48.
52. Ibid., 240. See the interesting argument in this connection made against the convertibility of the transcendentals (313–14) and its anthropological implications for the primacy of will or desire over ratiocination (e.g., 184, 232).

reality as a unity, since at the root of it was no longer a metaphysics of unity, but a free act of the Creator creating everything after its own nature."[53] This "gap" of freedom makes God irreducible to relations with creatures as remaining free in sovereign grace; it leaves creatures ever baffled for their own good and to their promised eternal delight at the freedom of God in giving life and world and eternal life. In turn, knowledge of this "gap" in faith fundamentally and hierarchically reorders creaturely desire according to Augustine's *ordo caritatis*: love is only love and not lust if one loves God above all and therefore one's neighbor as oneself—that is, loves self and neighbor as God loves them together, as His freely willed creatures whose paths have providentially crossed in God's agenda for Beloved Community.[54] I greet these themes from Augustine, as Wisse renders them, with great appreciation.

Yet there remain several relevant problematics in Wisse's treatise now to be explored. First, I need at least to mention the Calvinist themes (and confusions) of Reformation theology that avowedly provide the lenses for Wisse's Reformed reading of the bishop of Hippo.[55] That is to say, Wisse takes *De Trinitate* to be sharply focused as a rhetorical work persuading the Platonists of his day about the necessity of salvation in Christ,[56] so that the treatise must be read strategically as disestablishing the Platonic continuity between the inner self and the divine in order compellingly to present Christ with His salvation as the Word from God that comes to the self from outside the self.[57] It suffices for present purposes to make note of this "Calvinizing reading" and point to its contemporary target in the participationist scheme of Radical Orthodoxy that, as Wisse charges, evades the historical event of encounter with and transformation by the *verbum externum*: "In a Christology along the lines of a participatory metaphysics the incarnation becomes a mere illustration of the ontological structure of reality stripping the incarnation of its historicity and unicity."[58] I will deal with some "Calvinizing" confusion regarding deification later on, though it should be noted here that to his credit Wisse transcends confessionalistic partisanship and explicitly identifies the mutual deficit of Catholic and Protestant appropriations of Augustine in that they have torn apart what Augustine holds together: the creature's natural desire for the good and the necessity of radical grace to redeem desire gone fatally astray into lust.[59]

53. Ibid., 237.
54. Ibid., 190; see also 208, 218–19, 223, 314.
55. Ibid., 307.
56. Ibid., 196.
57. Ibid., 260.
58. Ibid., 249; see also 167, 249–50.
59. Ibid., 300.

Second, there is the very interesting case, already mentioned, that Wisse makes that Augustine's strong reading of simplicity as trinitarian unintelligibility is not only not Platonizing but also the very antidote to Platonism. What is all the more interesting in this connection, then, is the lineage that Wisse traces from Neoplatonism's philosophy of mind to modern idealism's philosophy of self-consciousness, as I have from time to time alluded to in detecting the genesis of modern idealism in the ancient metaphysics of "thought thinking and willing itself."

Third, there is Wisse's exegetical argument that it is the introduction of strong simplicity in book 5 of *De Trinitate* that creates the problem introduced at the beginning of book 6 about how to take the Pauline "Christ the power and wisdom of God," a problem that is then resolved in book 7. I will treat these themes in order. But I begin with the decisive difficulty, already mentioned, of Augustine's admitted inability to grasp the nature-person distinction of Eastern trinitarian personalism, which is, however, in Wisse's view the great virtue at work in Augustine's "defunctionalizing" of the doctrine of the Trinity![60]

As is well known, in *De Trinitate* 5.5.10 Augustine confesses that the Greek distinction *mia ousia treis hypostaseis* eludes him, since in Latin both *ousia* and *hypostasis* are translated interchangeably and synonymously with *substantia* or *essentia*. If we say "one being and three substances" or "one substance and three beings," we therefore articulate nothing but the nonsense of an evident contradiction, and a blasphemous one at that, implying, as it seems, tritheism. So we do not know, Augustine concluded, what we are talking about when we speak the Three: "Three *what*?" Discussing this crucial passage, Wisse holds that more is at stake than incomprehension. Equality, as opposed to subordinationism, is at stake. At Nicaea (not to mention at 1 Cor. 8:6), he says, "the language of origin that was typical of subordinationist terminology was retained in a more or less unproblematic way: the Father was still called the *origio* of the Trinity, although this implies, if pushed hard enough, because interpreted as an *a se* statement, that the Son is substantially different from the Father. . . . This is precisely the point where Augustine feels himself pushed by the logic of the Arian opponents."[61] And the result of this pressure—though Wisse in approving of its salutary effect on Augustine seems innocent of the entire struggle between the times of Nicaea and Constantinople to affirm *homoousios* in such a way that it did not efface the personal difference between Father and Son—is something very much akin to the modalist view, as

60. Ibid., 52, 61, 68–69.
61. Ibid., 58.

mentioned above, of the anti-Arian Marcellus of Ancyra finally repudiated at Constantinople.[62]

"The oneness of God is not guaranteed by Augustine by an appeal to the Father as the *origin* of the Trinity," Wisse writes, "but through an appeal to the one essence that is shared by all three 'persons'"; indeed, Augustine "deconstructs" the concept of the monarchy of the Father by way of his strong doctrine of simplicity, as introduced in book 5.[63] Divine "substance" is given that specialized meaning of radical simplicity by denying to it accidents; just this negation of accidental properties is what makes it divine, *esse ipsum*.[64] And just this introduction of the radical simplicity of protological metaphysics is what creates the conundrum in light of Paul's proclamation of Christ as the wisdom and power of God that opens book 6.[65] The resolution of the conundrum in book 7 grounds Wisse's Protestant reading of the Pauline text in 1 Corinthians 1:24: here power and wisdom are extrinsic gifts, not intrinsic divine attributes,[66] although, be it noted, neither Wisse nor Augustine connects this reading of power and wisdom as extrinsic gifts to the prototrinitarianism of 1 Corinthians 8:6.

In place, then, of the Eastern distinction between *ousia* and *hypostasis* Wisse, in the name of Augustine, demolishes not only the monarchy of the Father but also the very notion of *hypostasis* as a concrete way of being, personal being as opposed to being generically. And in doing this, he must remythologize the abstraction *ousia* or *natura* as if it were something real and indeed an agent. Augustine identifies *esse* and *subsistere*, a move said to be a "precursor to Aquinas' *definition* of God as *ipsum esse subsistens*."[67] In a related passage directed against Nyssa, Wisse comments, "The Trinitarian persons cannot be three hypostases in the sense of one essence subsisting in three persons, because this violates the simplicity of God and turns the one essence that is God into three subsisting Gods."[68] From this violation of simplicity, tritheism at worst, subordinationism at best follows. But instead, Wisse citing Augustine, God "is called being truly and properly in such a way that perhaps only God ought to be called being. He alone truly is, because he is unchanging," as is indicated by the divine Name, I AM HE WHO IS.[69]

---

62. On this, see Paul R. Hinlicky, *Divine Complexity: The Rise of Creedal Christianity* (Minneapolis: Fortress, 2009), 207–12.

63. Wisse, *Trinitarian Theology*, 59; see also 297.

64. Ibid., 54–55.

65. Ibid., 63.

66. Ibid., 68.

67. Ibid., 74 (emphasis added).

68. Ibid.

69. Ibid.

I will pass over the possibility that Augustine's formulation anticipates Spinoza's doctrine of God as the one true Substance. Discussing Richard Cross's attempt, parallel to those of Ratzinger, Ayres, and Williams discussed above, to harmonize Augustine and Nyssa, Wisse articulates well enough the alternative view of strong trinitarian personalism to his own substance-sans-accidents ontology:

> The three persons turn out to be three concrete instantiations of that single divine essence. . . . The single divine essence is merely a concept. The persons should really be distinct centres of action. . . . [But] appeal to the unity of action among the divine persons . . . would be far too weak because, for Augustine, God must not only be one in the sense of a unity of action but also in the sense of being numerically one . . . a "single entity."[70]

In that case it would not suffice merely to affirm that the *opera Dei ad extra indivisa sunt*; rather, each work would have to be the same work indifferently expressing the numerically same deity, a natural substance without accidents.

Let us pause to count the cost of these moves made in the name of Augustine. First, personhood is resolved back into being, which in turn is re-mythologized as an actually existing something that acts, albeit simply, acting wholly and purely in timelessly actualizing itself and expressing this self-actualization in the refraction of creatures in time and space—the barely disguised emanationism of Neoplatonism. Second, divine unity is taken not as the mystery of personal communion in holy love that can reach outside of its divine blessedness to include and overcome the creature's unblessed-ness, but rather as the indivisibility of being perfectly to which the unblessed creature may ascend, if she can (by grace, of course). Third, the knowledge of God at work through Christ in the Spirit becomes only a sign of something else, signifying an ineffability beyond understanding. All this, Wisse requires, with the argument teased out of Augustine, "that relative predicates (*relative* or *ad aliquid* expressions) are meaningless without underlying substantial predicates (*ad se* expressions)."[71] What is the same, a genus with only one member is no longer a genus but a singularity,[72] the numerically one, unique, and incomparable God Who Is God to God (*ad se*), and as such "underly-ing" God taken relatively (*ad aliquid*) as Father, or Son, or Holy Spirit to one another and to us. In this way, as Wisse repeatedly reminds, Augustine is the author of a strict and strong differentiation between the economic Trinity

70. Ibid., 83.
71. Ibid., 66–67.
72. Ibid., 72.

and the ontological Trinity, the latter being a "concrete otherness that cannot be scrutinized in thought."[73]

In the process, the metaphysical achievement—indeed, revolution—of Nicene theology that takes the economic Trinity of revelation as the truthful, fitting, but not necessary self-giving of the eternal God by God in God to the creation for the sake of the coming Beloved Community is tossed aside with an uncomprehending Marcellianism. Because of the essentially modalist cast of Wisse's thought, let me add to this list of costs that the Eastern doctrine of deification can only be taken as proffering an impossible salvation of fusing together divine and human natures rather than as the christological union of the incarnate Son with our humanity by which the Spirit, beginning with baptism, brings believers forth from death to the waiting arms of the heavenly Father. (Perhaps "Christification,"[74] if understood in terms of strong trinitarian personalism, would give a clearer account of deification or "participation.") Finally, let us note one more reification, the notion of Trinity itself, the "Trinity as a whole" over against patrology.[75] Rather than being useful theological shorthand for the God of the gospel who sends His Son in the Spirit in order to unite us with Christ and bring us to the Father, the "Trinity" itself now becomes reified and turned into a subject and agent as such (a collective agency, so to say, of equal somethings, as required by Wisse's rejection of the monarchy of the Father as the origin and principle of unity in the Three).

These criticisms aside, what remains to be discussed is the striking lineage, mentioned above, that Wisse traces from Neoplatonism to modern idealism, a genealogy that militates against the "participatory" ontologies advocated today in newly fashionable Platonist readings of Thomas. In Wisse's words, "I have tried to turn Augustine's argument [for trinitarian simplicity] into a critique of a specific type of Western metaphysics" according to which (since Hegel) absolute transcendence mediates itself by becoming visible in incomplete and partial ways and then affirms itself in this self-diremption as the totality of being.[76] As we can gather from the foregoing, Wisse's account of Augustine's trinitarian "irrationalism" categorically blocks the way here, "defunctionalizing" this use of the Trinity to map the being of the world as God's own process. Augustine's deliberate trinitarian irrationalism cannot be functionalized along the lines of God's history with the world but iterates

---

73. Ibid., 92.

74. Jordan Cooper, *Christification: A Lutheran Approach to Theosis* (Eugene, OR: Wipf & Stock, 2014).

75. Wisse, *Trinitarian Theology*, 69.

76. Ibid., 249.

the Wholly Other God, on whose concrete revelation salvation depends. Here I will sketch out these claims about the lineage of idealism.

First, "Fichte is much closer to Plotinus than to Augustine. In Plotinus, the soul realizes . . . its self-identity through its return into the world soul, the Nous"; but Augustine's account of self-knowledge "is not, as in Fichte and Plotinus, the ontological identity of the knower and the known in a higher unity, but a kind of epistemic access" of the lost creature to itself—that is, to its own frustrated desire for happiness and peace.[77] "This epistemic access is obscured through sin," not by the self-diffusion of the One into the many.[78] A similar differentiation is provided by Wisse from Pannenberg's more Hegelian idealism in the "dialectical character of his theology. The notion of the whole as the all-encompassing concept leads to the self-differentiation of this Absolute in that which is infinite and what is not. . . . The self-differentiation of the Absolute is then united again in an all-encompassing reconciliation as the moment of the Spirit"; but, Wisse continues, "This is different in Augustine," for whom the Holy Trinity is not "thought thinking and willing itself" writ large but "inconceivable and unique."[79]

Second, the basic idea in Plotinus is that "all knowledge presupposes a certain multiplicity," so that "the One as the One cannot be known"; knowledge then can be nothing but "going upwards along the chain of being towards greater unity and less multiplicity. . . . [Thus,] having knowledge of something is to become one with it, that is, to participate in its being."[80] Augustine breaks with Plotinus at each and every point. What is acknowledged in faith as unknowable and incomprehensible is not the One as One—that is, the ontological One beyond the numerical One—but rather the One as the surd Three; knowledge is a graced ascent on account of a prior, gracious condescension to the sinner in the flesh, the humility of God in Christ over against the *superbia* of the ascending creature in the power of its mind. This downward movement of grace breaches the imagined continuity of the cyclical scheme of descent and return. Graced ascent in the Spirit consequently does not abolish multiplicity or finitude but rather harmonizes multiplicity in charity and imparts to finitude the blessed vision of God that in seeing so adheres to God that *non posse peccare*. Knowing God is not substantial union with God but rather is learning to love God as the really Different, whom creatures ought to love; union with God is not to participate in God's being but rather to become a citizen of the *civitas Dei*.

77. Ibid., 162–63.
78. Ibid., 163.
79. Ibid., 223.
80. Ibid., 236.

So, third, against every kind of idealism, then, "truth does not consist in being identical with the object, or participating in a level of being that encompasses the subject and object in a unifying structure, but a relationship between subject and object presupposing a persistent and positively evaluated distance."[81] For just this reason, "Augustine's negative theology is also more negative than Plotinus',"[82] although, granted, "Augustine pushes the language of simplicity to such a degree that it almost stops making sense." But in fact "it is precisely the revelation of this Trinity that makes Augustine's theology more negative than Plotinus'"[83]—provided that we take the sheer "irrationalism" that presents divine life as One that is Three and vice versa as the right understanding of the divine self-revelation that is the gospel. Although breaching the idealistic continuity of the divine with the human mind is all to the good, and requiring instead the fellowship of love between the ontologically different Creator and creatures is even better, Augustine's account of the Trinity as a surd erects one mistake upon another.

So there is a definite value in this strong differentiation of Augustinian trinitarianism from its modern colonization by idealist metaphysics of the sovereign self. And Wisse has contributed greatly in showing this lineage and differentiating it from Augustine. But the costs of Wisse's trinitarian "irrationalism" are both too high and unnecessary.[84] The mystery of God's holy being can be recognized and protected from profanation in other ways that do not turn the Trinity itself into a Gordian knot that supposedly blocks the way of proud rationalism's ascent at the price of perpetuating Augustine's misunderstanding of the *mia ousia treis hypostaseis*. In the process Wisse has shown, however, that critics of the Régnon thesis such as Ayres have not made their case except by harmonizing strong and weak doctrines of divine simplicity, when in fact these two versions of the account of divine unity move in opposing directions. According to my eschatological reading of Zechariah 14:9, divine unity cannot be taken without further ado as the (natural) presupposition of revealed theology; rather, it must be taken as the revealed goal of the Beloved Community for the creation to which God freely determines Himself in the missions of His Son and Spirit. The weak simplicity

81. Ibid., 237.
82. Ibid., 90.
83. Ibid., 91.
84. This Wisse himself should realize from his approving discussion of Lossky (ibid., 302–9), which highlights the essence-energies distinction as corresponding to Wisse's own Augustinian distinction between immanent and economic Trinity. But Lossky distinguishes in order to relate. All the more Wisse could and should have learned from Lossky the more fundamental trinitarian distinction of nature and person. See Vladimir Lossky, *In the Image and Likeness of God*, ed. John H. Erickson and Thomas E. Bird (Crestwood, NY: St. Vladimir's Seminary Press, 1985).

that must be presupposed here thinks of the Three as able, competent, and willing (powerful, wise, and good) to achieve this goal by way of a consistent perichoresis, which is as such their sublime and ontological unity. This is not in any case a philosophical insight into timeless indivisibility as the ground of being but rather a theological observation, description, and inference from their historical agency, as Nyssa argued in *On Not Three Gods*.[85] This difference in epistemic access is decisive.

Moreover, as the Cappadocians learned in their battle with Eunomius, there are important christological matters at stake that require the weaker version of simplicity. Chalcedonian Christology is not only, or even chiefly, about the distinction of the two natures, which is but one pole of its doctrine. The gospel's Christology tells instead of a union of the natures in terms of trinitarian personalism—that is, of a hypostatic or personal union, as the Fifth Ecumenical Council clarified Chalcedon in pronouncing that One of the divine Three suffered in His own human soul and body. At this christological juncture, then, I will call into evidence the christological alternative to Wisse's Augustinian assimilation of person to nature from the illuminating study of these issues by John Meyendorff in his *Christ in Eastern Christian Thought*.[86]

The Personal Union

The christological problem, properly speaking, begins with the realization of post-Chalcedonian theology that if the incarnation of the eternal Son is true— that is, if "He who was rich for our sakes became poor" as also "He who knew no sin was made to be sin"—then "characteristics of the human nature have in fact been added to those of the divine nature" (76). In Christ God the Son acquires extrinsic properties and makes them His own. Yet prima facie "the incoherence" of this bald assertion is evident. If the divine Son is a hypostasis, as Constantinople had affirmed in the formula *mia ousia treis hypostaseis*, what then can the human "nature" be that He acquires in the *assumptio carnis*? If it is its own hypostasis, say, as nineteenth-century liberalism imagined and is still sought today in quests for a historical Jesus, a "personality," the "man behind the myth," then we would have two persons in close affiliation, the son of Mary and the Son of God, and Jesus son of Mary would be at best the brightest of the saints, like us in all things though better in holiness and

85. Hinlicky, *Divine Complexity*, 231–32.

86. John Meyendorff, *Christ in Eastern Christian Thought* (Crestwood, NY: St. Vladimir's Seminary Press, 1987). Henceforth, citations from this book are followed by page numbers in parentheses in the main text.

so a model for us to imitate in our own ascent. In a true union, by contrast, Jesus's soul and body must from His conception be enhypostasized—that is, concretely formed *in* the hypostasis of the eternal Son, so that the figure of the man *on* a messianic mission who appears in the gospel narrative is the mystery of the Son of God coming in the flesh to make us, with our sin and death, His own so that in Him we become God's own children by the same Spirit. For this latter view of Christ as saving Lord, an even clearer distinction between person and nature is required if Christology following Chalcedon is to be and to remain a function of trinitarianism rather than become a modalist alternative to it on account of a not-yet-baptized notion of nature. The need was, Meyendorff puts it, to "apply to the theology of the incarnation the concepts that the Cappadocian Fathers had used to express the mystery of the Trinity" (76), namely, the strong distinction of person from nature.

This passage from divine ontology to economy of the incarnation was not "without its difficulties" (76). Basically, "the hypostasis designated the 'who' and the nature the 'what'" (76), but the possibilities for applying christologically this distinction of who and what seem problematic. If one takes hypostasis as a nature with certain characteristics, then we end up with two persons in Christ, one with divine and another with human characteristics, as Nestorians take it. If one takes hypostasis as an existence by itself, an independent and autonomous subsistence, then one ends up with three unrelated but personally allied deities, tritheism. If one takes "the Thomist position that the divine hypostases are but 'relations' within the divine essence" (76), then the christological affirmation that One of the Three suffered implies "the passion of the divine nature itself" (77); in order to avoid that inference, one finds in Christ a human "ego" who suffered in coordination with the simple and impassible divine person that supposits it: back to Nestorianism. Surveying these unhappy possibilities, Meyendorff then makes the significant observation that none of these untoward consequences can be avoided so long as the metaphysical choices are "defined within the sole framework of the Aristotelian or Platonic opposition of abstract and concrete" (77). In particular, the trinitarian notion of "hypostasis cannot be reduced to that of 'particular' nor to that of 'relation.' The hypostasis is not the product of nature: it is that in which nature exists, the very principle of its existence" (77). Or, as I have been saying, the person is what is real in the world in freely instantiating or exercising possibilities of its nature.

A trinitarian hypostasis is the particular way of being that is essentially related to other ways of particular being such as to constitute a common life and organic whole, and thus a corresponding singular claim to the title of the one true God. In this divine life the Son cannot be the Son that He is apart from His Father and their Spirit, and it is precisely as such that He became flesh and dwelt among us once and for all, sent from His Father and endowed with His Spirit, acquiring human properties in order to give divine gifts.

So Meyendorff: "Such a conception of hypostasis can be applied to Christology, since it implies the existence of a fully human existence, without any limitation, 'enhypostasized' in the Word, who is a divine hypostasis" (77). The Logos, that is to say, takes to Himself all that is human and makes it in the incarnation His way of being the Son on earth as in heaven. This is the man Jesus, born of Mary Theotokos, who lives His human life enhypostasized in the divine Son—that is, indiscernibly in the very same relation to His Father and their Spirit as eternally and hence as the same Person, the Son. This conception of hypostasis, and its distinction from that of nature, which is enhypostasized into it, Meyendorff points out immediately, "assumes that God, as personal being, is not totally bound to his own nature; . . . God can personally and freely assume a fully human existence while remaining God, whose nature remains completely transcendent" (77). In the Son's becoming flesh, "human nature had become as fully *his own* as the divine nature . . . because his hypostasis is not a mere product of the divine nature but is an entity ontologically distinct from the nature, the ego that 'possesses' the divine nature and 'assumes' the human nature" (77). That is what makes the personal union the free obedience of the eternal Son from eternity and in time, as Philippians 2 teaches.

Unlike a quasi-mythological view of nature as an agent enacting a set of possibilities as its teleology, the person is free to love (or not), wisely (or not), the subject of a nature that can also freely "add" to itself properties of other things or persons in its lived history and indeed—in the case of the infinitely capacious divine nature—add to itself other natures. So Christ the incarnate Son not only may make me His own along with all humanity but also may take responsibility upon Himself for my lethal properties—my folly, pride, despair, angst, hatred, and all the rest that ruins me as creature of God—just as He may give me in turn as a gift for my own personal possessing in faith His own righteousness acquired in the obedience of His lived faith to death, even death on a cross. This "joyful exchange" may and indeed must be said against all Platonic or Aristotelian tendencies to reify nature, although Meyendorff passes over this implication in discreet, ecumenical silence. But clearly the distinction means that nature, just like the so-called gods and lords of which it is the abstraction, has no real existence except as hypostasized—that is, instantiated in the actual life choices of a personal life's journey. That is the demythologization worked by the gospel! To be sure, this means that the person of Christ the incarnate Son in turn is *the* miracle just as is this Person's work in the joyful exchange. The human nature in Christ is that set of human possibilities that had been from His conception hypostasized in the eternal Son. The unique person of Christ the incarnate Son is the mystery of the Word made flesh, flesh now "deified by his energies . . . the source of divine life, because it is deified not simply by grace [as Nestorians thought] but because it is the Word's own flesh" (78). To this the Reformation theologian must only add the Pauline "likeness of sinful flesh" (Rom. 8:3) of the One who, though He knew no sin, was made to be sin (2 Cor. 5:21).

If these christological reasons do not provide reason enough to embrace trinitarian personalism, at least they make unmistakably clear the enduring validity of the Régnon thesis, in spite of all ecumenical goodwill and the justified desire to gloss over the seemingly subtle differences in trinitarian theology between East and West. In our urgent situation today in Euro-American post-Christendom, systematic theology requires courage, clarity, and coherence and also an honest reckoning that pays the price for hard theological decisions. Nothing is off the table, as though orthodoxy were not itself the Spirit's work in progress, whose truth is not in its own power to confirm, but only in the power of the one true God, to whom it ever points in claiming to speak about Him truthfully. The great Augustine has many other virtues still relevant for theology today, above all his theology of the Beloved Community. Not among these, however, is his undermining of the monarchy of the Father by an uncomprehending fear of subordinationism that led in the course of centuries to the disastrous Carolingian theology of the *filioque*.[87] But rather his notion of the Spirit as the *vinculum caritatis* who binds the Father and the Son in love and thus believers to the Son (provided that we take this insight as the personal work of the Spirit)—this personal work of the Spirit as the One who unifies the sign and the thing signified (the *epiclesis*)[88] provides for a clarification of the Eastern doctrine of theosis, not as dissolution of humanity into the ocean of divinity as Wisse fears,[89] but as "Christification," as the Spirit's work of *conformitas Christi*.

Christological Apophaticism: The Coincidence of Opposites in Christ Crucified

I bring this chapter now to a close, recasting its inquiry by way of the distinction that has again become current in theology between *apophasis* and

---

87. Richard S. Haugh, *Photius and the Carolingians: The Trinitarian Controversy* (Belmont, MA: Nordland, 1975).

88. Hinlicky, *Beloved Community*, 328–35.

89. Wisse, *Trinitarian Theology*, 276.

kataphasis, in Latin the *via negativa* and the *via eminentiae* respectively, given the instability of analogy as an attempted synthesis of what remains a dialectic, a *sic et non* in theology. If we recast, then, the working distinction (1) between simplicity as a putative protological insight on one side, and as a rule to honor the singularity of the Triune God on the other, or, (2) between strong simplicity that asserts ontologically the timeless self-identity of God as the act of His own being beyond even numerical oneness, and weak simplicity that asserts ontologically the eternal becoming of God in the circulation of personal subjects of divine perfections in a consistent perichoresis, we would have to say that strong simplicity delivers a kataphatic natural theology. It claims an insight, however austere. Ascending from below, it accords divinity to the perfection of being, whatever that may be, to the sheer *actus purus*, properly denominated as Being Itself. Despite the austerity, this is rigorously kataphatic theology in holding to *esse ipsum subsistens*. This, as we heard Thomas affirm, is the most proper name of God—that is, the one, literally true statement regarding God that depicts God as sheer event and utter bliss beyond even numerical oneness. Correspondingly, this very kataphasis is what can and does make the cosmos lucid by way of the analogicity of being, so that everything, so far as it is, points to God hidden in unsearchable light.

And yet, Thomas hedges his bets in the Dionysian direction of an ultimate apophaticism, as I have pointed to the definite instability of his doctrine so far as he realized that the ontological One is One beyond a numerical one, since a numerical one entails distinction from another one and thus implies multiplicity. So a One beyond oneness is the ultimate reference at which human thinking is halted. Indeed, if the Thomist analogy of being speaks in this way of "a similarity within an even greater dissimilarity," as I will discuss in detail in the final chapter, we cannot but end in silence before an ultimately unknown divinity, denying also the literal truth of *esse ipsum subsistens*, affirming but a Not-Nothing. I referred to this earlier as the unstable, if not unprincipled, oscillation in Thomas's teaching that trades back and forth in a dialectic of univocity and equivocity that is not rescued by renaming it as analogicity. It is in any case exceedingly difficult to sustain a kataphatic natural theology. The last great effort in Euro-American modernity was Leibniz's *Theodicy*, and he felt compelled to follow Scotus more than Thomas in attributing free choice to God in the same sense as we speak of freedom in creatures, in order to affirm the lucidity of the cosmos as the best of all possible worlds in the face of rising gnostic pessimism. Even though sharing the anti-gnostic outlook, it was to avoid such an apparently unseemly affirmation of this troubled earth as the best possible world that Thomas hedged. We do not finally know and cannot fathom God's inscrutable choices but only, like Job, bow in silence before the whirlwind.

We would correspondingly have to say that weak simplicity is an apophatic revealed theology, Nicholas Cusanus's learned ignorance that asserts from below, but after the fact, the infinite incomprehensibility of the One who has truly come to us and reveals as the Three of the gospel narrative. That is to say, weak simplicity permits a correspondingly weak theology of the natural, one that sees in the retrospect of faith *Deus absconditus* apart from God predicated and so revealed in Christ, *Deus incarnatus*. Because it sees what it sees as light shining in the darkness (John 1:5), it sustains disciplined silence regarding things in the dark, unless and until the heavens are rent (Mark 1:10) and, *Hunc audite!* (Mark 9:7), God speaks from the silence (Ignatius, *To the Magnesians* 8; cf. Ignatius, *To the Ephesians* 19) as the Father of the Son on whom the Spirit rests.

Such silence can, of course, become sterile if it forgets that it arises out of faith in the revealed God and instead takes on a life of its own, casting negation upon negation in a dialectic of negativity that results in mere atheism (in place of mere theism) that no longer lives expecting a Word from God or the fulfillment of God's Word. Yet it can be the fertile silence of faith that is listening—silence, then, that is broken, as when Simeon sings, "Master, now you are dismissing your servant in peace, according to your word" (Luke 2:29). That is to say, in the light of nature even the unknown God can be taken in faith as a promise of knowledge, as a tacit word awaiting fulfillment rather than frustration, just as world and life in the light of nature can be taken as a tacit gift of a not-yet-known Giver (as Rom. 1:20 actually means). In any event, if a weak natural theology (better: Christian theology of nature) hears in faith a Word from God, it becomes in knowing and confessing that Word a kataphatic theology, knowledge in faith of the *Deus incarnatus*.

Despite that knowledge, however, this revealed theology remains, so far as it is theology thought and expressed by creatures, an *apophasis* that continues to follow after what it does not take into possession but rather possesses in the ecstatic existence of faith ("having, as having not"). So for the sake of true reference to God in His self-revelation it qualifies its affirmations with negations in an ongoing dialectic, even as the God who reveals Himself in the Crucified Man at the same time hides Himself (Mark 15:33–39) until this light of grace passes into the fullness of the light of glory. In sum, then, here we have a certain *sic et non* dialectic of *apophasis* and *kataphasis* in which all kataphatic statements are statements taken in faith in a Word spoken as God's and yet qualified as true only if God shows them to be true, as God alone is able to do. This circle is a virtuous one, however, revolving around the uniqueness that is signed by the word "God." This reserve of *sic et non* in theology points to the holy singularity of God and respects it. Theology can never, not in all eternity, say or comprehend how its affirmations are true, since the truth of its statements is the business of the One who alone can make them true, not only "for me" but also for all at the eschaton of judgment. Then will Zechariah 14:9 be fulfilled to human sight and infinite wonder, but not ever to comprehension.

I cannot do justice to Knut Alfsvåg's incredibly rich and profound study, from which I have drawn in the preceding paragraphs, *What No Mind Has Conceived: On the Significance of Christological Apophaticism.*[90] It is a major work deserving of careful study and broad discussion. For our present purpose, however, I call attention to one theme in particular that runs through it, the foregoing christological affirmation that keeps apophaticism from descending into nihilism. And I will point in this respect to a certain ambiguity in Alfsvåg's presentation as it appears from the perspective of the present inquiry in its argument on behalf of a rule of weak simplicity in theology.

Concerning the latter, it suffices to say that Alfsvåg does not work explicitly with a notion of the diversity of simplicities as laid out in preceding chapters. This lacuna accounts for the cursory and unsatisfying account of Thomas Aquinas in the book, which ignores Thomas's strong simplicity of God's perfection of being as *actus purus*[91] yet lifts up precisely the same doctrine in Nicholas Cusanus.[92] The strength of the notion for theology, in either case, is to account for the *esse Deum dare*, for the utter generosity of divine being. For Alfsvåg, however, it is much more a matter of how we access such a doctrine rather than whether the doctrine of simplicity is ontologically strong or weak, and for a number of reasons he finds the negative way of Cusanus preferable to the way of analogy in Thomas. I am in any case not so much troubled here by the critique of Thomas that Alfsvåg issues, with which I concur:

> Thomas tries to solve the problem *Christo remoto* through a definable dialectics of continuity in discontinuity where the human perspective is left with a relative independence. From the point of view of a Christian apophaticism, the problem of Thomas's doctrine of analogy is thus not that he tries to explore the conditions under which a predication of the divine is after all possible, but that he has lost the understanding of why this condition always will have to be seen as a given.[93]

The givenness of the condition is the apophatic realization that only God can speak of God, just as God comes only from God; it is the kataphatic confession

90. Knut Alfsvåg, *What No Mind Has Conceived: On the Significance of Christological Apophaticism* (Leuven: Peeters, 2010).
91. Ibid., 104–9.
92. Ibid., 148–49.
93. Ibid., 107.

that God has spoken in Christ before we can ever speak in response. In this way, the omnicausality of God the Giver from the origin of the world is derived theologically rather than cosmologically, as argued above in chapter 2. On this critique of Thomas's unstable synthesis of equivocity and univocity in the doctrine of analogical predication of God as the kataphatic-cosmological *esse ipsum subsistens*, Alfsvåg and I agree.

Rather, as the reader by now is well aware, I am troubled by the Nietzschean objection to the tendency in natural theology to define God negatively by the trick of reifying a Nothing that issues in Christianity as popular Platonism. I argue that the distinction being worked out in this book between strong and weak simplicity—that is, between a putative metaphysical insight and a divine command not to take the revealed name of God in vain—can guard against this optical illusion of negativity because the prohibition qualifies a prior affirmation, "I am the LORD your God who brought you up . . ." Alfsvåg in fact acknowledges my worry in the first pages of his book: "Is the outcome of the apophatic approach rather a weakening of the basic Christo-logical assumptions of Christianity, drawing also the understanding of Christ into a never-ending maelstrom of rejection and counter-rejection?"[94] If, as the question implies, the answer is "not necessarily," a rule version of weak simplicity would, I venture, strengthen Alfsvåg's case by clarifying the deep problem with any *Christo remoto* methodology that does not begin to make kataphatic affirmation until the silence has been broken with the Word from God concerning His Son (Rom. 1:2–3).

In happy fact, however, Alfsvåg's great contribution (with one exception)[95] is to trace the christological qualification of the dialectic of negativity—or is it the apophatic qualification of Christology?—through three major figures:

94. Ibid., 3.
95. In a brief introductory discussion of Gregory of Nyssa, Alfsvåg pegs "the untroubled combination of apophaticism and *homoousios*-Christology" as "particularly interesting" for his project, as indeed it is generally. He then goes on to unpack this "combination" as follows. "The idea that the incarnation should lead to a knowledge of what God is or is not that allows for conclusions concerning internal relationships in God, for example the Father-Son relation-ship, is totally unacceptable to Gregory for philosophical and theological reasons; he thus maintains a strict distinction between the immanent and the economic Trinity" (ibid., 43). This is a (remarkably Augustinian?) misreading of Nyssa in a book that otherwise is daunting in its scope, nuance, and sophistication. I can only suggest that the typically Western assimilation of the "who" question to the "what" question causes Alfsvåg to claim Nyssa's agnosticism regarding "internal relations in God," when the Eunomian denial of the ontological or im-manent Trinity, including the monarchy of the Father, is what Nyssa spent a career fighting. This misreading, I submit, is evidence that the distinction that I am advocating between strong and weak versions of simplicity in this book can helpfully clarify what Alfsvåg is concerned to say. See Wisse's much more accurate *Auseinandersetzung* between Augustine and Nyssa (*Trinitarian Theology*, 70–75).

Maximus the Confessor, Nicolas Cusanus, and Martin Luther. The following palette of citations gives the picture for Maximus. "The true meaning of incarnation and resurrection as the key to all there is, is therefore available only to those who have followed the apophatic path toward the divine through rejection of passion and intellection, thus letting themselves be prepared for the blessedness of deification as resurrection from the dead. . . . [In this way,] Christ is the key to the universe as the means of its creation and recapitulation."[96] Because of this way of "Christification," "the dialectic between the kataphatic and the apophatic seems to have a different structure in Maximus than in Dionysius. The profoundly Christological understanding of apophaticism in Maximus" still leads, as it did Pseudo-Dionysius, to the "silence of the knowledge of the unknown."[97] The Platonic tendency, Alfsvåg acknowledges, is still powerful. Yet because of his stronger christological orientation, "apophasis is to Maximus even more important as a qualification of the affirmative . . . [it] is not primarily [understood] as the end of theology; to an even greater extent, it is the proper beginning."[98] The implication is that "in Maximus' view, a non-incarnational apophaticism will not after all move beyond the level of preparation."[99] I will return to this formulation of the proper apophatic move as one of "qualification of the affirmative," as it seems to me that speaking of an apophatic Christology (rather than a christological apophaticism that still tends toward the silence of the unknown as its goal) better anticipates the promised doxologies of the Beloved Community.

The other (aliud) is the "this, but not that" that characterizes finite existence in the world. The Not-Other (non aliud) is the Infinite, which is every such other and at the same time not, the Infinite in whom all opposites, or others, coincide. This is a true, rather than false, infinite; an inclusive, not a delimited, infinity (as we may recall from the pre-Socratics). This teaching of Cusanus on the co-incomprehensibility of God and the world, Alfsvåg points out, "qualifies knowledge without nullifying it; what Cusanus aims at, is certainly not skepticism" but rather something (as I would say) like pragmatism's view that knowledge is always in medias res, with "room for improvement in the sense of further approximation to the truth." As we and all others of the world are embraced in the infinity of the Not-Other, then, God is not such as to be one object of our knowledge like other objects in the world but rather is the true subject in our knowing of all others. All others coincide in God as His creatures on the way to the Beloved Community. In this framework,

96. Alfsvåg, What No Mind, 67.
97. Ibid., 69.
98. Ibid., 70.
99. Ibid., 87.

for Alfsvåg, the hypostatic or personal union of divine and human natures in Christ is the paradigmatic coincidence of the two natures as a "union of what is different [creatures] with what is not [God]."[100] The *coincidentia oppositorum* thus ceases to be a metaphysical illusion of heavenly harmony and instead receives "Christological foundation" as "the union of Creator and creature without confusion and composition beyond all understanding"; this union presents us—creatures with our feet on the earth—with Jesus, the new Adam, the "perfection of creation in the way that all things would rest in him as their perfection. He would then exist with God above all time and prior to all things, and could thus appear in the fullness of time" on the earth.[101] As such, the "Christological and soteriological" claim of Cusanus's apophaticism is "basic": "*coincidentia oppositorum* is conceived as a reflection of the coincidence of what is created with what is not in Chalcedonian Christology."[102]

To this, I would add, if Chalcedonian Christology is, as I have argued, a function of trinitarian personalism, we get the Holy Spirit as the subject in knowledge of the object, Jesus Christ the Son of God, before the audience of God the Father, whose kingdom comes.[103] That note leads us to the last major figure studied in Alfsvåg's book, Martin Luther, in whom the gradual christological transformation of apophaticism that he has been tracing comes to a climax. The kataphatic exuberance of Luther's theology of the Word and revelation is well known, yet it remains, as Alfsvåg shows, deeply and consistently qualified apophatically. "Admittedly, God has presented himself through his word. But the emphasis on discontinuity is maintained in that this word is not supported by anything in the experienced world; on the contrary, it exposes the world of the senses as being mere appearance. . . . [A] God construed on the terms of experience and finality, is no God . . . one

100. Ibid., 138.
101. Ibid., 139.
102. Ibid., 156. This christological rendering of the teaching on the coincidence of opposites is crucial in that it tears the notion of harmony away from the metaphysical illusion of heavenly peace supposedly backgrounding this veil of tears. That is to say, christologically rendered, the coincidence ceases to function analogically to point to heaven and comes to function paradoxically to point to God who comes to earth to die on a cross for us who are not in harmony. See H. Lawrence Bond, "Nicolas of Cusa and the Reconstruction of Theology: The Centrality of Christology in the Coincidence of Opposites," in *Contemporary Reflections on the Medieval Christian Tradition: Essays in Honor of Ray C. Petry*, ed. George H. Shriver (Durham, NC: Duke University Press, 1974), 81–94. In his verbal fistfight with Slavoj Žižek, John Milbank takes the coincidence of opposites as the peace of God that infinitely saturates the cosmos, if we would but in faith dare to envision it; he is rightly devastated by Žižek's retort, "I in my atheism am a better Christian." See the account in Brent Adkins and Paul R. Hinlicky, *Rethinking Philosophy and Theology with Deleuze: A New Cartography* (London: Bloomsbury Academic, 2013), 133–41.
103. Hinlicky, *Beloved Community*, 82–84.

will have to adhere to the unknown as revealed in his word by trust only."[104] Alfsvåg's formulation here may be overly Bultmannian and as such create logical difficulties that beggar intelligibility; one has to have some reason to regard an "unknown" revealed in her, his, or its word for all our trust *as God.* Otherwise, one may fall for any who "come in my name saying, 'I am He'" (Mark 13:6). The virtuous circle of Word and Spirit is needed here. Luther, in the same writing to which Alfsvåg here recurs (the *Heidelberg Disputation*), does not simply reject kataphatic ontotheology built up by the way of eminence on the basis of Romans 1:20. The One who is powerful, wise, and good enough to create all that is not God *is* the one true God. Rather, Luther says that creatures know this true power, wisdom, and goodness that make God the worthy Creator of this creation falsely. This knowledge is misused by the theologians of glory who do not want to know this very God in and as Christ crucified.[105]

Notwithstanding this nuance, Alfsvåg is surely right in his basic contention that Luther's apophatically qualified Christology is a prophetic assault on the human *securitas* that treats appearances as reality and fails to see the reality of God for us fraudulent beings in the stone of stumbling that is the Crucified One; so we have failed as theologians of the cross if we have failed to love "death and hell as the means by which faith is purified."[106] This, says Alfsvåg, points to Luther's "understanding of negativity that is Christologically informed in a way that he does not find in [Pseudo-]Dionysius."[107] Alternately formulated, "Apart from his insistence on the importance of a Christological qualification of negativity as the believer's experience of the cross, his understanding of the unknown as characterized mainly by [God's] creativity also sets him apart from some of his predecessors."[108] The reference here is to Luther's purpose clause that again links the apophatic move to a kataphatic affirmation and functions as a kind of rule for proper speaking of Christ crucified: "God kills *in order to* make alive."

From a place of profound appreciation for this argument, which I wish to make also my own—if I properly understand it—I must ask, "Which is it? Is it negativity that is qualified by Christology, or Christology that is qualified

104. Alfsvåg, *What No Mind*, 204.

105. Martin Luther, *Luther's Works: The American Edition*, ed. Jaroslav Pelikan and Helmut T. Lehmann (St. Louis: Concordia; Philadelphia: Fortress, 1955–86), 31:55.

106. Alfsvåg, *What No Mind*, 204.

107. Ibid., 205–6. See also Paul Rorem, "The Uplifting Spirituality of Pseudo-Dionysius," in *Christian Spirituality: Origins to the Twelfth Century*, ed. Bernard McGinn, John Meyendorff, and Jean Leclerq (New York: Crossroad, 1985), 132–51; Rorem, "Martin Luther's Christocentric Critique of Pseudo-Dionysian Spirituality," *Lutheran Quarterly* 11, no. 3 (August 1997): 291–307.

108. Alfsvåg, *What No Mind*, 207.

by an apophatic reserve?" In order to answer this question in the latter way, we must have a univocal Christology that says of the crucified man, "This *is* the Son of God" (see Mark 15:39), just as by extension it says of the blessed bread of the Lord's Supper, "This *is* the Body of Christ." *Est*, not *significat*. *Est*, we know not how, yet *est* that works a catachrestic metaphor to force a new meaning to occur in the world.[109] The professed ignorance ("we know not how") expresses the apophatic reserve, precisely specified, that qualifies the kataphatic christological affirmation. Not *significat*, which signs a reality other than itself, far away in heaven, making of the blessed loaf a similitude rather than the paradoxical present gift of the Giver, making of the Crucified Man, who cried His dereliction to the Father, who had abandoned him, an undialectical analogue of a heavenly being rather than the Lamb of God given to take way the sin of the world. So much, I expect, Alfsvåg and I agree on.

By contrast, however, if we were to prefer the alternative formulation of a "christological apophaticism," the danger, as it seems to me, is that the *est* is thereby made into an equivocation by an endless dialectic of negativity "drawing also the understanding of Christ into a never-ending maelstrom of rejections and counter-rejections," against Alfsvåg's express intentions. While it may be that *in divinis* the law of contradiction does not apply, here on the earth it surely does if we creatures are to speak meaningfully, also in theology. If Christology tells of the God who comes to us who are on the earth, we avoid the logical law of noncontradiction at the cost of sheer vacuity; that is, we may say, "This *is* the Son of God," sure, but so is everything and anything else. Rather, the "coming" of God in Christ is to be apophatically qualified, deliteralized, and decoded (which "demythologization" is what theology as hermeneutics is) to tell of the self-surpassing movement from the wrath of the God of love over the ruin of His creation to the mercy of the love of God that redeems and fulfills this "ruin of Joseph" (Amos 6:6). In the next chapter I pursue this correlation of the rule version of weak simplicity with apophatic Christology in some distinction from the great Karl Barth's teaching on the analogy of faith so far as it conceals a subtle but persistent Nestorianism along these latter lines.

109. Janet Martin Soskice, *Metaphor and Religious Language* (Oxford: Clarendon, 1987), 58–63.

4

Analogy and the
Communicatio Idiomatum

Analogia Entis?

"There are two distinct concepts," Henry of Ghent argued against Avicenna's univocity of the concept of being, namely, "the being of God and the being of creatures, that cannot be further reduced and [instead] are related by analogy."[1] The "analogy of being" thus emerges as a doctrine from the tradition of Thomism that appeals to the ontological claim of Thomas that all the many creatures, each in its own way, reflect in the mere acts of their beings the sheer act of being that is their Creator. Sheer being is, in this context, a perfection; it is better to be than not to be,[2] and to be absolutely is to be perfectly. As the creature exists finitely and so compositely, so analogously the Creator exists simply and thus infinitely. As the creature grows into its natural perfection, so analogously the Creator is always already its own natural perfection in actuality; correspondingly, the ultimate goal of the creature's desire for perfection is

---

1. John Marenbon, *Medieval Philosophy: An Historical and Philosophical Introduction* (London: Routledge, 2007), 276. I am grateful here to Hans Zorn for helpful comments clarifying Thomas's position in relation to Henry of Ghent and that of later versions of Thomism.

2. In the *Confessions* Augustine recalls that this innate conviction guided him as an inner light during the time of his wandering. It is to be noted that it is an axiological conviction.

to adhere to God's perfect being. It may achieve this by becoming the similitude of the Creator in the perfection of eternal life. Indeed, already now insofar as each creature reflects in some way its Creator, it already participates by this analogy in His goodness, albeit partially and imperfectly in its temporal life. As the Creator is Being itself and Goodness itself and Truth itself and Beauty itself, in Him one and the same, so the creature, so far as it exists at all, is in some way good, true, and beautiful, a reflection of God though in diverse ways as the manifold creature in relation to the One who is Creator.

As we have seen in the previous chapters, this descending doctrine of analogy from the pure actuality of He Who Is to the imperfect actuality of creatures affirms the goodness, truth, and beauty, albeit finite and diversified, of this existing creation composed of many against the perennial danger in Christianity of gnostic dualism; it identifies creation as good and the worthy object of divine redemption and fulfillment. The descending analogy of being is, then, a corollary of strong simplicity: since God as God is the perfect identity of essence and existence, imperfect creatures are known as like God in their being so far as they actualize, and as yet imperfectly realize, their essences.

Can we ascend in this way to any notion of what God is? To do so would make simplicity something like a superessence—God is essentially *actus purus*—that properly qualifies everything else that might be said of God by way of creaturely language. We do not as a rule ascend from creaturely perfections to God's essence, but by aid of this ascending analogy of being we can point to similarities between creature and Creator within the always greater dissimilarity signified by *actus purus*—the sheer, impersonal, and incomprehensible divine act of being. To the extent that this holds for Thomism (beginning with Henry of Ghent),[3] if not precisely yet for Thomas, it appears that the ascending analogy of being "is guilty of talking about God's essence, which is to exist, in two opposed ways: to indicate God's unboundedness and unknowability, and also to explain something that we all know—that we and all things around us exist"[4] as proper, thus proportionate effects of the divine *actus purus*. This equivocation, under the name of analogy, is the root of the peculiar oscillation that attends the strong doctrine of simplicity in the alternately apophatic and kataphatic faces that it shows: the "appeal to analogy softens the edge of [Thomas's] negative theology, but does not remove it."[5]

The descending *analogia entis,* then, is a Thomist slogan (the phrase itself does not occur in Thomas) articulating Thomas's justly famed maxim,

3. Marenbon, *Medieval Philosophy*, 276.
4. Ibid., 240.
5. Ibid., 238.

Gratia non destruit, sed supponit et perfecit naturam. I regard the anti-gnostic intention in this thought as roughly equivalent to my own articulation of the singular cognitive claim of Christian theology: *God is to be identified as the One who is freely determined to redeem and fulfill His creation through the missions of His Son and Spirit.*[6] The way by which I have come to this parallel claim is via Karl Barth and his successors in evangelical theology Eberhard Jüngel and Robert Jenson. And indeed, what is of particular interest today is that this claim for *analogia entis* was renewed, revised, and revitalized in the twentieth century by the Jesuit theologian Erich Przywara, who worked it out in implicit and explicit dialogue with Karl Barth, who in turn developed his counterproposal for the analogy of faith (*analogia fidei*).[7]

Barth came within a hair's breadth of Przywara's doctrine when he described faith as the human being's obedient act and decision that corresponds to God's free act and decision in Christ for humanity. This analogy also sees, then, a similarity within an even greater dissimilarity. To be sure, as a miraculous gift of capacity to the incapacitated, faith's analogy to its object consists in a true knowledge of God as ectype to archetype, as its human copy, replication, and confession. In this connection, Barth can even cite in support Luther's *in fide ipsa Christus adest*, although, as we will see, Luther's statement has the slightly different import of baptismal unification by the Spirit—that is, of the believer's conformation to Christ by way of the joyful exchange. For Barth, in any event, in faith in the present Christ a certain and clear knowledge of God comes about in the believing creature like the clarity and certainty with which God knows Himself in His Word. This likeness of the known in the knower in the thought and speech of the believing creature suffices to discern the spirits, though it is not and cannot be perfectly adequate to God because of the ever-greater dissimilarity.

Barth makes this latter point eschatologically, appealing to 1 Corinthians 13:12, where this knowing in faith is characterized as seeing through a glass but dimly until faith gives way to sight eschatologically, when the believer will know even as she has been known. Yet the eschatological account that Barth provides of the dissimilarity seems to imply something that Przywara could not metaphysically embrace, namely, a knowing *fully* as we have been known. On metaphysical grounds, such knowing fully could never be admitted, *finitum non capax infiniti*

6. Paul R. Hinlicky, *Beloved Community: Critical Dogmatics after Christendom* (Grand Rapids: Eerdmans, 2015), 42–55.

7. The following summarizes Karl Barth, *CD* I/1, 236–45 (Karl Barth, *Church Dogmatics*, trans. G. W. Bromiley, ed. G. W. Bromiley and T. F. Torrance, 4 vols. [Edinburgh: T&T Clark, 1975]). Henceforth, citations from this work are referenced in the main text by parentheses with "*CD*" followed by volume and part and then page numbers, as in the present instance.

(unless, be it noted, the full knowledge in question were parsed as personal understanding in distinction from metaphysical comprehension). Otherwise, it would abolish the distinction between Creator and creature, as understood in the doctrine of strong simplicity; it would indicate a fusion of the finite with the infinite rather than a similitude. So, indeed, we face a real conundrum here if fully knowing can be explicated only in terms of natures rather than in terms of persons in community. It is striking, in any case, how vigorously Barth at the end of this discussion rejected Przywara's charge of passivity induced by alleged "theopanism," speaking instead in Thomistic accents of God's gift as enabling and empowering the creature's own agency. The difference, then, between Przywara and Barth seems to be between protological and eschatological accounts of analogy, or of ascending and descending accounts of analogy.

Indeed, in a solid and illuminating study, Keith Johnson has shown that, contrary to Hans Urs von Balthasar's attempt to harmonize these two doctrines of analogy, Barth never abandoned his critique of Przywara's ascending analogy of being, insofar as he continued to regard it as the stalking horse of natural theology, the intellectual form of works-righteousness.[8] And it would seem to be the case that if (1) I become analogous to God by dint of my acting to realize my essence, and if (2) my knowledge of God and correspondingly my own essence also come by way of my own reflection and decision and act according to the natural light, "It is better to be than not to be." And if, further, (3) I am as such a member of a fallen humanity that "wants to be God and does not want God to be God" (Luther), I am, then, in double jeopardy by the analogy of being of thinking idolatrously about God in seeking a righteousness of my own (Phil. 3:9). Johnson shows that Barth mitigated this criticism, however, as Przywara moved to a more explicitly christological explication of the analogy of being and as another Catholic theologian, Gottlieb Söhngen, also responding to Barth, argued that the ascending analogy of being is *within* the descending analogy of faith.[9] Söhngen's move would here parallel David Burrell's acknowledgment, as we recall from previous chapters and further to be discussed below, that Thomas's philosophical "distinction" between perfect and imperfect being in fact borrows from revealed theology's knowledge of God as Creator of all that is other than God; Söhngen extends this borrowing to apply also to the proper relation of the two natures in Christ, as replicated in the believer's obedience of faith.

John R. Betz, at least at moments, appears to agree with Johnson. In his outstanding introduction to the translation into English of Erich Przywara's

8. Keith L. Johnson, *Karl Barth and the* Analogia Entis (London: T&T Clark, 2011).
9. Ibid., 170–81.

Analogia Entis, he argues that, in his *Auseinandersetzung* with Karl Barth over the doctrine of analogy, Przywara "brings us to a metaphysical crossroads, for 'either one identifies the mutable and finite with what is immutable and infinite,' as inevitably happens with both pantheism and theopanism, or one recognizes the actual state of affairs that the *philosophia perennis* describes by the '*analogia entis*.'"[10] This is indeed a crossroads, though not exactly, I am arguing, in the way that Betz imagines, since, minimally, the incarnation tells of the divine Logos, who did not only "associate" with "what is immutable and infinite" but "*became* flesh"; and who, at the decisive juncture of His incarnate sojourn decided in the obedience of faith that it was better for Him *not* to be (Mark 14:34–37) for the sake of others, utterly emptying Himself in obedience "to the point of death—even death on a cross" (Phil. 2:7–8). Such divine becoming and acquisition thereby of extrinsic properties to the extremity of assuming the death of sinful humanity under the curse of divine law violates strong simplicity, so that one or the other must bend and give way. That objection to Betz's putative fork in the road will be evident enough from the preceding chapters and will be argued further in this chapter: there is a tendency toward trinitarian modalism, and a corresponding christological Nestorianism, wherever strong simplicity functions axiomatically to delimit proper thought concerning God. We ought rather to learn what the oneness of God is from God's act in Christ, God surpassing God to reconcile the world to Himself by no longer counting its trespasses (2 Cor. 5:19).[11] This would give us a weak doctrine of simplicity that qualifies the incarnation and cross of the Son of God as ineffable mystery with respect to the question of efficient causality, "How can this be?" Weak simplicity, in other words, defers to the God to whom all things are possible, even though not all things are wise or good.

So, as opposed to the apparent (and all-too-convenient in these gray days of "ecumenical winter") agreement of Johnson and Betz on a fork in the road between Protestant and Catholic doctrines of analogy, I wish in this chapter to query, *Tertium non datur?* And I will answer that there is indeed a third way, which is the patristic *commercium admirabile*, the wondrous exchange of properties in Christ that Luther rephrased to stress the existential import of patristic Christology, the *fröhliche Wechsel*, the "joyful exchange."[12] That

10. John R. Betz, introduction to *Analogia Entis: Metaphysics; Original Structure and Universal Rhythm*, by Erich Przywara, trans. John R. Betz and David Bentley Hart (Grand Rapids: Eerdmans, 2014), 53.

11. Hinlicky, *Beloved Community*, 691–711.

12. See further Paul R. Hinlicky, *Paths Not Taken: Fates of Theology from Luther through Leibniz* (Grand Rapids: Eerdmans, 2009), 145–50.

third christological way will agree with Thomas on the redemption of the creature and fulfillment of nature, and with Barth on the correspondence of faith in Christ to the Creator, who is also the redeemer and fulfiller—whose creation, in other words, is eschatological from the origin on. But it will differ from both in articulating this position christologically in terms of the unity of person rather than as a dialectic of the two natures, where "person" is used in Christology in exactly the same sense as in the trinitarian distinction, *mia ousia treis hypostaseis*. Here the needed dialectic in theology transposes from the modalist dialectic of divinity and humanity to the trinitarian dialectic of Word and Spirit.

I said that Betz "at moments" appears to agree with Johnson. In fact, there is something odd about this apparent agreement, which seems to me more a matter of confessionalistic posturing than deep agreement. So, for the present, the claim that I wish to engage at this juncture is Betz's own contemporary argument for what is in fact his surprisingly qualified and refreshingly iconoclastic doctrine of analogy (in distinction from the rich and complex thought of Przywara in its own complex development, consideration of which would take us too far afield from the present purpose of uncovering the christological cost of the analogy of being). Suffice it to say that this restriction to Betz's introduction is justified for several reasons.

First, Przywara's own incessant invocation of "theopanism," the theological equivalent of Spinoza's philosophical pantheism, to capture Luther's (and Barth's) theology is too crude by far. It is as crude as Protestants or Scotists accusing Thomas *simpliciter* of Aristotelian naturalism; hermeneutically, it is the equivalent of it in merely polemical theology. Moreover, we have it on good apostolic authority that the eschatological goal, in conformity with the eschatological sense of Zechariah 14:9, arrives when God becomes *panta en pasin* (1 Cor. 15:28)—"theopanism," if you will. In this light, the actual problem in early Protestantism[13] (and in this not discontinuous with scholastic precedents) is that something like a "theopanist" *Alleinwirksamkeit Gottes* might be justly attributed to Huldrych Zwingli's (neo-Thomist!) doctrine of providence.[14] But in this theopanist vein Zwingli wrote *against* Luther's view in the latter's *The Bondage of the Will* for conceding too much "freedom" to creatures "in things below us"—that is, as "secondary causes" cooperating with the Creator, whether by His general or special providence. Thus, however melodramatically the polemical Luther expressed himself, his own position,

---

13. For the following, see Paul R. Hinlicky, *Luther and the Beloved Community: A Path for Christian Theology after Christendom* (Grand Rapids: Eerdmans, 2010), 139–78.

14. Ulrich Gäbler, *Huldrych Zwingli: His Life and Work*, trans. Ruth C. L. Gritsch (Philadelphia: Fortress, 1986), 37, 148.

like that of Augustine, from whom he drew, is that God is the cause of all causes but not the maker of all choices, *Alleswirksamkeit Gottes*—that is, the "omnicausality" of Thomas![15] It would be too tedious by far to sort out Przywara's errors in the interpretation of Luther (dependent as they are on what German Lutherans of his day were saying about Luther), while Betz, as we will see, is more nuanced than to reduce theology in Luther's tradition to modern pantheism or, for that matter following Kerr, to assume a seamless continuity of Thomas with what Thomists say about him.

Indeed, second, Betz more or less openly allows that Przywara's *analogia entis* is not pure Thomistic theology but rather a notion stemming from Thomas that undergoes a series of subtle revisions (not least by fuller integration with the teaching of the Fourth Lateran Council on analogy, as already mentioned).[16] Indeed, centrally in Betz's telling, "[Karl] Barth's criticisms caused Przywara to think more deeply about his own position," resulting in a more theocentric rather than cosmological orientation and a firmer focus on "Christ as the measure of the relation between God and creation."[17] (How much of the Reformation–Counter-Reformation confessional tension at once dissolves when we see in the new Adam the cosmic-christological "analogy of being"!)

Third, along the same lines, this admitted revisionism is also poised by Betz against the popular, if not predominant, self-bootstrapping naturalism (Molinism) associated with the analogy of being from the hyperconfessionalized Catholicism of the modern period; with von Balthasar, Betz regards this (nigh-universal modern) interpretation of Thomas as a "misuse of Catholic theology."[18] Pertinently, then, once again let me reiterate what was said at the outset of this book: if we are to take what Lutherans say about Luther *cum grano salis*, the same might be said, with Fergus Kerr, concerning what Thomists have said about Thomas.

Fourth, and most refreshingly as a result of the preceding revisionisms, Przywara's analogy of being now appears in Betz's rendering as Heidegger's partner in *Destruktion*, smashing the idols of ontotheology (see the discussion, in this connection, of Burrell in chap. 2). "Indeed, lacking none of the deconstructive or iconoclastic zeal one finds in Heidegger, Barth, or Marion,

---

15. Betz, "Introduction," 71–72. The only difference is that Luther does not shrink from the implication that God, whose creative presence in the creature enables its own acts, just so enables also the wicked acts of the sinner, who remains God's creature, and in this way God "hardens the heart of Pharaoh" by causing him to act on his wicked desires, freely willed.

16. Ibid., 72–74.

17. Ibid., 115.

18. Ibid., 101.

the point of Przywara's *analogia entis* and his own animating pathos is precisely to clear away all conceptual idols, to demolish every foundation that the creature by virtue of its being or its thought would presume to have in itself, to *loosen* our grasp on being, and to point through the *mystery* of creaturely being to the profounder, even more inscrutable mystery of God, leaving no foundations but for the creature to cling to God over the depths of its own nothingness."[19] If that is so, I cannot resist the shameless observation that it would not be unjustified historically to say that, via Heidegger's critique of ontotheology (and "theopanism" notwithstanding), Betz's Przywara has caught up with Luther's initiating theological program: "The sum and substance of this letter [Romans] is: to pull down, to pluck up, and to destroy all wisdom and righteousness of the flesh (i.e., of whatever importance they may be in the sight of men and even in our own eyes), no matter how heartily and sincerely they may be practiced, and to implant, and make large the reality of sin (however unconscious we may be of its existence)."[20] Just this project of Luther, we know today, inspired the early Heidegger's own break with the reactionary, neo-scholastic, hyperconfessionalized, and polemical antimodernism in which he had been schooled.[21] Unlike Luther, however, Heidegger the iconoclast never found his way forward to Christ, the God-man and icon of the new Adam given into death for us idolaters (however unconscious we remain of our true plight) that in the Spirit we might be returned to the Father as beloved children in new and living likeness to God.

In a rich footnote, however, Betz surpasses such confessionalistic posturing to offer the following insightful analysis of an ecumenical way forward, following a sample from Thomas's own "fascinating conjunction of the protological and the eschatological"[22] with respect to the biblical similitude of creature to Creator, the *imago Dei*. Along the lines of Bonhoeffer's view of the biblical account of the origin as "hope projected backwards," Betz acknowledges that the "likeness of Genesis 1:26 could be understood as a proleptic likeness, that is, as a promise, which is to be effected historically through Christ and His Spirit,"[23] as 1 John 3:2 would indicate. Thomas "unfortunately" does not pursue the question of the relation of the protological and the eschatological

---

19. Ibid., 82.

20. Martin Luther, *Luther: Lectures on Romans*, ed. and trans. Wilhelm Pauck, Library of Christian Classics (Philadelphia: Westminster, 1961), 3.

21. Benjamin D. Crowe, *Heidegger's Religious Origins: Destruction and Authenticity* (Bloomington: Indiana University Press, 2006).

22. Betz, "Introduction," 41.

23. Ibid.

similitude so posed. But the question that arises for us today is "not *whether* there is an analogy of being . . . [but] whether the analogy is to be affirmed already as a matter of protology (in spite of the subsequent reality of sin) as a terminus a quo (which not even the reality of sin can destroy), or whether the analogy is to be affirmed only eschatologically, as terminus ad quem, which is produced only through faith in Christ and the work of the Spirit."[24] These two possibilities reflect the tendencies of the divided confessions, with Przywara following Thomas already in affirming the analogy on the level of nature, *analogia entis*, but Barth following Luther in taking analogy eschatologically, hence in the present only as a matter of faith, *analogia fidei*. "But perhaps," Betz concludes in a deft stroke, "the whole debate is best resolved simply by positing the traditional Orthodox distinction between 'image' and 'likeness'—which does not confuse but makes explicit the difference between nature and grace."[25]

In that case, we could say in Protestant lingo that the "image" is the universal calling of God to humanity to respond to His creative command and blessing and so arise to its task as God's covenant partner in the care and development of creation by becoming "like" God in creative, other-regarding love. For both Catholic and Protestant traditions, then, we could further affirm that the corruption of sin destroys the likeness even as the image—that is, the divine calling as God's *creatio continua* persists indelibly, providing the basis for human dignity and justice in a corrupt world (Gen. 9:2) no matter how filled that image becomes with unlikeness to God. In other words, only the human person (as image of God) can sin (become unlike God). In such a world that is laboring, groaning, sighing under corruption (Rom. 8), Christ comes as the new Adam and true *imago Dei*, the being in the world, icon not idol, who is the concrete, person-at-work analogy between God and humanity. It is His mind (Phil. 2:5), then, that believers have and are to have by the impartation of His Spirit.

This suggestion from Betz illustrates afresh the old bromide that as divided Christians draw closer to Christ, they are drawn closer to one another. Indeed, as Betz rightly concludes, the contrasting "emphases" between the Protestant "*novelty* of revelation" and the Catholic "total mystery of the being of the cosmos . . . need not—and ultimately cannot—be opposed."[26] With that honest recognition of difference and hopeful sketch of ultimate ecumenical convergence in mind, I wish now to turn to the interim "choice," as Betz in the same passage requires of us, regarding how to order these

24. Ibid., 42.
25. Ibid. This is the very move in theological anthropology that I make in my systematic theology.
26. Ibid., 115.

contrasting emphases on similitude. I will argue, with (selective) help from Eberhard Jüngel and Karl Barth, that the matter of analogy or similitude in the biblical matrix of faith is a matter not of the disclosure of being but rather of a causal alteration of being, "new creation," that nevertheless proleptically brings, and promises to bring about fully, the Pauline "redemption of our bodies"—that is, the redemption and fulfillment of the common body, creation. Creation from the outset is thus eschatologically oriented and new creation, taken as the "redemption of our bodies" (Rom. 8:23), is *creatio ex vetere*.[27] The disruptive new creation is *creatio ex vetere*. But in order to get there, some ground must be cleared on the convoluted matter bequeathed to us from Heidegger: ontotheology. Here I will appreciate (equally selective) help from Duns Scotus.

Vindicating Univocity

The distinction between strong and weak versions of simplicity, as argued in the preceding chapters, is one between a putative metaphysical insight into the timeless self-identity of divine and perfect nature and a theological acknowledgment of the singularity claimed by and for the God of the gospel, the Father of the Son in the Spirit, taken as the one true God coming to the earth, by the knowledge of Jesus Christ and Him crucified. I am now extending this analysis into the realm of theological language. Corresponding to the foregoing differentiation, I will argue in this section for a weak version of similitude for referring to the God of the gospel in human language. According to strong simplicity, proper theological language comes by the extended similitude of analogy. This works by way of a comparison proceeding from the greater known to the lesser known; for example, "Scotus is to Thomas as Leibniz is to Spinoza." Such analogy clarifies (at least in certain circles!) the reference to the lesser known, as in "A is to B (a better-known relation) as C is to D (a lesser-known one)." Thus, in the example just given, the familiar medieval disagreement between Thomas and Scotus illuminates a less familiar early modern one (in the perhaps unlikely event that neomedievalists should become curious about early moderns). Yet this parenthetical note made about "certain circles" also indicates the sensitivity of strong similitude to its presupposed, often unnoted, and in that case necessarily unexplicated and unwarranted context. What we assume as familiar and even take for granted as knowledge "in our circles" is in fact tacit; unnoticed, it may not obtain

27. John Polkinghorne, *The Faith of a Physicist: Reflections of a Bottom-Up Thinker* (Princeton: Princeton University Press, 1994), 167–69.

for others, who then cannot understand the clarification that we intend by comparatively applying a relation that we (but not everyone else) know(s) to one that we do not know.

In weak similitude just this problem of context and epistemic access is lifted up and problematized. This has the force of relativizing strong claims on behalf of similitude, as if just so they acquired timeless and universal insight into correspondingly timeless and universal truth. The realization that all creaturely speech, theological too, moves from "our circle" of limited vision and sinful egocentricity to new ones—that is, begins from some particular fund of tacit knowledge *in medias res*—not only blunts the force of the claim that similitude as such (say, as opposed to literal representation) is *the* way to *the* theological language. It means little to say, on reflection, that all our language for God is metaphorical when all our language about everything is metaphorical to one degree or another. But, further complicating the strong claim for similitude is that metaphor is deciphered and understood precisely when its literal reference (n.b., not "representation") to something in the world is grasped, as in Janet Soskice's humorous illustration: if I say, "Don't touch the *live* wire!" and you would reply, "It's not really *alive*. That's only a metaphor," well, you would *literally* be dead by electrocution when you picked up the only *metaphorically* "live" wire.[28]

These complications are enough epistemologically to relativize claims for similitude as *the* key, semantical and ontological, to the problem of language for anything, let alone for the singularity that is God. But further, for Christian theology the complication is even more dramatic. In revealed theology the direction of the "movement" (*meta-phora*, or *trans-latio*, after all, is transition, change, motion) in the peculiar metaphors of the gospel is reversed from the presumed ascent of natural theology "from below to above" (to put it, ahem, metaphorically). Here the speech is about the free and gracious movement of God, who comes to creatures "from above to below," as it were, in human language. Here consequently the central questions of theological similitude become "How does the unfamiliar make itself known to us (revelation), how does it establish access (faith) and create a context (*ecclesia*) in which it can be understood and thus intelligently believed and lived?" And here, as we will see, the peculiar type of metaphor technically named "catachresis" (i.e., the paradox that asserts on the basis of semantical univocity what to all appearances is a contradiction in order to generate a new meaning in the world) is key to the language of the God of the gospel: Christ *crucified*, and the resurrection *of the body* (to register those gospel

28. Janet Martin Soskice, *Metaphor and Religious Language* (Oxford: Clarendon, 1987), 70.

metaphors of catachresis that bracket 1 Corinthians in its first and fifteenth chapters, respectively).

To appreciate the catachrestical metaphor, then, we need theologically to rehabilitate univocity and thus transcend the misleading binary between so-called literal and so-called metaphorical discourse in theology. In his disputes with contemporary Thomists who hold to the tall tale of the fall from Thomas into nihilism that begins with Duns Scotus, Richard Cross rightly objects to accusations that (1) the use of univocal concepts entails the posit of a univocal reality, "being as such"; and (2) as such subordinates God and creation to this common reality, "being as such," as to a genus, which perforce makes God a specific individual entity of being and thus the ontotheological idol of a being alongside other beings, albeit best and brightest; and (3) that univocity thus undermines perception of the analogicity of being that provides the only means metaphysically to articulate the strong distinction of Creator from creature.

In response to these accusations, Cross points out that treating concepts as reality—that is, logical and semantical claims *de dicto* as if they were epistemic or metaphysical claims *de re*—is historically a blunder with which Scotus cannot justly be charged, even as the very accusation instead betrays a realist understanding of concepts superimposed from the side of the accusers. Moreover, as Thomas himself knows, the "analogy of being" (as above, a Thomism, since this formula is not found in Thomas himself) in regard to God is so thin as to be evanescent (i.e., claiming the sheer similarity of existence between God and creature that itself must always be bracketed by an ever-greater dissimilarity). Consequently, as Thomas already knows, the way of analogy ultimately breaks down and ends with Pseudo-Dionysius in apophatic silence before the Unknown and Unknowable One, who is beyond numerical oneness (since numerical oneness entails multiplicity as its antonym) and thus an ontological One that is inconceivable to us in its negatively defined indivisibility. But, then, so far as the doctrine of analogy seeks the middle way between negation and eminence, it ultimately fails; negativity prevails in the hyperdialectical form of negating also the negations to point silently to the One beyond being and nonbeing as Not-Nothing.

Consequently, Cross argues, some version of eminence based on univocity is required if speech concerning God is not finally to be empty. To put the critique positively, in Cross's own words, "If *all* we know are negations, then we will not be able to distinguish God from non-being. If, contrariwise, we know negations that are proper to God, this can be the case only on the basis of some positive and specific understanding that we have of God [i.e., the divine perfections]."[29] The way of eminence, of course, perfects these positive or kataphatic attributions

29. Richard Cross, *Duns Scotus on God* (Burlington, VT: Ashgate, 2005), 259.

by eliminating creaturely imperfections. It too is an "eliminative method," though it begins with positive-because-univocal affirmations—for example, as I would imagine, the doxological attribution of "the kingdom, the power, and the glory" to God alone in the conclusion of the Lord's Prayer. The *soli* in *soli Deo gloria*, then, is the apophatic or "eliminative" qualification of the attribution of majesty to God; it exemplifies, in terms of the present argument, the rule version of weak simplicity that we respect in our speech the holy singularity of the one true God so far as we claim this title for the God of the gospel. "If we are to be so robustly apophatic as to exclude even this sort of eliminative method, then it will be hard to see how any speculative or systematic theological project could get off the ground. And we would certainly be more apophatic than is warranted by the Christian theological tradition. To pursue cataphatic theology is not to be naively anthropomorphic."[30]

In historical fact, the aforementioned string of Thomist accusations against Scotist univocity depends on a series of historical and philosophical decisions: Aristotle's objection to Platonic forms; Avicenna's definition of Aristotle's distinction between the methodological questions "Does it exist?" and "What is it?" into notions of existence and essence respectively; Thomas's utilization of Avicenna's conceptual distinction between essence and existence to articulate the metaphysical difference between necessary and contingent ways of being; and ultimately, as mentioned, the integration of these decisions with the dogmatic decree of the Fourth Lateran Council in 1215.[31] That papal council not only articulated the principle of analogy as setting similarity within an ever-greater dissimilarity, but also, not accidentally, construed the trinitarian doctrine as a virtual quaternity—that is, "plac[ing] behind the persons a '*res non generans neque genita nec procedens*' (a *thing* not begetting nor begotten nor proceeding) [that] really transforms the persons into mere modalities *kat' epinoian* (existing for thought), or into inner processes in God."[32] These moves, I am arguing, are correlative.

30. Ibid.
31. The Lateran Councils are not ecumenical councils but papal councils. In addition to the trinitarian quaternity mentioned above, we have to thank the Fourth Lateran Council for (1) authorizing the temporal sword's persecution of heretics and (2) the doctrine of eucharistic transubstantiation. See Henry Bettenson, ed., *Documents of the Christian Church* (London: Oxford University Press, 1947), 188–89, 210–11.
32. Adolph von Harnack, *History of Dogma*, trans. Neil Buchanan, 7 vols. (New York: Dover, 1961), 6:183. To this Western turn to a modalist doctrine of quaternity, Harnack put the acute question, "Or is it still a doctrine of the Trinity, when the immanent thinking and the immanent willing in God are defined and objectified as *generare* and *spirare* (begetting and breathing)?" (6:183–84). Harnack further comments,

In Thomism the doctrine [of the Trinity] still had a relation to the idea of the world, in so far as the hypostasis of the Son was not sharply marked off from the world-idea in God

Each one of these steps, which are relevant for grasping the contextual sense of the claims for strong simplicity and the corresponding doctrine of the analogy of being, is disputable. They are not, theologically, irreversible canonical decisions like the combination of Old and New Testaments against dualism and docetism; or the *homoousios* against Arianism and, with the refined distinction between *ousia* and *hypostasis*, against modalism; or salvation by grace against Celestius and Pelagius; or the unity of Christ's person against Nestorianism and the duality of His natures against monophysitism. Going to the heart of the matter regarding the strong Creator/creature distinction, then, Cross rightly registers a procedural protest against the imperiousness of the Thomist accusations: It is not "required that we identify God with his own act of existence. There are plenty of other ways of identifying God as necessary and creatures as contingent," any of which may sustain David Burrell's "distinction."[33]

One of these other ways is the way of semantical univocity. Univocity, according to Scotus, characterizes a concept that is "one in such a way that the unity is sufficient for a contradiction when it is affirmed and denied of the same thing."[34] Univocity gives us the logical power to contradict, to affirm this over against that, hence to speak concretely also with respect to God as something in the world, biblically, as His Word: "Thus says the LORD, the God of Israel, 'Let my people go!'" (Exod. 5:1) and, again, "Whoever listens to you listens to me" (Luke 10:16). This is so because under univocity, as Scotus understands it, Creator and creature can fall under the extension of the same concept—say, for example, goodness—even though in reality they differ by a qualitatively infinite magnitude in goodness, since the Creator has access to goodness in an unbounded way with respect to creatures, while any creature's goodness is extrinsically conferred, finitely possessed, and ever vulnerable to loss by incursions of actual evil.

If I say, for example, that because God is God in having infinite possibilities for good, and wills out of this infinite treasury of goods life, righteousness, and peace for His creature, it follows that I can also say concretely here on the earth that this Creator God is against, say, Stalin's gulag or the Atlantic slave trade. These may be identified theologically as finite and historical instantiations of the evil that actually contradicts God's will for good and hinders the

---

[i.e., the mediating Logos of Neoplatonism via the emanationist scheme in Avicenna]. Thomism was also necessarily obliged to retain its leaning to Modalism, as the concept of God did not at bottom admit of the assumption of distinctions in God, but reduced the distinctions to relations, which themselves again had to be neutralised. The Scotist School, on the other hand, kept the persons sharply asunder. (6:183)

33. Richard Cross, "Idolatry and Religious Language," *Faith and Philosophy* 25, no. 2 (April 2008): 192.

34. Cross, *Duns Scotus on God*, 251.

coming of His reign on the earth—that is, that blocks the stream from that infinite treasury of good in God, out of which He continually works the work of His good creation. Urgently, then, I cannot let such knowledge of God's good will and purpose for good on the earth die the death of a thousand apophatic qualifications on the grounds that there is some good, however dim, also in the gulag or on the caravel, that their evil is solely a privation of the perfection that they ought to be rather than a genuine contradiction of God in actual evil. I cannot be consoled with the putative knowledge that God as such and most properly speaking is good beyond any such creaturely knowledge of the finite, earthly measures of good in opposition to evil.

In fact, all similitudes, even the thinnest one of all in the analogy of being, depend for their sense (again, not as mental replicas adequate to extramental things but rather as references, as successfully pointing to and thus identifying something in the extramental world for creatures to act on) on a baseline of semantical univocity, if metaphorical predications are to avoid, on the one side, vacuous equivocation and, on the other side, an ultimate apophaticism, really, with respect to the God of the gospel, a final theological agnosticism. Just this latter danger attends the doctrine of the analogy of being, which, strictly speaking, affirms only *that* God is, as in a kind of tautology, and cannot specify *what* this really existing God is as something real or good or wise in the world, since strong simplicity requires the real resolution into undifferentiated unity of all such distinctions implied by the plurality of attributes predicated of God by His creatures—even though it is by predicates that we otherwise specify *what* in the world we are talking about. But of the God of the gospel we can and must say, "Christ is the power of God and the wisdom of God"; and in Paul's weakly simple way, we at once qualify this affirmation thusly: "For God's foolishness is wiser than human wisdom, and God's weakness is stronger than human strength" (1 Cor. 1:24b–25).

In the same way, the God who says at the burning bush, "I am THE ONE WHO IS," reveals His name in order to reveal His identity in the course of His history with His people, who are, not accidentally but precisely, the Hebrew refuse of the world: "I am THE ONE WHO IS, *your God, who*[35] *brought you up out of the land of Egypt, out of the house of bondage.* . . . Have no other god; engrave no images of your own for me; do not abuse my Name, but remember it and what I have done for you on the Sabbath" (see Exod. 20:1–8). If we adopt a philosophical theory that actually disables such divine self-predication, accompanied as it is by the election of the rejected and the

35. On relative clauses as identifying descriptions of the agent, see Robert W. Jenson, *The Triune Identity: God according to the Gospel* (Philadelphia: Fortress, 1982), 1–20.

correspondingly sharp warnings against self-chosen and self-invented predications, we are in double jeopardy of losing the revealed God and overlooking
His concrete election (i.e., His choice) and at the same time replacing Him not
only with gross "ontotheological" idols but also with a subtle, abstract, and
highly refined "One." That would be what Cross, following Scotus, tags as the
"vicious abstraction" of *esse ipsum subsistens*, Being itself, the reification of
a No-Thing. Under univocity, to the contrary, all the tensions in predicating
God that attend the biblical narrative, summed up centrally in Jesus's cry of
dereliction (Matt. 27:46; Mark 15:34), become the fertile ground for knowing
God in His motion of grace, from the wrath of His love to the mercy of His
love (Hosea 11:8–9). But under analogy, these tensions have to be disqualified,
attributed not to the God who complexly comes to us by the Spirit's proclamation of the crucified Messiah, Son of the Father, savior of the perishing,
but instead to varying creaturely projections, reflecting varying creaturely
states, none of which touch the vicious abstraction itself in its ineffable bliss.

Burrell expressly correlates his strong claim for analogy against univocity with his strong version of ontological simplicity, saying that the oneness
of God is the ontological identity of essence and existence in God rather
than a merely numerical reduction from polytheism to monotheism. Burrell's
overriding (and, let me concur, justified) contemporary concern to align the
Abrahamic religions against arrogant secularism (quite in parallel, as we have
seen, to Nasr), however, overcomes sober judgment. Whether or not Judaism
and Islam agree with him on ontological as opposed to a merely numerical
monotheism, I dare not venture a judgment, though I will voice my working
suspicion that these religions are just as conflicted as Christianity in regard
to scriptural and metaphysical accounts of God's oneness (think of Spinoza's
dismissal from the synagogue or Al-Ghazali's repudiation of the "incoherence
of the philosophers"). At least for Christian trinitarianism, however, it must
be questioned whether Burrell's decision for protological simplicity does anything more than valorize a philosophical choice for persistence over change,
for cosmic order over *creatio continua*, for *prisca theologia* and *philosophia
perennis* against the novelty of the gospel, for the reification of a No-Thing
rather than deliverance from "ontotheological idolatry" or, rather, deliverance to the Creator, who is inseparable from His free determinations by His
Son and Spirit to redeem and fulfill his groaning creation, Jews, Muslims,
and us wicked Christians too. Of course, Burrell would rejoin: God as pure
actuality represents to the contrary the greatest possible theological choice
for activity over stasis.

In this post-Christendom age we Euro-American Christians, still divided
and mutually anathematizing, should intend orthodoxy rather than claim

it as our self-evident possession. Unless we in principle acknowledge the vulnerabilities that attend all our partisan claims to truth, as received, and penitently look for ways to move forward the real theological argument embedded in, but also distorted by, those partisan traditions, we de facto identify our particular philosophical preferences or our special confessional idioms with the truth of the gospel, as in the lamentable scapegoating of Scotism by contemporary Thomists for the modern loss of all good—itself a gross narrative and an eminently disputable oversimplification. To this complaint, I would further add now from my Lutheran perspective that there are several specific disadvantages theologically with particularities of Thomas's doctrine of simplicity visible in the corresponding doctrine of analogy, as tacitly acknowledged in Betz's revisionism (but also, be it again noted, that on questions of the Christian doctrine of sin and grace I will, for the same Lutheran reasons, align with Thomas over Scotus as also Augustine over John Cassian).[36] Here I will enumerate the difficulties by way of summing up this section on rehabilitating univocity.

First, apropos of Cross's argument for semantical univocity, logical argument in theology depends on clear and consistently applied concepts (as Thomas, above all, also knows), without which theology as knowledgeable discourse (Scotus: *scientia*) about God turns into fog and mirrors—for example, as in today's carefree plunge into equivocity[37] under the name of metaphorical theology, celebrated with an academic kind of gallows humor as some new diversity; in fact it but obfuscates the loss of the chief cognitive claim of the God of the gospel to be the one true God in exchange for a happy relapse into polytheism, a new and abject enthrallment to "many so-called gods and lords."[38]

36. In exemplary articles Bruce D. Marshall has pointed to these convergences: "Faith and Reason Reconsidered: Aquinas and Luther on Deciding What Is True," *The Thomist* 63 (1999): 1–48; "Justification as Declaration and Deification," *International Journal of Systematic Theology* 4, no. 1 (March 2002): 3–28.

37. R. Kendall Soulen, *The Divine Name(s) and the Holy Trinity*, vol. 1, *Distinguishing the Voices* (Louisville: Westminster John Knox, 2011), 238–40.

38. But note the counterwitness from within this camp of Vítor Westhelle, *After Heresy: Colonial Practices and Post-Colonial Theologies* (Eugene, OR: Cascade, 2010). What is remarkable about Westhelle's book is its resistance from within the world of contemporary contextual theologies to the plunge into practical polytheism. According to Westhelle, biblical narrative functions subversively to give liberating expression to the experience of "subalterns" ("others who are under or beneath" [130]). Westhelle struggles therefore against a mere plurality of subaltern genitive and adjectival theologies. Nor does he resign himself to apophatic silence, gesturing to a place above the fray. Indeed, he would unite these postcolonial theological subversions, not in one common representation of the Infinite, who remains essentially *Deus absconditus*, but rather in the usage of the principles of *sola Scriptura* and the Chalcedonian *communicatio idiomatum* as rules for "expressing the gospel in the dialectic of a particular context" (163) to refer to the saving God of the Bible.

Second, there are other factors (as Burrell acknowledges, indeed insists on in his other polemic against so-called analytic theology) covertly at work in Thomas's presentation of so-called natural theology, namely, his secret "interjection" of dogma from revealed theology that in fact works as a hidden axiom. Not least of this borrowing is the Creator/creature distinction itself, which Aristotle does not know and Avicenna compromises (to al-Ghazali's objection;[39] incidentally, this is the same critique of covert borrowing from revealed theology that I have made of the Lutheran Leibniz in his conflicts with Spinoza and Hobbes).[40] In the same way, Augustine's correlative principle of natural light, that "it is better to be than not to be," conceals a biblical judgment of value derived from Genesis 1. This may well be a profound truth of the revealed doctrine of creation, as in the refrain "And God saw that it was good" running through the seven days of Genesis 1, but it is not an indisputable (think of Buddhism) axiom of philosophical thought. What else is our gnostic nihilism today than the renewed contestation of that revealed truth about the goodness of finite being in Genesis 1?

Third, there are good reasons, as already alluded to, for regarding "being" as nothing but a "vicious abstraction" (the equivalent of the claim that trinitarian *ousia* is nothing real in itself but a conception of what qualifies as the one true God, who really is, according to Christian doctrine, the Father of the Son in the Spirit and as such the free Creator of all that is not God). Of course, to challenge Aristotelian actualism in this way is to deny that essences in no way exist except as actualized (they *do* exist as possibilities in the infinite treasury of the divine intelligence, pressing there, as Leibniz imagined, for admission to existence in the world). It is further to make being, as an abstraction, into a highest genus—that is, into a classification of things or persons that are there in space and time. In this alternative metaphysics, being as such, then, is *not* the ineffable reality of perfect persistence that is grasped in the notion of *actus purus* with its attendant presuppositions in Aristotle's prioritization of actuality over possibility. Furthermore, subordinating God and creature to a common concept of being in thought is not the same as subordinating God and creature to a common reality that exists as such apart from the mind's conception of it and thus as something exterior to both. Indeed, the appearance of this subordination is created by the imposition of the notion of Being itself as the really real onto Scotus's struggle for logical clarity in conceptual discourse about God, whose holy "being" we cannot begin to

39. Borrowing from Josef Pieper's observation that "creation is the hidden element in the *philosophy* of St. Thomas" (David Burrell, "Creator/Creatures Relation: 'The Distinction' vs. 'Onto-theology,'" *Faith and Philosophy* 25, no. 2 [April 2008]: 179).
40. Hinlicky, *Paths Not Taken*, 223–59.

distinguish from that of creatures in the fallen world unless conceptually we use the notion "existence" univocally, for being there in a world. Then it becomes clear that God exists *for us*, as antecedently God mysteriously exists *for God* in the eternal plentitude of tri-personal love, the eternal *world* of the Beloved Community. It is this God who comes from God in the free decision from the origin in action to redeem and fulfill a world of genuine others. That is to say, God exists for God in the freedom to love wisely that is the eternal circulation of the Father and the Son in the Spirit, and it is as such that the Triune God freely spirals forth *ad extra* to achieve a world of creatures in the coming of the Beloved Community.[41]

In this formulation, note, we use the term "exist" univocally, and accordingly we cannot speak of "God" in the vicious abstractions of a worldless, timeless, spaceless *ousia*, *physis*, *natura*, *substantia*, *essentia*, and so on but can speak of "God" only as the Father of the Son on whom He breathes the Spirit, taken in faith as the one true God, who as such comes to us. If this strong and kataphatic trinitarian personalism is "ontotheology," so be it. Heidegger is not the pope, nor ought genuinely Catholic theology follow Heidegger's critique of ontotheology uncritically, which is in fact a path to atheism, since it does not pass through the *Destruktion* to the new creation in Christ, to the trinitarianism that is, as Jüngel has so powerfully argued, beyond atheism and theism. Victim as Heidegger was of neo-scholasticism, trinitarianism in the way enunciated in this book was not even in his purview. Yet trinitarianism does not merely "associate" God with creatures "ontotheologically"; it makes creation, incarnation, and resurrection the signature of the one true God. Taken univocally, then, the *egeneto* in *kai ho logos sarx egeneto* tells of personal change (not substantial mutation), the divine acquisition of extrinsic properties by the movement of the eternal Son into the time and space of creatures to make it His own henceforth and forever more. If that is clear, the catachrestic metaphor of paradox launches responsible Christian discourse about God or it is not actually initiated at all, "so that the cross of Christ might not be emptied of its power. For the message about the cross is foolishness to those who are perishing, but to us who are being saved it is the power of God" (1 Cor. 1:17–18).

Sorting Out Paradox and Similitude

If the foregoing is cogently argued, Eberhard Jüngel has rightly affirmed that "the cross of Jesus Christ is the ground and measure of the formation

41. Hinlicky, *Beloved Community*, 861–64.

of metaphors which are appropriate to God."[42] Where this admittedly odd standard of orthodoxy is in force, which reiterates Paul's call at the outset of 1 Corinthians (2:2) to know nothing but Christ and Him crucified, it hastens on through all the difficulties of the *ecclesia* living as new creation in the still unredeemed world to tell properly of the resurrection of the body, the redemption of the creation, and the renewal of the world envisioned as our promised future, when Gòd will become all things to everyone (1 Cor. 15:28). Thus Jüngel argues that the theological metaphor, rightly deciphered, brings about a "gain to being" that "expands the horizon of the world in such a way that we may speak of the renewal of the world."[43] In this formulation, Jüngel attempts to order the paradox of the cross to the similitude of new creation. This ordering is motivated by Jüngel's entirely proper desire to secure a redemptive relationship of the interruptive word of the cross to the world in which we live, so that the world fallen into godlessness is contradicted redemptively and thus made anew to be seen as the blessed creature of God on the way to righteousness, life, and peace. The apparent contradiction of this world by the paradox of the cross of the Messiah brings in its wake a new affirmation of the world, vindicating the simile of creation: as the potter to the clay, so the One who vindicated the crucified Jesus is to the world that crucified Him: "Behold, I make all things new!"

If that is right, the issue will be, just as Betz suggested, whether this attempted ordering renders creation itself an eschatological notion, a work in progress advancing from the promise of the origin to the consummation of the Beloved Community, or, alternatively, if this ordering fails, whether redemption can be no more than a disclosure of a creation that already is given, possessing the goodness in which it is divinely regarded though somehow lost from conscious awareness.

Yet, at the same, Jüngel senses a difficulty with the paradox of the Messiah's cross. He qualified his formulation of the strange contradiction in terms, "Christ crucified," with the *ubi et quando Deo visum est* of Augsburg Confession V: "A theological metaphor can only have this [redemptive] effect, however, because of the renewing power of the Spirit of God."[44] It is in the hands of the Spirit that the paradox of contradiction, "Christ crucified,"

42. Eberhard Jüngel, *Theological Essays I*, trans. J. B. Webster (Edinburgh: T&T Clark, 1989), 65. The following four paragraphs are adapted from Paul R. Hinlicky, "Metaphorical Truth and the Language of Christian Theology," in *Indicative of Grace—Imperative of Freedom: Essays in Honour of Eberhard Jüngel in His 80th Year*, ed. R. David Nelson (London: Bloomsbury, 2014), 89–100.
43. Jüngel, *Theological Essays*, 71.
44. Ibid.

effects a salutary, not desperate, slaying of the old Adam and brings forth the similitude of the newborn child of God. The Spirit working through the Word, that is to say, not only effects a *translatio* in words that discloses being as creation but also effects a valid verbal predication of new birth in creatures. In other words, the Spirit's proclamation of the paradox works causally, not merely disclosively. It discloses because it enunciates first of all a *translatio* of things. So Luther had argued against Latomus, upon which argument Jüngel here is drawing:

> *Et in hac translatione* non solum est verborum, sed et rerum metaphora. *Nam vere peccata nostra a nobis translata sunt a posita super ipsum, ut omnis qui hoc credit, vere nulla peccata habeat, sed translata super Christum, absorpta in ipso, eum amplius non damnent.*

And in this transference [that Christ was made to be sin, 2 Cor. 5:21] it is *not only a metaphor of words but of things*. For truly our sins are transferred from us and placed on Him, so that all who believe Him truly have no sins but they are transferred onto Him, absorbed in Him, no longer damning him.[45]

For Luther, the exchange of things concerns first of all Christ, and only so also the believer. It is Christ who came once for all and thus still comes by the Word and the Spirit as the Lamb of God to take away the sin of the world. Only so can this Word incarnate say and regard the auditor as forgiven and freed as a matter of truth, no matter how she feels or actually is one way or another. Luther's *metaphora rerum* concerns Christ, who comes to the sinner. If that christological priority is clear, the next question is whether the power

45. Martin Luther, *D. Martin Luthers Werke: Kritische Gesamtausgabe* (Weimar: Hermann Böhlau, 1883–2007), 8:87; cf. Martin Luther, *Luther's Works: The American Edition*, ed. Jaroslav Pelikan and Helmut T. Lehmann (St. Louis: Concordia; Philadelphia: Fortress, 1955–86), 32:200. See the compelling analysis by Anna Vind, "Christus factus est peccatum metaphorice: Über die theologische Verwendung rhetorischer Figuren bei Luther unter Einbeziehung Quintilians," in *Creator Est Creatura: Luthers Christologie als Lehre von der Idiomenkommunikation*, ed. Oswald Bayer and Benjamin Gleede (Berlin: de Gruyter, 2007), 95–124. Her conclusion about Luther on metaphor comports with my own conclusion about Jüngel's effort (which she mentions in this connection) in the present book. "Der Begriff der Metaphor ist zu eng, um den Inhalt sowohl der kontroversen Textstelle aus dem *Antilatomus* als auch der Schrift *Vom Abendmahl Christi* sowie der Disputationen wiederzugeben. Das Wesentliche ist nicht bloss der Metaphor, sondern es ist die Bereicherung der Sprache überhaupt, die die Erneuerung durch den Schmuck der Rede, durch den ornatus, bewirkt . . . es bei Luther um etwas geht, was ausserhalb von Quintilians Horizont liegt" (123), namely, the *non solum est verborum, sed et rerum metaphora*. In the same volume see my treatment of Luther on metaphor, "Luther's Anti-Docetism in the Disputatio de divinitate et humanitate Christi (1540)" (Bayer and Gleede, *Creator Est Creatura*, 147–66). In his 1974 essay "Metaphorical Truth," Jüngel drew on the Luther texts that Vind analyzes (*Theological Essays* [repr., London: Bloomsbury T&T Clark, 2014], 16–71).

to become the child of God can have "this effect" *in* the believer merely by saying so, "Abracadabra!"—that is, apart from the corresponding "translating" power, if I may so put it, of the Spirit of God working a corresponding death and resurrection in the auditor. The faith to receive the crucified Messiah, who bore our sins in order to make us right, then, is itself gift, the gift of new birth into the likeness of God. To be sure, this effect is worked by none other than the Spirit of Jesus Christ, whom the Son breathes upon the auditor just as the Father had breathed upon Him—that is, the Spirit who now sheds the costly love of God abroad in human hearts that have been convicted concerning sin, and righteousness, and judgment (John 16:8–11). Consequently, in the Spirit-given reality of repentant faith sin is yielded to Christ, who bears it away, and in turn His righteousness truly becomes the believer's own, just as if she had done it herself rather than received it as Another's self-giving gift. But such is the nature of gift: unmerited, it nevertheless truly becomes one's own, one's own possession in the ecstatic sense of "having, as having not." Just this new and personal appropriation of Christ's righteousness as one's own is the Spirit-given *translatio rerum* of the human subject; it is the faith that justifies. Faith, in its own specific way of being as death to sin and resurrection to newness of life by appropriating Christ, who repossesses sin in offering Himself, thus corresponds to the specific way of being that is told by the metaphor "Christ crucified," namely, that new thing-and-meaning in the world that is the Son, who came not to be served but to serve and lay down His life as a ransom for many (Mark 10:45). This correspondence of possessing faith to giving God is, or could be taken as, Barth's "analogy of faith," as I will shortly discuss further.

Clearly the divine Word—returning from his source in Luther to Jüngel himself—works as catachrestic metaphor in the ordered sequence that passes from paradox to simile, from contradiction to similitude, from the death of the sinner to the newborn child of God; the motion reflects Luther's crucial purpose clause, "God kills *in order to* make alive" as God surpasses God in God's motion from the wrath of His love to the mercy of His love. Another way to pose the question about how Jüngel thinks this movement to occur, then, is to ask, "Can the metaphor fail in this progression—for example, can it blind and harden (Mark 4:11–12) as well as enlighten and redeem?" Arguably, it *can* fail in the sequence that Jüngel, following Luther, intends, precisely if and when the disruptive metaphor of paradox is thought to work "on its own," so to speak, as if it were routine similitude. This takes the paradox of contradiction out of the Spirit's hands and puts it back into the keeping of business as usual. It is thought to work routinely on its own, doing business as usual when the dissonance of paradox is muted by annulling univocity in principle, thus defanging the catachrestic metaphor of contradiction that generates new meaning and reality in the world. So the paradox "Christ crucified"—that is, the victor became victim in order to become victorious for us—that thus tells of a horizontal passage is turned into simile that supposedly discloses how the world really is, anchored in Being itself where grace is everything by analogy and therefore nothing real in particular. The horizontal passage is transposed into a vertical simultaneity.

Just so, the intended progression through contradiction to similitude is obscured. In this case, if not taken in the Spirit by faith as the contradiction in terms, "Christ crucified," this kerygma has to be taken out of the Spirit, in bad faith, disclosing something like "To be Christ is to be victim" or "The victims of the world are Christ." Not a little contemporary theology, right and left, views the matter in just this way, forgetting that a mere disclosure of timeless truth—even the truth that God is love, or that the loving God sympathizes with the victims, or that the love of God is (merely) revealed on the cross—can be, in Paul's or Luther's sense, nothing but law: a divine truth that crushes me in my impotent lovelessness and leaves me there, dead in my sins, be it as victim or as victimizer.

It is important to see why we may come to such perverse theology that divinizes victimization or victimizes the divine—and justly offends alike those who struggle against victimization and those who hope in God's vindication of victims. We mute the paradox in this way, making it into an illuminating disclosure of some supposedly deeper truth of our world, because we take ourselves, the human auditors of this strange announcement, as having by nature rather than by personal transformation of repentance and faith epistemic access and corresponding aptitude to process this information in comparison to, and thus as part of, all that we already know. We have access and acquire aptitude as members of a system of beings ordered as cosmos who regularly learn the lesser known in terms of what is already familiar. We presume to learn accordingly what it is to be Christ crucified by our all-too-familiar experience of victimization. "Christ crucified"—for good or ill, victimization is the deepest truth of our world. Self-hatred, as the history of popular Christianity amply documents, becomes the religious work that brings us close to the divine, while for elite culture "pleasure is in the perception of a momentary radiance, before the door of disappointment is finally shut on us."[46]

The alternative to this perverse but ever-popular theology—and the reason why the mature Luther left behind the easily misunderstood rhetoric of his

46. Frank Kermode, *The Genesis of Secrecy: On the Interpretation of Narrative* (Cambridge, MA: Harvard University Press, 1979), 145.

early "theology of the cross" to learn to speak of the Crucified One in the Spirit as truly His Father's victory for us, be we victimizers or victims—is that the metaphorical Word works as the Spirit intends in progressing through contradiction to similitude. If that is so, it is the humanity of Jesus Christ, univocally taken as something to which we can point in the world *sub Pontio Pilato*, that is the "vestige" of the God who is tri-personal love on the way to us all. We may speak this way because Christ Jesus is this way. That is to say, He does not signify as to Another than Himself, but rather He *is* the Son of God in the flesh, the *translatio rerum* on the basis of which we speak the gospel in a *translatio verborum*.

Jesus as Vestige of the Trinity

This chapter's argument has been leading to the christological thesis, now to be argued, that it is the one Lord Jesus Christ who is the new Adam and true analogue of His Father, "through whom all things are and through whom we exist" (1 Cor. 8:6). This christologically parsed analogy of being, moreover, corresponds to the weak version of simplicity that allows for robust trinitarian personalism, as argued in the preceding chapters. A reprise of Jüngel's argument from his magnum opus, *God as the Mystery of the World*, for the *man* Jesus—that is, for the cruciform *humanity* of the incarnate Son—is now in order.[47] It is in order because Jüngel's very title, *God as the Mystery of the World*, is borrowed from Przywara and because, in some Lutheran distinction from Barth as already argued by Bonhoeffer,[48] the mystery revealed in Christ is not found in a dialectic of the two natures but in the unity of the person of Christ as seen in the figure of the gospel narrative, historically and critically understood.[49] This makes the human figure Jesus in His personal relations to

47. The rest of this section is a synopsis of Eberhard Jüngel, *God as the Mystery of the World: On the Foundation of the Theology of the Crucified One in the Dispute between Theism and Atheism*, trans. Darrell L. Guder (Grand Rapids: Eerdmans, 1983), 343–67.

48. Michael P. DeJonge, *Bonhoeffer's Theological Formation: Berlin, Barth, and Protestant Theology* (Oxford: Oxford University Press, 2012), 56–82. See also Paul R. Hinlicky, "Verbum Externum: Dietrich Bonhoeffer's Bethel Confession," in *God Speaks to Us: Dietrich Bonhoeffer's Biblical Hermeneutics*, ed. Ralf K. Wüstenberg and Jens Zimmermann, International Bonhoeffer Interpretations 5 (Frankfurt: Peter Lang, 2013), 189–215.

49. Assuredly, the mature Barth, following upon the new articulation of the doctrine of election in *Church Dogmatics* II/2, increasingly moved in the direction of a one-subject Christology, as Bruce L. McCormack argues in *Orthodox and Modern: Studies in the Theology of Karl Barth* (Grand Rapids: Baker Academic, 2008), 201–31. However, I do not fully concur with McCormack's account of the way in which Greek metaphysics is to be overcome, and hence also on the correct way to take or to revise the doctrine of deification.

the Father and the Spirit on earth, as per the gospel narrative historically and critically understood, that "vestige" of the Trinity that Augustine, looking for love in all the wrong places, sought in creatures but never found (if Wisse is right, deliberately so, as a kind of cautionary tale).

In fact, Jüngel argues, Jesus's history with God and with us is the "root" of the Triune knowledge of God. This is, of course, true historically and critically. Whether it is also true ontologically is an interesting and difficult question.[50] Does God become triune because of His history with the man Jesus? If so, then, logically a divine Subject prior to and apart from His history with Jesus is being presupposed, so the question is begged how one might ever know and account for this prior subjectivity. This question begging is the fatal flaw in the Hegelian doctrine of the Trinity, which by way of natural light identifies this prior subjectivity of God as such with creativity and derives God's history with us by logical deduction *Christo remoto*. But the patristic doctrine of the Trinity, which I am retrieving here, denies this and insists that God the eternal Trinity becomes Creator in a free and costly self-determination that is intelligible after the fact as the resolve to redeem and fulfill by the missions from the Father of the Son and the Spirit. This self-determination in the antecedent subjectivity of God is thus to be understood as the subjectivity of the eternal Beloved Community. Suffice it to say, then, by way of preface to this reprise of Jüngel's valuable argument for the specific humanity of Jesus as the place in the world (as I am taking it) where the eternally Triune God becomes this same God for us—as we are and not where we ought to be—that for weak simplicity the ontological Trinity is to be understood as the antecedent condition for the possibility of the economic Trinity, nothing more and nothing less. It comes to knowledge as the after-the-fact reflection of faith on the freedom in this revealed God's self-determination by the Son and Spirit to redeem and fulfill—that is to say, as acknowledgment of the monarchy of the Father, the subject of power in the harmony of power, wisdom, and love. That the ultimate power should become through Jesus Christ our Father too is indeed Jüngel's mystery of the world.

What is at issue, to begin with, is not the "being" of God so much as the "life" or "vitality" of God—an initial differentiation of the "living God of the Bible" from the god of the philosophers. But this vitality of God comes as a surprise, namely, the surprise of the living deity that is compossible with bearing the opposite of life, death, not pathetically but victoriously, for the sake of new life. This bearing of death by the living God for the sake of new life can be successfully articulated, however, only by way of the trinitarian

50. I am grateful to David Bruner for helping me to sharpen the question here.

distinction of persons according to which One of the Three suffered. The unitarian alternative is to say either that God has not come in the flesh but remains above, invulnerable by nature (theism), or that God has emptied Himself into the flesh, died to remain dead and buried, arising only in the philosophical comprehension of the world come of age (Hegelianism). But the differentiation of God from God at the heart of the gospel narrative is the root of the doctrine of the Trinity, which in turn is the theologically understood soteriology of the divine union of life with death for the sake of new life.

At this juncture, Jüngel clears up a series of contemporary Lutheran confusions according to which Luther's distinction between God hidden and God preached is taken to consign theology of the Trinity to impractical or even dangerous curiosity—prying into the hidden being of God, presumptuously mapping the incomprehensible One hidden in majesty, as opposed to the simple gospel preached of the heavenly Father and the man Jesus, who shows us what God is like. This Lutheran confusion, to be sure, does not stand up to Luther's own robust trinitarianism, which manifestly takes Trinity as the God preached, *Hunc audite!* (Mark 9:7); the Father who declares to faith, "Listen to Him!" must be taken as truthful to us as true to Himself in the self-donation of the Word incarnate and self-communication by the Spirit from the Father of the Son. Otherwise, the economic Trinity of the gospel narrative can only be taken as a charade, as in modalism. By the same token, this affirmation of the truthfulness of God in His self-revelation for us is *all* that the classic doctrine of the immanent and ontological Trinity claims. It serves to back up the economic Trinity of revelation as the truthful claim of the one true God, who is not reducible to the relations with creatures that He goes on to acquire in creating a world in order to redeem and fulfill it. It is not, accordingly, an invitation, let alone license for all sorts of extraneous speculation that removes us from the action of the gospel narrative.

Indebted as contemporary theology is to Karl Barth for this renewal of the doctrine of the Trinity, Jüngel in the next step of his argument corrects a tendency of Barth, in keeping with the Reformed *extra Calvinisticum*, to disassociate divine self-revelation from the earthly language that bears only a creaturely and extrinsic witness to it. As we will see, it is a subtle but significant correction of Barth that can take the earthly man, Jesus, and the earthy biblical speech about Him as understood today by historical science, as the vestige of the Trinity. Revelation has worldly speech as part of it, Jüngel argues, just as theology is comprised of worldly thinking. As human language-cum-thinking is the epitome of human historicity, this particular language regarding this particular history is made special—that is, sanctified—by the event of revelation that commandeers it and makes it its very own speech.

Thus the man Jesus, as preacher and as preached and as understood, is and can be the vestige of the Trinity. The externality of the *verbum externum* is found not, as in Barth, in the eternal Son's transcendence of the man Jesus but rather in the eternal Son's being the man Jesus, crucified for our sins but raised for our justification, as proclaimed in the normative witness of prophetic and apostolic Scriptures and understood historically and critically in modern theology.

With the ground cleared in this way, Jüngel makes his central claim about the man Jesus. It is the event of His crucifixion as the would-be Son of God and of the resurrection of the crucified Jesus as God's self-identification with Him that requires the differentiation of God from God that is the historical genesis of the trinitarian understanding of God's being. Indeed, just this differentiation is what makes revelation a divine event, namely, the event of divine persons interacting for us and for our salvation: the Father, who sends; the Son, who freely goes; and their "confrontation" at Golgotha and reconciliation in the Spirit on the third day. Divine nature is thus rendered here not only as event, as in Barth, but more specifically as a *social* event of persons living a communion in face of genuine opposition that would sunder the communion. What else could the incorporation of human sin and death present, interposing the divine blessedness of the Beloved Community? This genuine contradiction requires us to probe the proclamation of God in Jesus's ministry as that which brought Him to His *particular* death that constitutes the precondition of His resurrection.

In the light, then, of the divine event for us of Jesus's passage through death to resurrection, Jüngel next turns to His ministry. Jesus inaugurated fellowship with God, creating a new society. We can validate this claim historically by critical knowledge of the Lord's Prayer as Jesus's own statement of faith that also spells out faith as a specific way of relating to God in the world. Likewise, critical knowledge of Jesus's parables corroborates this specific way of faith that Jesus announces and blesses. The parables bring about a new obviousness of the grace of God that effects reconciliation in the world when it is received in faith. However, this putative new obviousness of grace also elicits the hostility of the representatives of the old and still predominant obviousness of the law that operates not by the logic of election and gift but rather by the logic of reward and punishment. According to the law, justice requires that each one get what is one's due. This opposition of grace as free gift and law as just reward (or punishment) is carried out in, on, and against Jesus's person in that the proclaimer of God's grace also embodies it in His fellowship with the undeserving—the tax collectors and sinners.

This scene of battle in Jesus's person has nothing to do with the unfortunate category ("too much anthropology, too little theology") of His so-called messianic self-consciousness. On the contrary, what stands out in Jesus is His total other-consciousness. His self-relation, or personhood, is "enhypostatically" to relate wholly to His Father God as the Father God has related to Him, the beloved Son, thus in filial obedience of love and trust. Yet what is not at all obvious in the world where the *lex talionis* and the quid pro quo prevail is that this man who thus inaugurates a new fellowship with God according to grace is Himself divine grace in the way of being the Father's Son. He seems instead to embody something that is not His own to give: Who is this man to forgive sins (cf. Mark 2:7)? What is rather more obvious is His mere humanity in gross contradiction to high claims in the name of God, presumptuously addressed as the heavenly Father. Defenseless before this objection, the man Jesus can do nothing but display His total openness to and reliance on His Father God in giving up His body, embodying at once these poles that He has united in His history: God's grace and human sin. Yet, in just this purity of heart, Jüngel argues, Jesus manifests royal freedom as freedom from self for others, just as God the king, according to His proclamation, majestically gives a world to creatures at great cost and no benefit to Himself. So Jesus the man for others (Bonhoeffer) lives as man in analogy to the majestic generosity of God that He proclaims, whose society He inaugurates with tax collectors and sinners and finally embodies in His self-oblation.

The anomaly of high claims about God and Jesus's own lowly appearance brings a new wrinkle to His conflict with the law. He does not magically or sovereignly annul the law but rather sets the law against the law. The holy law of God, in Jesus's proclamation, in fact demands what should be obvious in a world that is and knows itself as God's creation: love is the rule of life where grace gives the gift of life. But insofar as law in its act and performance *demands* what should be obvious, neither God who gives nor creation as gift is or can be obvious. Rather, the law motivates what is not obvious, love, by threat of punishment and hope of reward, extorting an obedience that can only be grudging, servile, and self-justifying rather than carefree, filial, and liberated from self-regard. In this way, law as demand contradicts law as royal command of life and gracious blessing. In just this way, however, the law by requiring what ought to be obvious, love, reinforces the oblivion of grace and insinuates the very inordinate self-love (in fear of punishment and hope of reward) that is at heart a faithless despair of the gracious love of God for the anxious, self-justifying self. So one loves not for the sake of the other but rather for the sake of self, not freely but by extortion. One loves lovelessly, even rapaciously, because one does not first love oneself with the majestic love of God for the self with all others.

In response to this demand of the law in a world oblivious to the grace of God, where instead what is obvious is reward and punishment according to justice, Jesus forces a confrontation by sovereignly forgiving sins. It is a lordly act that gives precisely what is not deserved; it releases from debt so that to all appearances the forgiven debt goes unpaid, disrupting the economy of things in the demand for reparation. In just this subversion of the legal order, Jesus battles as a Lord goes out to battle. Yet He battles not with annulment, by the fiat of a *deus exlex*; instead, He battles with the law's own ethical claim for love, which He has in fact made His own and embodies in the mercy of love for sinners. So in Jesus, the law battles against the law; that is, Jesus battles sin with the mercy, rather than the wrath, of love. For the root of sin is the faithless despair of the love of God for the self that one actually is, hopelessly imprisoned as a historical self in "the hell of the irrevocable."[51] What the holy law of God demands is love, even if the sinner, curved into herself, can only love lovelessly so that, even despairing of her bondage, the sinner can only try to quit this fate by a renewed hope of reward and fear of punishment that insinuates once again the sinful self. Coming from outside of this trap, the forgiving love of Jesus satisfies the law's demand for love with mercy and so fulfills its ethical demand. In just this true obedience to the true claim of the law of God for love in the world of His creating, Jesus is the absolutely free human being whose freedom to love sinners concretely enables God to be near again as Father, the One who gladly gives all without scruple. This free man is, Jüngel writes, thus the analogue of the God of grace.

This historical appearance of Jesus as the image of God is not the end of the story but only its precipitation. Sins forgiven do not dissolve into thin air—"Abracadabra!" Rather, the sins that Jesus freely forgives in merciful fulfillment of the law of love become His own, not as the One who did the sins but as the One who releases others from them. The hell of the irrevocable is not made to disappear with the wave of a wand. But in making His own the sinners and tax collectors who believed Him in His word of forgiveness, Jesus takes the burden from them and takes it on Himself, *translatio rerum*. They are released from their sins because He becomes burdened by them. Thus in His passion, the law that punishes sin and does not reward it is brought into final conflict with the law—that is to say, the ethical content of the law—that is love, also to "real, not fictitious sinners."

51. Josiah Royce, *The Problem of Christianity* (Washington, DC: Catholic University of America Press, 2001), 162–63, 169, 175.

The mercy of love is made to conflict in Jesus's passion with the juridical requirement that lovelessness be rejected and suffer condemnation. That is why Paul says that Christ died accursed and why the Gospel of Mark portrays the dying Jesus as forsaken by God, the very depiction of eternal death. This sight of the forsaken Son of God would be nothing but sheer terror, however, a revelation (a mere disclosure) of the wrath of timeless and eternal love against our lovelessness, but for the two decisive words added, "for us." These two words tell of the divine and voluntary love hidden in the Godforsaken death. This "for us" concerning Jesus, who died for our sins in the obedience of filial trust but was raised for our justification, is possible, then, only because of a further event, one that interprets Jesus's Godforsaken death positively—that is, as divine, voluntary love "for us." The "for us" is not obvious in the darkness of Good Friday; it is rather the Easter confession of faith in the Crucified One as God's Son, who loved us and gave Himself for us, indeed was given by the Father for us and attested by the Spirit to us. Easter brings this recognition because it was the causal change in the order of being organized as cosmos, the initiation of new creation. As such, Easter is the origin of Christian faith in the crucified Jesus as the Holy One made to be sin, though he knew no sin, that in Him we might become the righteousness of God (2 Cor. 5:21).

Theologically interpreted, then, whatever happened between Jesus and God on the cross is that which identifies Christianity by giving the good reason for its christological faith. This is, as Hegel saw, a "difficult thought" that is consequently often evaded. Hegel's great achievement was to face rather than evade the thought—even if his solution of the speculative Good Friday is itself finally judged as another evasion.[52] Unlike Hegel, however, we should not understand the self-differentiation of the Son and the Father in this event of the Son's passage through death to new life as something forced on God from without. This movement is not a negative dialectics, so to say, but rather a positive dialectic of love loving the unlovely to make them loved and lovable again.[53] Only such a holy and divine motive can differentiate God from God and enact this differentiation for us as grace, as free gift, the deed of generosity, not the need of greed. Theologically interpreted, then, resurrection is not an intervention, a comic ending pasted on at the end by a *deus ex machina*, only covering up the tragedy of negative dialectics. Resurrection must be understood, following Barth, as a truthful event—more precisely,

---

52. Thanks to Rob Saler for this observation.

53. For the exposition of "positive dialectics" against Hegel and with Giorgio Agamben, see Brent Adkins and Paul R. Hinlicky, *Rethinking Philosophy and Theology with Deleuze: A New Cartography* (London: Bloomsbury Academic, 2013), 179–86.

according to Jüngel, as an advent into the world of the eternal event of God's tri-personal life.

God comes from God, then, into the world of creatures fallen under the corruption of sin and subjected to the law of reward and punishment that requires love, but love that can be true only when it is free and freely given. Jesus's self-giving to God as for us gives freely to the unworthy what the law justly demands of them, at once satisfying the law's juridical condemnation and rendering its mechanism of reward and punishment inoperative. Jesus's self-donation fulfills the law by reinstating the majesty of God who gives. And so, Jesus's suffering of our objective godlessness in this way cannot but be understood as God interposing with God for us.

> In that God differentiates himself and *thus*, in unity with the crucified Jesus, suffers as God the Son being forsaken by God the Father, he is God the Reconciler. God reconciles the world with himself in that in the death of Jesus he encounters himself as *God the Father* and *God the Son* without becoming disunited in himself. On the contrary, in the encounter of God with God, of Father and Son, God reveals himself as the one who he is. He is God the Spirit, who lets the Father and the Son be one in the death of Jesus, in true distinction, in this encounter. This "chain of love" (*vinculum caritatis*) emphasizes God's eternal being in the death of Jesus. Thus God is differentiated in a threefold way in his unity: in the encounter of Father and Son, related to each other as Spirit. But in the fatal encounter, God remains *one* God. For he remains as Father and the Son in the Spirit: the one "event God."[54]

Thus it is that the *man* Jesus, as known in His personal obedience of Spirit-endowed faith in the Father, is the vestige of the Trinity, the new Adam, the similitude of God.

The Analogy of Faith as Union with Christ

In spite of a certain christological correction mentioned above, the foregoing argument from Jüngel is profoundly indebted to the fresh start given to theology in Luther's tradition by Karl Barth. The matter may be put this way: if it is the human individual Jesus, as known in His Gethsemane decision to give Himself to His Abba Father for us, who is the "vestige" of the Trinity, then another analogy, which purports christologically to say something like "Jesus is to God as the eternal Son is to the eternal Father," falters fatally. It falters in implying, or tacitly assuming, two sons, related to each other in a

---

54. Jüngel, *God as the Mystery*, 368.

kind of allegory. There is a human son of Mary who is said, then, to be the one and only on the earth like the eternal Son of the Father. But if Jüngel is right, the man Jesus is not discernible in this way from the eternal Son; Jesus *is* the eternal Son in His *coming*, to be sure, sent to us from the Father, God from God when made known to us as such, by the Spirit's free grant of faith, beginning with Mary His mother. It is thus the other way around. The eternal Son becomes known in and indeed *as* this cruciform humanity, or not at all. In the statement "Jesus, the crucified Messiah, is the Son of God," the "is" is an *est*, not a *significat*. If not, the paradox cannot work to generate the new meaning in the world that Jesus is the Son *in that* He came not to be served but to serve and lay down *His* life (not the life of His analogue) for others. In that case, of course, we have to think of an eternal Son who *can* come, enter time, and take up space, acquiring "accidental" properties. Moreover, according to Jüngel's argument, it is as this particular human individual in His dramatic history with His Father and their Spirit, as told in the gospel narrative (and understood historically and critically), that the sense of His personal identification as the Son makes sense to begin with. (How else would one know of an eternal Son of the Father in the Spirit as Another to whom Jesus points?)

To be sure, it is also true, as Barth held, that we cannot argue from history to theology, from below to above; in equal fact, Jüngel's revision of Barth does not make this mistake. For Jüngel, too, we cannot know Jesus as this human individual in His Gethsemane obedience of filial faith except as the Father identifies our sin and death with Him, and then again our justification and life with Him, sending the Spirit to so proclaim Him to us: crucified Jesus for us, then, as risen and present for us as indeed only One who is truly God and truly human can be. There is a dialectic here, as Barth requires, but it is not between divine and human natures in the person of Christ. Rather, it is a dialectic between the Word and the Spirit, where the Word points to the Spirit's baptism with fire by which we receive the gift of faith to receive the gift of the Word incarnate. The Spirit in turn points to the way He first led the Word incarnate through death to life in order to be recognized as the *Holy* Spirit of *Jesus* and His *Father* amid all the other so-called lords, gods, and spirits at work in the world. That trinitarian dialectic of Word and Spirit (not, then, a supposedly Chalcedonian dialectic of divine and human natures dancing around each other but never uniting) in turn stipulates that Chalcedonian Christology is a function of the doctrine of the Trinity, as the Fifth Ecumenical Council made clear. We know Jesus Christ the Son of God in *the unity of His person*, a unity that unites His death for our sins and resurrection for our justification, as the very Son of the Father who comes for us in the Spirit working through the gospel concerning Him.

This accent of trinitarian Christology is important if we are to move past the dead-end impasse between the analogy of being and the analogy of faith. In fact, what we have from Keith Johnson's and John Betz's apparent agreement to disagree is a (false) alternative in that it is posed on the level of anthropology, where a choice between creation and new creation is being forced on us. Christologically, however, we are to see in Jesus Christ the Son of God the new Adam, who is the true icon or analogue of God, through whom all things are made and in whom all things hold together. If we begin anthropologically, however, with a self-imagined construction, driven by the dialectic of negation, of divine and human natures, we can never again unite them. Either one will disappear into another, as in monophysitism, or, as in Nestorianism, Christ will be taken as a federation of two sons, closely allied. If instead we begin our reflection christologically with the figure of the gospel narrative, we begin with what later theology called the *prosōpon*, the concrete phenomenon that is the man who forgives sins and the Son sent by the heavenly Father to become poor and a servant. When we begin reflection thusly with the *prosōpon* that is the man Christ Jesus in His horizontal passage from kenosis to obedience to humiliation through shameful death to glorious vindication, exaltation, and promised parousia, we can distinguish without confusion or separation God, who eternally gives in Jesus's innocent self-donation, and the creature, who evermore receives in Jesus's birth, baptism, and resurrection, just as we can also identify that divine person, God in the concrete way of being Son as Him who suffered for us, in distinction from and relation to the persons of the Father, who sent Him, and the Spirit, who led Him and then vindicated Him. Moreover, such distinguishing and relating is important, as we will see, because it provides for a thicker account of divine attributes that allows us to say in Christ what in the world we are talking about when we speak in the name of God and confess the name of God before others in our own earthly words and earthly works. That thicker account begins with the pioneering new start made by Karl Barth with his justly celebrated account in *Church Dogmatics* II/1 of God's perfections as the freedom to love, to which we shortly turn.

Bruce McCormack has, I think, rightly argued that Barth's *Church Dogmatics* is not well understood if one takes this massive work as internally consistent in every respect rather than a work in progress, ever and again starting afresh. In particular, he holds that it is a misleading oversimplification to characterize Barth's Christology as "Chalcedonian," in the sense pilloried above—that is, as tacitly Nestorian until and unless corrected by the Fifth Council at Constantinople,[55] an argument contemporized above all by Robert Jenson.[56] Piotr Małysz has pointed out to me,[57] along these lines, that Barth is not so easily pigeonholed as if still captive to the Augustinian/ Thomistic notion of impersonal knowing and willing of the simple God in Its sheer actuality. Instead, for Barth, God is emphatically an "I" (CD II/1, 268), indeed a Person (CD II/1, 284), and even more than that an "overflowing" and "personifying" Person who "risks" himself for humanity (CD II/2, 163). Accordingly, it is necessary to be cautious in interpreting Barth's dialectic of veiling and unveiling (see further below), which seems to make of the humanity of Jesus a veil of the unveiling Son of God but actually intends to secure the objectivity of the knowledge of God; later in the Church Dogmatics (CD III/2, 218) the description of the humanity of Jesus as a veil seems to be jettisoned for the notion of "copy" (i.e., analogue). Yet here too, to perceive what may seem to be nothing but a string of analogies—that is, the human Jesus copies the eternal Son, who is the eternal copy of the Father—is to overlook Barth's intention, which was to affirm that Jesus in His ethical relations with fellow creatures copies the trinitarian communion of the Father and the Son. I am grateful to Małysz for these important nuances in Barth interpretation, which we should happily receive. If Barth is indeed on the road to a one-subject Christology, that is all to the good, provided that we keep to this trajectory. That would mean recovering the trihypostatic life of God as the framework of Christology—a social, not psychological, Trinity.

This in particular is what I faulted Barth for in my book Paths Not Taken: not that he fails to take God as Person (which is all to the good), but that he fails (consistently and radically) yet to take God as tri-personal in the strong sense, as a social not psychological event.[58] So Barth polemicized in Church Dogmatics I/1 against the "tritheistic weaknesses of Melanchthon's concept of person" (CD I/1, 365)—Melanchthon appears here in his familiar role as Protestant theology's favorite whipping boy—in favor of Barth's well-known tri-modal rendering of the doctrine of the Three. Once again, the polemic is entertaining: "It would be pagan mythology to present the work of God in the form of a dramatic entry and exit of now one and now another of the divine persons, of the surging up and down of half or totally individualized powers or forms or ideas, of a shifting co-existence and competition of the three hypostases" (CD I/1, 374). I faulted Barth's modal account of trinitarian

55. McCormack, Orthodox and Modern, 232–33.
56. Robert W. Jenson, Unbaptized God: The Basic Flaw in Ecumenical Theology (Minneapolis: Fortress, 1992), 120–24.
57. Personal correspondence, January 25, 2015.
58. Hinlicky, Paths Not Taken, 55–57.

relations for its tacit adaptation of the account from German idealism—if Wisse is right, itself descended from Plotinus—of the self-positing subject. Correspondingly, in the same book I faulted Barth's more mature theology of God's freedom to love for its omission of the third perfection, wisdom; this omission reflects, I argued, an inadequate trinitarianism and indeed a binitarian tendency in Barth's theology[59]—the tendency descended from Augustine in thinking of the Holy Spirit as an impersonal bond of love between the Father and the Son rather than as the divine agent who unites the sign with the thing signified.

This binitarian tendency can also be detected in Jüngel. Recall the final citation in the preceding section, which concluded (with emphasis now added), "Thus God is differentiated in a threefold way in his unity: in the encounter of Father and Son, related to each other *as* Spirit. But in the fatal encounter, God remains *one* God. For he remains as Father and the Son *in* the Spirit: the one 'event God.'"[60] "As Spirit" does not mean the same as "in the Spirit." The latter accords personhood to the Holy Spirit, in whom the Father and the Son mutually indwell, as the divine agent who unites the sign with the thing signified. This is personhood in the same sense as ascribed to the Father and the Son, and it evokes the culmination of the development of the doctrine of the Trinity at the Council of Constantinople, having the personal Spirit eternally complete the triad, rather than the cosmos as in Platonist schemes of emanation. By contrast, the former, "as the Spirit," assimilates in the fashion of Western modalism the persons of the Father and the Son to a cipher for divine nature, impersonal spirit, even if that cipher is interpreted as love. In that case, the Spirit becomes the impersonal eros that binds the Father and the Son, not the divine Person who mediates their personal differences by His own personal, other-regarding love.

But this is the personal work of the Spirit, especially as articulated in the economy of salvation where the epiclesis *Veni, Creator Spiritus* beseeches, as for our salvation itself, the unification of the sign with the thing signified. Otherwise, the Son takes upon Himself, likewise personally, the sin and death of the fallen creation and thus becomes the just object of the wrath of the Father's love against lovelessness. What kind of terrifying wisdom is that! What a crushing act of power that would be! Were that the end of the story, sign un-united with the thing signified in eternal Godforsakenness, God would be divided indeed against God evermore, truly not one either for God or for us. But in eternity the other-regarding love of the Spirit of God binds

59. Ibid., 128–42.
60. Jüngel, *God as the Mystery*, 368.

the beloved Son by returning Him to the Father in praise of His deity, as also He binds the Father to the Son from whom, as from Another, He receives the acclamation "Abba, Father!" So again the Spirit is at work in time, by raising the crucified Son, in whom the sinners of the world have been united in love, and presenting Him, bonded together now with them by this other-regarding love of the Spirit in which the Son has loved them, to the Father as *indeed* the beloved Son, in whom the Father is well pleased. So the Spirit completes the circle of the eternal life of perichoresis in time as in eternity. So the unity of the Triune God is lived, risked, jeopardized for us, and so also, if the promise vouchsafed in the resurrection proves true, triumphant for us and for all.

If we think along these lines of a consistent account of divine oneness as personal perichoresis, we must distribute the divine perfections personally in order to tell what in the world we are talking about when we speak of God. We assign all possibilities to the almighty Father; we assign the wisdom that saves the world from its own wisdom by the folly of the cross to the Son, the Word incarnate; and we assign love that qualifies power with wisdom and wisdom with power to the Spirit, who unites the Son and the Father as sign to thing signified. Then we would formulate: God who gives is the freedom to love wisely and well. The binitarian tendency at work in Barth's account of divine perfections as the freedom to love, by contrast, assigns the perfection of love to the Son instead of to the Spirit breathed upon Him; it consequently makes the Spirit nugatory even as it overlooks the wisdom of God that is the saving folly of Christ crucified for the fallen world. That is to say, neglecting divine wisdom as one of the three mutually qualifying perfections of the Triune God causes us to overlook the disruption of God's paradoxical wisdom, Christ crucified, and to proceed naturally, all too naturally, to similitude apart from personal unification with Christ that comes by dying with Him in the Spirit's baptism. But we have gotten ahead of ourselves. Let us pause in this (immanent!) critique of Barth first to appreciate Barth's accomplishment.

In coming to the traditional topic in dogmatics of the divine perfections, Barth announces programmatically that the dynamic being of the Triune God consists in the freedom to love (*CD* II/1, 322–47). This freedom to love is the life that God lives out in relation to creatures, so that to know God is to know Him ever and ever again in new ways of surprising love. It is unique to God to be identical with the multitude of His perfections in this dynamic way. "Perfections," be it noted, is plural not singular, yet just so forms a unity of the many in God. God is at one and the same time unity and multiplicity, so that the attributes combine to provide the concrete characterization of divine unity, describing *what* God is. Divine perfection is not to be understood, as the dogmatic traditions tend to understand, as unity in God's self-relation but plurality in relation to creation. Rather, God is true to Himself as unity and multiplicity also in His relation to the creation. This relation is Jesus Christ. As such, He is the "Lord of glory," whom the foolish rulers of this age crucified in their wisdom, which is in truth an ignorance of God's wisdom, hidden from the ages but now revealed in Christ not only as His glory but also "for our glory" (1 Cor. 2:6–8).

In this light, Barth inveighs, how spectral seems the *actus purus* that tells divine unity without multiplicity! That tells of the One *without* the many glories of His name! But the Lord is one with His glories, just as without the Lord the glories dissolve into so many incoherent multiplicities, a pantheon of ultimate values often at odds one with another: power versus goodness, justice versus mercy, transcendence versus immanence, and so on. Giving little other than the familiar philosophical choice between chaos and cosmos, such reversions to polytheism take the rule from the one God and distribute it into a plurality of cults and a multitude of idols; they dissolve the oneness of God in His coming reign into a multiplicity of appearances concealing a hidden, protological unity. (This sophisticated polytheism, as I am arguing, reappears in Christian doctrine as trinitarian modalism, which sees the Trinity as an economy of appearances only, not seeing that God is true to Himself in His economic outreach to the creation and so the one true God in revelation as He is in Himself.) The fear is palpable in a Eunomius, an Occam, or a Biel, Barth notes, that a plurality of perfections in God (like trinitarian personalism) violates simplicity. So also in more recent times, Friedrich Schleiermacher taught that the ascriptions that creatures make to God befall only them, not God in transcendent simplicity. Even John of Damascus and John Calvin, seeking to avoid this awkward combination of economic polytheism and drastic ontological monotheism, only met the challenge halfway in theorizing a divine "accommodation" corresponding to a discreet pious silence about the true object spoken in theology on account of the creaturely limitations infecting even the language of revelation.

In order to escape this dead end, what is needed is a critique of the one-sided *simplicitas* of the supposedly divine *essentia nuda*, the ghostly idol devouring the richness of God's glories in the real multitude of His perfections, the glories of His name. This critique is not of unity for the sake of multiplicity in a mere inversion, then, of the ghostly idol in heaven in exchange for a plurality of images on the earth. It is the one true God, who is not reducible to His relations to creatures, who is already antecedently in His own life a unity in multiplicity and multiplicity in unity. The needed critique comes rather when we learn the what of God from the who of God in determining how Christian theology is to speak of the perfections ascribed to Him and so concretely to say what in the world we are talking about when we say the word "God." So a solution like that of Gregory Palamas, which virtually separates the streaming energies from the hidden essence-source of God from which they radiate, is no solution. We seek instead, Barth says, a simple complexity or a complex simplicity, a dialectic of unity and multiplicity that befits the living and dynamic whatness of the God made known in the witness of Holy Scripture. So likewise the needed dialectic does not affirm multiplicity at the expense of simplicity. Instead, we need to overcome the entire Greek cosmological framework of the One and the Many that forces these false choices upon us. And we can make this break on the grounds that the One no less than the Many is in fact one and the same divine being, thought *in relation to us*; it is One in relation to us no less than Many in relation to us. It is an optical illusion, then, to imagine that in reality we ascend by the several paths of eminence or negation to the Absolute One as is claimed. In either way, we only achieve "our" One or "our" Many. With this realization, the whole house of cards built up in the Christian Platonist synthesis is collapsing today. But in Christian theology willing to make a fresh start, what God is must be learned from who God is—that is, from the Father, who gives and communicates Himself in Christ as freedom to love.

The divine perfections, then, will be thought of as the attributes of freedom and of love in the dialectic of their mutual qualification of one another in the life of the Father and the Son. This is emphatically not to be understood in the traditional way of dogmatics as varying lists of absolute and relative attributes. Because of the optical illusion that has us think that we can think an absolute absolutely rather than relatively—that is, in relation to us—the instability of equivocation takes form as a dialectic of negativity. As a result, such divisions of God's perfections always ultimately resolve in favor of an impersonal absolute who just happens also to be related to a world, our reification of a No-Thing that itself must finally be negated to a Not-Nothing ad infinitum. Barth's attributes of freedom, to be sure, encompass the Christian concerns articulated under the traditional metaphysical attributes pointing to the irreducibility of God to His external relations. Barth's attributes of love likewise encompass the traditional moral attributes of God pointing to the reality of His external relations to creatures. But the dialectic of freedom and love that Barth proposes overcomes the cosmological framework of the One and the Many because it is understood as a dialectic internal to the eternal life of the Triune God and therefore and as such also true in the external relations that this same God acquires in creating.

So, rather than flat-footed sets classifying attributes of God metaphysical and moral, this dialectical movement of God as freedom to love constitutes the perfection of His holy being as *event*. As event, this dialectic of freedom and love is kindred to the dialectic of "veiling and unveiling" in revelation that Barth had established from the beginning of the *Church Dogmatics*. "In a gracious sovereign act," as Bruce McCormack captures the kinship, "God takes up the language of human witnesses and makes it to conform to Himself. God must therefore speak when spoken of by human witnesses if such witness is to reach its goal. He must reveal Himself in and through the 'veil' of human language."[61] These parallel dialectics of veiling and unveiling and freedom to love accordingly parse the same event of God from different angles. God is the one Subject in its own eternal act of being, of God speaking in freedom and God spoken as loved, as such also "repeated" in its temporal act of revelation. The way to theological speech, then, is neither a way of negation nor a way of eminence, nor is it the attempted synthesis of these two ascents in the analogy of being. The way to theological speech is by the ontology of act—that is, the method of *Nachdenken* that follows in thought after the divine Subject who is revealed exercising freedom in His deed of love. The deed of love, however, is veiled in the human being Jesus and the human language by which He is attested and only unveils where and when the Subject sovereignly and graciously acts in freedom to make it known (this latter is, of course, a tacit but unexplicated reference to the Spirit).

As McCormack further analyzes, corresponding to the divine Subject who loves in freedom is the faith that freely loves in turn. Indeed, "It is at this point that the inherently dialectical character of the *analogia fidei* is clearly seen. . . . God unveils Himself by veiling Himself in human language. In truth, the *Realdialektik* of veiling and unveiling is the motor that drives Barth's doctrine of analogy and makes it possible."[62] Faith corresponds to revelation, for in analogy to God's free act of love in Christ, faith freely receives and so acts in love to the neighbor in turn. McCormack points out that, so construed, the analogy of faith, as the human correspondence to the divine Subject who loves in freedom, (1) does not posit such a relationship as inherent in creation, especially the fallen creation that we now know as "nature," and (2) denies that any human act of would-be ascent can trigger God's free act of love (which would then cease to be free and gift and become merit and reward). God's free act of love is the event that generates faith; it is the occasion of faith and faith consequently never becomes a human habit, a possession, a predicate of the human subject. Faith, for our salvation, remains decentered

61. Bruce McCormack, *Karl Barth's Critically Realistic Dialectical Theology: Its Genesis and Development, 1909–1936* (Oxford: Clarendon; New York: Oxford University Press, 1995), 18.
62. Ibid.

and ecstatic, relying always on an alien righteousness, communicated externally by the Word of God, which is the free subjectivity of God the Son, guaranteed as God's act alone precisely by the human veil and stumbling block that otherwise barricades our access as ascent. Here, and here alone, through the stumbling block of the veil, God unveils Himself where and when He pleases.[63]

Notice in the foregoing Barth's take on personhood *as subject* that unveils the (dare I say, noumenal) freedom in the action of love. On the model of Martin Buber's "I-Thou" as opposed to "I-it" relations, itself modeled on Kant's distinction between theoretical and practical knowledge, the one Subject that is God in the free event of His love for others evokes a corresponding Thou of faith, which is freed to love in turn. All would be well with this if the faith under examination were the faith that comes about when the Spirit proclaims Christ, folly to our natural eyes, as God's power and wisdom. Then faith would consist in the "Christification," so to say, of the auditor; that is, faith would be that unification with Christ's crucified and risen Person that consists in dying to sin and rising to newness of life by the Spirit's baptism. One could then say truthfully with the apostle Paul, "It is no longer I who live, but it is Christ who lives in me; and the life I now live in the flesh I live by the faith/faithfulness of the Son of God, who loved me and gave himself for me" (Gal. 2:20 AT). Here Jüngel's vestige is operative: in the relations of this historical individual, Jesus, to His Father and their Spirit, faith is achieved for us and so also in us, if and when the Spirit pleases in His other-regarding love to communicate His own relation to Jesus also to creatures, thus relating them in Jesus to the Father as well. *Jesus* is the Christ, analogue of the Triune God, while "Christians"—that is, those who are "in Christ" by faith—in turn are His "little Christs" (Luther), sinners though they remain so far as they persist as members, if not citizens, of the apostate creation.

But if the analogy of faith is only slightly reoriented to say instead that Jesus is to God as the eternal Son is to eternal Father, we cannot then speak of a union, neither a personal union in Christ affirming that *Jesus* is the Christ nor a unification of believer with the person of Christ saying truthfully, and in spite of the persistence of sin in the life of the redeemed, that the Christian *is* in Christ. McCormack is right, of course, to maintain that from the early Barth's dialectic of veiling and unveiling onward a certain progression occurred, without abandoning dialectic, toward "the centrality of an incarnational Christology . . . [and] Barth's adoption of the ancient anhypostatic-enhypostatic model of Christology in May 1924 (together with his elaboration

63. Ibid., 17.

of a doctrine of the immanent Trinity)."[64] I will describe this development momentarily. But the troubling question that arises here is whether the tacit model of the one God as the *Subject* who manifests freedom in the moral act of love depends more on Kant's version of German idealism than the social trinitarianism of the Christian doctrine of God, whose freedom to love wisely makes Jesus, and the Christian in Christ Jesus, enhypostatic in reality, and not only in a way of talking.

This dispute here is a matter of considerable subtlety; it has to do with a distinction that I proposed in my systematic theology between taking the trinitarian Person as a "subject of free acts" or as a "patient-agent" of acts by way of the communal role it plays.[65] Another way of putting the dispute is whether in Christology the term "person" is being used in exactly the same way as in the doctrine of the Trinity, where the doctrine of the Trinity is socially rather than psychologically modeled. According to this, the person is a concrete way of being in relation to other persons, and it is a "chicken and egg" question to ask which comes first, person or community, since the terms are taken here as correlative. That precisely is the model of social trinitarianism. In the former way of a "subject of free acts," however, one invariably thinks of the psychological model of "mind thinking and willing itself," where there is and must be one Subject, divine Mind, in its act of coming to self-awareness and self-affirmation. This model is what creates the difficulty christologically. Since such modes of one psychological process are impossible to distribute, as if the individual Jesus *is* the moment in God's Mind of self-knowledge on the way to the Spirit as Mind's self-affirmation, one must regard Jesus in His human act of faith as the creature who signifies this modality of God's timelessly eternal self-knowledge, "Jesus who is to God," then, "as the eternal Son

---

64. Ibid., 19.

65. I am indebted to the Bonhoeffer scholar Michel DeJonge for his elaboration of Bonhoeffer's Lutheran critique of Barth's interpretation of Christology in a way that aligns the traditional *extra Calvinisticum* imputed by Lutherans to the Reformed tradition with Kantian transcendental subjectivity. Bonhoeffer located the externality of the divine Word not in the transcendent deity of the eternal Son, nor in a kerygmatic event making known the truth of timeless divine love (as in Bultmann), but rather in the one, undivided person figured in the incarnate humanity of the gospel narrative—not a what or a how but a who that is personally presented in speech and present in His Easter reality, as promised by the Spirit's Word and sacraments. Here "person" (as opposed to Barth's more Kantian "subject," as in the noumenal agency that is the condition for the possibility of the free moral act) means the unity of act and being that constitutes a narrative identity established by its course in space and time. Thus Jesus Christ unavoidably entails the history of the first-century Jew who came in the name of Israel's God but ended on the cross abandoned by the same. Here Christian theology finds the divine Son of God (cf. Mark 15:39) or not at all, and so also the wisdom of God or not at all—that is, in this ambiguity that is not humanly resolvable, as Bonhoeffer insisted, but only "from above" on the third day. See DeJonge, *Bonhoeffer's Theological Formation*, 71.

is to the Father." Here the christological *est* must be rendered as a *significat*. The man Jesus signifies that mode of divine Mind's eternal existence in self-knowledge. God's eternal self-knowledge in turn "repeats itself" in time by way of the creature Jesus, the veil who corresponds to God's self-knowledge where and when God in freedom so discloses. Since for Barth the creature can only veil God, including the creature Jesus, it is impossible to understand how the creature Jesus can at the same time unveil God. But that seems ultimately to be Barth's point (at least through the 1930s and again in the final installment of the *Church Dogmatics*, IV/4). The flesh, or humanity, of Jesus remains flesh, veiling, creature, *non capax infiniti*. It cannot and does not unveil God. It blocks this access. It only signifies. "The flesh profiteth nothing: the words that I speak unto you, they are spirit, and they are life" (John 6:63 KJV). It is indeed true that Paul says similarly that "the body is meant not for fornication but for the Lord"; yet it is also true that he adds immediately, "and the Lord [is meant] for the body" (1 Cor. 6:13).

In this light, the excellent McCormack has, I think, misconstrued (or perhaps followed Barth's misconstrual) of the "nature of the hypostatic union by means of a running debate with classical Lutheran Christology."[66] Let us see how. First, while it is certainly the case that Barth thinks that he has adopted the Christology of the ancient church, he has in fact only gotten to the *anhypostasis* and not yet reached the *enhypostasis* if the flesh of Jesus is and can be only veil, or, for that matter, copy—not the tangible, touchable, tastable being alongside other beings in the world that is full of grace and truth (John 1:14, 16; 1 John 1:1–3). That is to say, for Barth the primary import of classical Christology is the denial that Jesus has an autonomous human subjectivity. Moreover, it is to say that "the classical Lutheran Christology" also adopts the anhypostatic-enhypostatic Christology of the ancient church, precisely to exclude, as Barth also wishes to exclude, as McCormack puts it, "the tendency of Zwingli to reduce the affirmation that 'Christ has suffered' to a mere figure of speech."[67] Barth affirms, then, that the divine Person incarnate really suffers—not an abstracted human nature treated as if it were a separable patient; rather, the divine Person suffers in and as His *own* humanity. On this, there is no "debate" at all.

Second, it is also the teaching of the great Johann Gerhard, against the lesser Lutheran thinker Johannes Brenz and his school[68] (who is the real target of the McCormack-Barth critique under the title "classical" Lutheran Chris-

66. McCormack, *Barth's Critically Realistic Dialectical Theology*, 363.
67. Ibid., 364.
68. I treat this divergence between Brenz and Chemnitz/Gerhard extensively in my systematic theology, *Beloved Community*, 536–65, to which the reader is referred for the details.

tology), that this real suffering of Jesus Christ the Son of God is attributed to the divine Person incarnate—not directly to the divine nature but rather to the divine Person in union with His assumed humanity. To be sure, for Gerhard the communication can and does run also in the other direction, as the *enhypostasis* indicates. Indirectly, by way of the same divine Person who personally communicates, divine properties are attributed to the assumed humanity, so that it is true to say, as Luther himself had provocatively put it, "This *man* created the world."[69] It is such fulsome affirmation of the *enhypostasis* that Barth in fact declines with his doctrine of the veil of humanity (though not with respect to the divine *Logos ensarkos* from eternity, which he emphatically affirms). There was never a divine Logos that was not to become Jesus in the fullness of time. Even so, in denying the *Logos asarkos,* and affirming the *Logos ensarkos,* Barth keeps to the *extra Calvinisticum,* as if to say that God the Son is from all eternity veiled rather than revealed in His human flesh (contra, then, John 1:14, 16; 1 John 1:1–3).

Gerhard would certainly agree with McCormack's Barth that the union is a free and personal act, not a "physical" compounding; it is an ineffable personal act of appropriation, not some kind of impersonal hybridization or metamorphosis of natures. The personal union of natures, more precisely *communion* of natures by the personal act of the Son of God, is thus, as McCormack puts it for Barth, an "indirect union, mediated through the Person in whom both natures are grounded."[70] Yet there is a significant imprecision here. Barth affirms an indirect "union of natures," only to deny a "direct" one. But in fact the classical teaching on the *communicatio idiomatum* speaks about a *communion* of natural properties in the incarnate Person at work; this imprecision elides something important. In Christ there is not a union of natures but rather a personal communion of natures; the term "union" instead is reserved to explicate theologically the sense of the *egeneto* in *kai ho logos sarx egeneto*: the Logos did not metamorphosize into flesh but rather took human flesh, body and soul, into the unity of His own Person. This unity of Person in turn is unchanged and unchangeably the Son's eternally living personhood in relation to His Father and the Spirit, though now, in becoming flesh, this same personhood is lived out in the earthly sojourn named "Jesus." Thus from the apparent agreement with Barth and the ancient church on the personal nature of the union and corresponding communion of the natural properties, Gerhard would not have to draw the conclusion that McCormack's

69. Thesis 4 of Martin Luther, *Disputatio de divinitate et humanitate Christi* (1540) (Hinlicky, "Luther's Anti-Docetism," 182).

70. McCormack, *Barth's Critically Realistic Dialectical Theology*, 364.

Barth draws, namely, that the Lutheran teaching of a *personal* communion of natures in Christ wanted "the divine nature to be directly given to the human nature" as a divine victory overcoming the supposed "antithesis of God and humankind."[71]

But the monophysite smear misses the target. Gerhard, following Martin Chemnitz, who already took exception to Brenz's direct and undialectical and thus generic attribution of divinity to the humanity in Christ, explicitly spoke of the communication of natural properties in Christ as a free act, at the abiding disposal, so to say, of the divine Person in His henceforth and forever incarnate life. Thus, in terms of the ubiquity controversy where these christological questions were hammered out, they said that the incarnate Son is *ubivolipraesens*, "present where He wills"; the divine freedom of the personal Son of God, also in His incarnation, is thus opposed to Brenz's connatural ubiquitism of Christ's glorified body with its impersonal stretching of Jesus's body everywhere. With this stipulation from strong trinitarian personalism, Gerhard can affirm a free and personal communion of natures in Christ according to the personal will of the patient-agent, the Son of God, in carrying out the mission in His flesh from the Father in the power of the Spirit.

For Barth, as McCormack explains, the problematic antithesis between God and humanity that is resolved christologically is moral, not natural. It is overcome not by uniting the natures, then, but by the real predication to the Person incarnate of the sin, guilt, and punishment of humankind. Overcoming this antithesis of holy God and sinful humanity in the Person crucified for us, however, "in no way set aside the antithesis on the level of the relationship of the natures."[72] Antithesis? Is that not the merely negative construction of God's deity that Colin Gunton criticized? Why not the "distinction" between God who gives and the creature who receives and is thus enabled also to give? Would not a personal union in that case overcome the corruption of human nature in Adam, who wants to be God and does not want God to be God? Would it not set forth the new Adam, who trusts wholly in God the Giver to the extremity of obedient death for others, even death on a cross?

In any case, for McCormack's Barth, the divine deed of Christ cannot be attributed to the assumed human nature for the logical reason that "attributes and operations may only properly be predicated of persons or subjects. But there is no human subject here to whom divine attributes and operations might be attributed. . . . God is capable of the human, the relation cannot be

71. Ibid.
72. Ibid., 355–56.

reversed."[73] In this affirmation of the Reformed maxim *finitum non capax infiniti* we have perhaps reached, with McCormack's help, the deepest level of Barth's core convictions and commitments. Barth's dialectic of the finite and the infinite has to deny that the man Jesus simply *is* (= is enhypostasized in) the Son of God, all the while affirming that this particular (anhypostatic) veil of all possible veils in the world is nonetheless the one that witnesses the unveiled Son, where and when God pleases. Jesus is a sign that signifies the thing itself; an analogue, then, not a communion, a *significat* not an *est*. Jesus "is" the Son of God, then, in, and only in, the *event* of the divine Son's free self-revelation by way of His chosen sign, Jesus.

Clearly the concern for a necessary *sic et non* in Christology is the same in Gerhard and Chemnitz as in Barth. Knowledge of Jesus Christ the Son of God is the work and gift of the Spirit, not ever a human insight, not even an insight of the so-called historical Jesus. Barth in this way is materially close to the *ubivolipraesens* of Chemnitz and Brenz in affirming the *personal* nature of the union in Christ. If that is clear, let us proceed from this shared concern by excluding as equal and opposite errors Brenz's undialectical ubiquitism (the monophysite error) on the one side and Zwingli's Nestorianism on the other. In that case, the present argument is refined. It amounts to the proposal that Barth's avowed concern to safeguard Christ in our understanding from profanation would be better accomplished by the trinitarian dialectic of Word and Spirit than by his christological dialectic of flesh and spirit, human nature and divine, veiling and unveiling, freedom and love, and so forth, if the concern is in fact to block human claims to possess divinity like a prize. That is so because, despite its iconoclastic virtues, it becomes impossible according to Barth's dialectic of the two natures to see how this particular instance of human nature, Jesus of Nazareth, is either anointed in the Spirit or suffers for others on the cross if, as nothing but an abstract nature, this humanity has no properties of its own since it is not itself a "subject." But in fact this humanity can have properties that identify it in the world, since it is enhypostasized, albeit uniquely, in the divine Word. Jesus is real and concrete, the tangible (1 John 1:1–4) and thus one and only humanity of the Son of God.

Let us entertain a christological counterthesis to illustrate the precise difference in Christology being proposed. What if the human claim to speak God's Word in God's name or, more precisely, christologically, to speak in God's name *as* God's Word for the inclusion and life of beings such as us—what if this claim is laid upon the claimant as a lethal burden, not a privilege but a cross to carry? So heavy that it leads, humanly speaking, to final forsakenness and

73. Ibid., 366.

eternal death if nothing new can supervene to surpass that evident finality? In this case, the foolish wisdom of God in the contradiction of the Messiah's cross to our world's mendacity and vainglory blocks any and all human claims to possess divinity like a prize, if indeed the Lord of glory is crucified in its midst and remains, also in His exaltation, this same One crucified for others. In this case, on the other hand, what else suffices to bear the burden of the sin of the vainglorious world, the sin that is not one's own doing but rather all that is done to one and against one? What else but the mystery of the *communion* of natural properties in the divine Person become man, who has in truth from conception made this individual of human nature, Jesus of Nazareth, His own soul and body, never to be separated, even at the cost of the Spiritual death of the very Son of God—the Godforsaken separation of the Son incarnate in the likeness of sinful flesh from the Father? If the christological mystery is this human individual, Jesus, anointed in the Spirit to perish as the suffering Servant of the Lord so far as human and also the divine eyes of the Father can see, is it not only by the Spirit's preaching (Rom. 1:2–4) that the sign and thing signified are united again to re-present the same *persona, prosōpon, figura* in the world? So that if we see Jesus, more precisely if we see apocalyptically "how Jesus dies," we see the Son of God (Mark 15:39) ransoming us (Mark 10:45), whose revealed glory is therefore to have come down to the depths, into our hands, our mouth, our bosom (Mark 14:22–24)? Then our glory is, slowly and often painfully but all the same decisively, to be changed into His likeness (2 Cor. 3:18) by learning to think, as the Spirit teaches, of Jesus as God His Father thinks of the obedient Son who will be vindicated (Mark 8:33), just as Jesus Himself learned obedience, to think of Himself (Mark 10:45) in the obedience of faith (Mark 14:36).

If this line of christological reflection finds traction, it may be summed up as follows. The mystery of the incarnate Person (Mark 4:41) is not best exposited by the notion of subject. The modern subject is not the conceptual equivalent of the trinitarian Person. As subject, the eternal Son cannot really become, be, and remain forever and ever a human individual unless space is made for its pure actuality by making the humanity nothing but an anhypostatic shell—that is, an abstract nature that veils until it becomes transparent to the unveiled Son of God in the act of divine love for us. Barth has actually missed the fine point here of the old Christology that otherwise he has so powerfully retrieved. The denial that Jesus has a hypostasis of His own intends to exclude the Nestorian autonomy of the human nature enhypostasized in Adam, thus in order to affirm that Jesus qua human *is* the "Holy One" in our midst, enhypostasized in the eternal Son, so that the hypostasis of the man Jesus, mystery of God incarnate that He is, *is* the eternal Son in His own dear flesh. If this is right, then Barth's divine Subject assumes a human nature without a subjectivity of its own (anhypostatic) as but the vehicle or occasion of its self-disclosure as the loving act of God's freedom. Consequently, the divine wisdom that selects and forms this particular humanity is necessarily subordinated. It is but the blank slate by which the divine Logos speaks, in principle separable from it.

Barth would, of course, hotly contest this inference. Such sophisticated neodocetism certainly is not his intention. Yet how else are we to take Mc-Cormack's highly nuanced statement in this precise connection? Barth takes the "second Person of the Trinity in history, as a Subject who enters fully into the contradiction of human existence and overcomes it, without fear of historicizing revelation. The eternal Son is present in history indirectly, never becoming directly identical with the veil of human flesh in which he conceals Himself (since divine attributes are not properly predicated of the human nature)."[74] A subject manifests its natural properties in its free action; a divine subject does just this under the veil of an apparent humanity. The sign Jesus is to God as the eternal Son is to the eternal Father, the thing signified, if and when the eternal Son so unveils in the event of revelation occasioned by human words of witness to Jesus Christ, Himself *the* witness of God.

If McCormack is right, I do not see logically how the concept of subject—so far as Barth employs it as a conceptual equivalent to the trinitarian notion of person—can avoid oscillating in this way between a Nestorian double subjectivity in Christ (as the figure of Christ appears in the gospel narrative, sign pointing to thing signified) and an Apollinarian monophysitism (as in reality, theologically demythologized, the unveiling Son of God in the veil of His flesh). And it does not help to call this opportunistic oscillation a dialectic. The alternative afforded by weak simplicity is to think of the patient-agent Person of Christ as the eternal Son who freely takes to Himself human flesh, body and soul, to live on the earth His very life in relation to the Father and the Spirit, but now further in a newly forged relation of the mercy of love to lost and dying humanity.

We may leave the problem raised here to the Barth scholars and now return to the main argument that the analogy of faith is to be understood not as a witness external to the event of Christ for us but rather as a unification with the Christ who unites with sinners by His death and resurrection. Certainly the word concerning Christ comes to us from without as an external report of news that is good. However, it comes externally in order to re-form its auditor internally; it comes not on account of faith but for the sake of faith.

74. Ibid.

As Christ *is* the analogue of God by virtue of the personal communion of divine and human natures in and for His work of the mercy of love, so in Him in turn human beings really become Christified by His Spirit's gift of repentance and faith. This is to say that Christ is object of faith[75] in the sense of *fides Christo formata*—that is, not firstly or only or chiefly its paradigm, *fides caritate formata*; it is to say that His person at work for us is the mystery of the eternal Son, the second of the Three, who suffered for us in order to triumph in us. Barth, of course, intended nothing different in this respect, and I have been criticizing a certain concept, the noumenal Subject, and its corresponding grammar, a dialectical (i.e., Kantianized) *extra Calvinisticum*.

At the Mercy of the Spirit

If "subject" is understood as a social patient-agent, then, the christological problem appears quite differently. As Jesus is God in the way of being the Son of the Father in the Spirit, He has ever at His free disposal the capabilities and liabilities of divine and human natures to employ as the needs of His mission require, sent from the Father in the power of the Spirit to overcome death by death. This is what the personal communion of natures means; it is not the abstract and speculative nonsense of the Brenzians, making contradictory predications in general, such as "God suffers" or "human beings forgive sin," that annul the paradox rather than pass through it to the Spirit's intended similitude in the gift of new creation. But the personal communion of natures is the concrete interpenetration of human and divine passions and capabilities in the one Lord Jesus Christ at work in His mission. And it is thus the ground for speaking truthfully, "This man forgives sins," or "This Son of God dies on the cross," when such statements are put to work in the Spirit's work of working in us repentance and faith. Unification with Christ, analogous to the personal union in Christ, can accordingly consist in the joyful exchange of the Christ who unites with the believer by His gracious and unilateral exchange of predicates: "Give me your sin and take my righteousness; let go of your death and receive my life!" Christ is the One who so unifies Himself to faith that believes Him, and just so He brings about His new creation as something palpable, tangible, tastable, audible, and visible in the world: "*This* is my body given for you" where the "you" is the *ecclesia*, the chosen people of God.

You cannot have a communication of idioms, obviously, without idioms. Natures are conceptual sets of idioms by which we classify the things and

75. See further "Historicizing the Eschatological?" in Hinlicky, *Beloved Community*, 393–400.

persons that we encounter in the world. They are as such concepts abstracted from our experience of reality, and by induction and generalization they prevail so long as they prove useful for navigating reality. But if reified, concepts can become alternatives to experience of reality, worlds of ideas that serve instead to evade reality in a state of false consciousness rather than working efficiently to engage what is not in the mind. Even worse, fanatics can become intoxicated enough with their abstractions that they would force the reality of persons and things into them, remolding reality according to them, turning even the living God of the Bible, who meets us in His Word with its claim to truth, into a vicious abstraction. What violence has been done on the earth in the name of such supposed idealism! But in fact, our concepts swim in an ever-flowing historical stream of revision when they are working well to navigate reality, which stream is itself Heraclitus's river of continual change. Experienced resistance to our ideas rightly sends us back to the drawing board to find better ones with which to swim with and not against the stream in which we earthlings live and move and have our being.

This river of becoming is interpreted in Christian theology as God's *creatio continua*.[76] Each one's experience, in spite of sin, is received in faith as God's making the person to be redeemed and fulfilled in the Beloved Community. So my idioms as one called by God as His image concretely in my own biographical journey to become His likeness are the properties that I acquire in my life's way, whether for likeness or unlikeness to God. Likewise, the "I" who acquires properties is enhypostasized, beginning in Adam but turned by the Spirit into Christ. Abstractly considered, this can be a terrifying thought. I *am* my concrete biography. I cannot undo anything that I have done or failed to do. I own the deeds and the failures and the omissions whether I own up to them or not. Royce therefore called this reality of personhood betrayed and likeness to God lost "the hell of the irrevocable" and the "moral burden of the individual"[77] who has lost God's calling and filled the image of God that she is with waste and ruin instead. Unless another break into the strong man's house and bind him, she remains bound in Adam to the tyranny of that tyrant in its hell of the irrevocable. The One who breaks in to wrest free does so not with equal violence but rather with self-donating justice—the extraordinary justice of the One who took upon Himself our sin and death in order to give us His righteousness and life, just so prying free the tyrannous grip of the past and setting free for the destiny of the Beloved Community.

76. Hinlicky, *Beloved Community*, 740–61.
77. Royce, *Problem of Christianity*, 293.

The ancient church, following the lead of the Gospel of John, took the exchange of idioms in the person of Christ ontologically as the exchange of divine life for human mortality, though it must not be forgotten that in thinking ontologically this way death was regarded as the unnatural fruit of unnatural sin. In divine philanthropy the Logos became what we are in the likeness of sinful flesh in order that we might become what He is in the likeness of God. This is the root of the Eastern Christian doctrine of theosis or deification, which I have said is more precisely understood as the Spirit's work of Christification in working repentance and faith. It affirms that the image of God cannot be lost. That indelible stamp is indeed the reason why eternal death remains a real threat. The indelible image of God created for immortality can instead be filled with unlikeness to God that as a kind of weight—Jesus likens it to a millstone tied around the neck—drags one down to the dreariest depths, there to dwell forever with impenitent Dives, who is sorry only for his punishment but never for his sin.

It is to defeat this death to the Spirit that Christ the victor comes to be death of death and hell's destruction, giving life to the dead by dying our death, there at the nadir of despair, to give us His life. So John also knows about Pauline death as the wages of sin, even if his gospel focuses more on the abundance of eternal life giving itself to the dying. The apostle Paul in turn shares the Johannine thought of the ontological exchange and gift of eternal life for our sinful death, as when he writes of Him who, though He was rich, for our sakes became poor. Yet for Paul, the exchange is focused more on the moral matter of Christ's acquisition by the lived obedience of His faith[78] of that extraordinary justice that gives what is not deserved by virtue of His life of filial obedience for the sake of the unworthy. In just this obedience Christ is not only the incarnate Logos showing forth the Father's love but also the new Adam, who in exchanging His righteousness for our sin is the analogue on earth of God who gives. This person at work is one and the same, in a historical passage.

I may draw the threads of this chapter together as follows. Idioms, attributes, properties, and perfections are nature, not person, yet a person is concretely their idioms, both intrinsic (image, calling) and acquired (likeness, biography) in communion (fulfilled or breached) with other persons. The element of truth in the received doctrine of simplicity is that, as God is the singularity who creates all that is not God (recalling that this construal of deity is not a natural insight but rather a truth of revelation), and so strictly speaking beyond comparisons drawn from what is created, we cannot say

---

78. R. Michael Allen, *The Christ's Faith: A Dogmatic Account* (London: T&T Clark, 2009).

absolutely what the divine nature is, but only relatively what it is in relation to us. We can say only what this singularity is in its operations in relation to His creatures such as in faith we likewise take ourselves to be. To be sure, this limitation to knowledge of God's whatness—the privative, incommunicable attributes—bars the prying eyes of creatures. It leaves a "gap" of uncertainty, consequently, concerning the identity of the unknowable singularity with its supposedly knowable operations—how could we ever know that these are one and the same? Such is the worry about the received doctrine and its vulnerability to projection, whether of gross idols or of vicious abstractions projected onto the blank screen of the "gap."

But we have learned from Karl Barth (who learned from Luther's distinction of God hidden and revealed) that faith in the revealed God learns to trust God as truthful in His operations with us. Faith in the revealed and preached God closes the gap and in just this way learns to correspond to the God who first closes the gap in drawing near to us in His self-revelation, manifesting freedom to love. Consequently, an ultimate negation, a prohibition against ontotheological profaning of the Holy One Who Is, becomes in Barth the analogy of faith, corresponding to the Free One who loves in its own freedom to love others. The analogy of faith teaches us to qualify all proper speech about God as speech about the One who is free and so irreducible to the relations of love freely, but *only* freely, given by God in drawing near to us. This drawing near is the event of the man Jesus Christ, the analogue of God in the world in the freedom that He shows in loving others.

But is this event of Jesus Christ sheerly an assertion in the world? Is faith that corresponds to it blind? Must any explication of it by creatures that would understand its truthfulness to God as also to us consist in the attempt to unveil what is and must remain veiled? If so, we are left in the odd place of saying that of all the possible veils in the world, the man Jesus is the One where God's unveiling occurs, if and when God so wills. One fears that this too is a formalistic muddle, not the concrete mystery of the cross. How is this claim in its own way not a neodocetism that cannot say specifically why Jesus should be the veil or, for that matter, copy of God? Why is it that just Jesus's speaking of the God of grace brought Him in His concrete personal reality into conflict with regnant powers? From another angle: How does this pure, kerygmatic claim avoid being anything other than another human projection and thus new Christian idolatry? As this line of questioning indicates, treatment of Jesus as the surd of God's sovereign self-revelation is a dead end. We should instead specify this man, and not any other, not negatively as the veil that yields to unveiling, but affirmatively, as Jüngel's vestige of the Trinity.

We have learned from Jüngel that this christological analogy is precisely not obvious. It must be made obvious by a work of the Spirit. This invocation of the Spirit, however, is not miracle mongering. The christological similitude rather becomes obvious when its paradoxical power to challenge the obvious causes the scales to fall from our eyes (Acts 9:18; cf. Gal. 1:16). What is obvious is nothing but the apparently blasphemous claim of Jesus (Mark 14:62) to inaugurate fellowship with the God of grace for those undeserving according to the economy of the quid pro quo, for those who merit punishment instead of reward. Still, when this new obviousness of the God of grace breaks in and breaks up the old obviousness of the reign of merit, this claim for Jesus as the analogue of the God of grace can be followed from the hindsight of faith in His Easter vindication. So Jüngel in fact follows in thought, as we saw, by specifying the concrete humanity of Jesus as the person in the world in whom this conflict was adjudicated. It can be argued, then, that a world in which grace is not obvious is made known by way of the palpable contradiction to it played out in the life of one of us, Jesus, who is singularly Bonhoeffer's "Man for others." So far as that argument takes us, it gives reasons for adopting Christian faith in giving reasons for understanding Christian faith. As befits the claim of Jesus for the God of grace, this passage to the new obviousness of grace is itself a matter of grace that cannot be predicted or calculated but rather comes from God the Holy Spirit, who blows as He wills (John 3:8) when the gospel is proclaimed in its truth and purity. So the necessary dialectic to prevent the co-optation of God's gift for alien purposes is preserved in the trinitarian way of the nonidentical repetitions of the Father's grace by the Word incarnate and the free-moving Spirit.

But that means that in our language about God we are at the mercy of the Spirit. By His paradoxical predication of Christ crucified, the similitude of Christ, the new Adam, comes into force for us as for them for whom He died, bringing in its train the new obviousness of the *esse Deum dare*, albeit still in confrontation with the economy of the quid pro quo. "[Christ] must reign until he has put all his enemies under his feet" (1 Cor. 15:25), that last enemy being the death that claims to be the last word spoken over sinners, giving them their just deserts (1 Cor. 15:56–57). Just so, the tri-personhood of the God of the gospel is *understood* in faith as the promise of inclusion in the coming Beloved Community by virtue of that One of the Three who suffered for us and triumphs for us. This inclusion in the eternal life of God by incorporation into Christ is inaugurated by baptismal unification with the Son so that in the power of the Spirit we return with joy and thanksgiving to the Father, who has anticipated our arrival from the origin.

This, then, is the wisdom of God "for our glory" (1 Cor. 2:7) that was hidden from the regnant powers of this age, since otherwise "they would not have crucified the Lord of glory" (1 Cor. 2:8). But in the wisdom of God the Lord of glory gives and wants to give glory to us, that we might glory in Him who has taken from us the shame of our sin and the sting of our death. Trinitarian Christology must be able to say these things. It must be able to say that God is the freedom to love wisely in that the free love of God in Christ enacts as the folly of the cross that which is wiser than the world at its best. And it must be able to say that this free love of God in Christ is surprisingly wise in the joyful exchange of God's life for our death, Christ's righteousness for our sin, the Spirit's loving choice for us "not many wise, not many powerful, not many well born" (see 1 Cor. 1:26) in place of—no, in deepest resistance to—imperious projects of the *libido dominandi* for forcible unification on the earth that seduce and tyrannize with the false promise of the quid pro quo. Or will we remain so foolish in our wisdom not to count ourselves among these little ones?[79]

79. My dying father, patiently listening to his granddaughter explaining to him the wonders of her graduate education at Princeton Theological Seminary and the challenges that contemporary theology faces after Christendom, in all wonder confessed at the end of a rich life of pastoral ministry, "All I have is my poor, dumb Christian faith." He had the divine wisdom in this way to count himself among the little ones for whom the folly of God is wiser than the wisdom of the world.

Conclusion

And Christ Must Reign until . . . (1 Cor. 15:25)

The Counterthesis of Analytic Theology

In chapter 3 I argued against Lewis Ayres's contestation of the Régnon thesis, noting that his is the best contemporary historical case for a strong doctrine of protological simplicity, also in trinitarian doctrine. The best contemporary metaphysical case for simplicity as constitutive of the Christian doctrine of God is, in my reading, that of James Dolezal's *God without Parts*.[1] At the outset of his book he cites the Westminster Confession, that God is "most free, most absolute." I will return to the striking juxtaposition of freedom and absoluteness here shortly. But it is the use of the superlative "most" that at once strikes this reader as paradoxical. How can an absolute be better or best in absoluteness? If the superlative is rhetorically intensive, it but underscores that what is "most" absolute is so in relation to relative entities that lack absoluteness, like you and me. And, then, it is but relatively absolute, so to say, in spite of its rhetorically superlative appearance. As with "perfect being" theology, there is the danger here of an optical illusion: we attain an insight into perfection as such when in fact we only identify a perfection relative to us in the ways that we regard ourselves as imperfect beings. To say that God is the Creator of all that is not God, as Christian theology is

---

1. James E. Dolezal, *God without Parts: Divine Simplicity and the Metaphysics of God's Absoluteness* (Eugene, OR: Pickwick, 2011).

surely bound to say, is in reality already to have put God into a relationship, namely, with all that is not God. But Dolezal does not linger over such aporias of protological metaphysics.

Nor, until the final chapter, does he attend to the aforementioned juxtaposition, equally perplexing, of freedom and absoluteness in the passage cited from the Westminster Confession. In the end, to his credit, he faces the "difficulty" that has quietly accompanied his intervening case for strong simplicity as "*the ontologically sufficient condition for God's absoluteness*."[2] Since the "knotty question of how a simple God can be free with respect to creation"[3] resists any solution, however, in the end Dolezal makes a literal virtue of necessity. In a fashion reminiscent of Wisse's case for Augustine's defunctionalizing of the Trinity, he praises the resulting "incomprehensibility of God,"[4] as if the muddle that he has made of the Trinity were the mystery to be adored.

Celebration of a muddle that asserts a manifest contradiction,[5] according to the present argument, thus supplants the genuine mystery of God's eternal being in becoming that is capable of creation, incarnation, and inhabitation by the coming of the Beloved Community. I lift up Dolezal's book, nevertheless, as the best contemporary alternative to the present case for weak simplicity as a theological rule. That is not damning with faint praise. To the contrary, the book argues with unusual clarity and dauntless intellectual honesty for that which Mullins urged: the unvarnished radicalness of protological simplicity. Dolezal thus comes at length to this (in the present view, Christianly) fatal inference: "There has never been a temporal or logical moment in the divine life in which God stood volitionally open to other possible worlds";[6] that is to say, there is no third way in the doctrine of God between a libertarian freedom of arbitrary choice and the simple identity in God of intellection and volition. It is either Occam on to Descartes[7] or Thomas on to Dolezal's version of the Westminster Confession. Either/or!

2. Ibid., 2.

3. Ibid., xx.

4. Ibid., 210–12.

5. For detailed logical analysis of the muddle, which he calls a "deadlock," see Yann Schmitt, "The Deadlock of Absolute Divine Simplicity," *International Journal of the Philosophy of Religion* 74 (2013): 117–30. In brief, Schmitt holds that divine simplicity is not a univocal notion; that absolute simplicity denies to God any metaphysical complexity, while a moderate simplicity allows to God "parts"—that is, perfections, which are formally distinct from one another and from the being of God. The latter possibility for a weak doctrine of simplicity turns on Scotus's "formal distinction." Schmitt's dissection of strong simplicity runs in parallel with my theological criticisms of it.

6. Dolezal, *God without Parts*, 207.

7. For this genealogy, see the penetrating analysis by Dan Kaufman, "Divine Simplicity and the Eternal Truths in Descartes," *British Journal for the History of Philosophy* 11, no. 4 (2003): 553–79. Kaufman shows how Descartes's notorious doctrine of the divine creation

Given the simple identity of intellection and volition in the simple being of God, if God in fact wills to create a world, and foresees precisely this world in which I write these words and you read them, then God necessarily and eternally wills to do so as the byproduct, so to say, of God's own eternal act of being. If that is so, indeed "the difficulty is in understanding how such power to do otherwise [*than* create a world and thus *freely* to have in fact created one and so also free *now* to oppose the wayward acts of creatures under the ruinous power of sin] can be reconciled with the denial [by strong simplicity] that God exhibits any sense of passive potency."[8] Just this freedom of the One who has infinite access to all possibilities, including the permission of the sin that God actually opposes, can be admitted, however, in the weak simplicity advocated in this book that is now to be formulated as a theological rule in this conclusion. This "admission," however, is not a concession to be evaluated on the act/potency scheme; rather, it presupposes a revision of classical metaphysics by the gospel, such that to be God is to have infinite possibilities to give, as in Mark 10:27 and 14:36, as we behold in astonishment the God of the gospel surpassing God by the resurrection of His Crucified Son, put to death for our sins but raised for our justification.

Dolezal acknowledges, in following the Westminster Confession's juxtaposing of "most free, most absolute," that Christian doctrine requires us to say both that God is free in creation and that God is irreducible to His relation to creatures, that God is free in His love. That is most certainly true. But if divine simplicity is taken in the metaphysically strong sense of absoluteness, as insight into an ontological unity of timeless self-identity, it follows, if thought rigorously with Spinoza and without biblical anthropomorphism cluttering things up, that God and creation are simply the same act of being in the different modalities of *natura naturans* and *natura naturata*, respectively. Slamming on the brakes before driving over this cliff, Dolezal in the end can only assert an apparent contradiction, "most free, most absolute," and deny the implication that God by nature creates necessarily, if God in fact creates at all so that all is as it must be by the omnipotent will of God. "Oh the depths, oh the riches. . . . How inscrutable are His ways!" But before indulging in such parody of the apostle Paul, the muddle here should send us back to the drawing board.

One reason for ending up in this false dilemma can be found in Dolezal's rebuke of Occam and his followers for imputing a libertarian freedom of

---

of the eternal truths coheres with strong simplicity in the same way that eternal creation is a necessary implication of strong simplicity, if in fact there is a creation. So also then are eternal truths eternally created.

8. Dolezal, *God without Parts*, 209.

indifference to God as anthropomorphic, without a hint of recognition that intellection (on the model of God as Mind) is just as anthropomorphic (as also is the social model of the Trinity). None of our theological models escape anthropomorphism, especially not by the trick of vicious abstraction, which merely transposes and does not dispose of some myth or narrative telling God to us. These stories and figures of God are in historical fact the starting point of theologies; abstracting from them only succeeds in promoting the false consciousness that reifies the No-Thing. Surely for Christianity, in any case, God is love *ad intra* and thus also *ad extra*. So God as love may be disposed or inclined or motivated, but not necessitated, by His trinitarian being as the primordial Beloved Community to create—and, further, to create this world, on which the cross of Jesus stood, as the best of all possible worlds for reasons that infinitely transcend our comprehension (Rom. 11:33–35) but on revelation are nevertheless understandable in faith (Rom. 11:32) and followable in the lives of the just who live by their faith (Rom. 1:17).

Indeed, Paul's doxological acknowledgment of the depths and riches of God's inscrutable ways follows upon revelation and does not precede it as a metaphysical insight; it follows upon the revelation that is revelation precisely in enacting God's choices. Thus it comes about as an apophatic qualification of the revealed disposition, inclination, or motive of the God of love at work in His choices as made known in the economy: "God has imprisoned all in disobedience so that he may be merciful to all" (Rom. 11:32). But just such divine deliberation, resolve, and capacity to innovate in accordance with the faithful pursuit of a free divine self-determination, as Romans 11 details in the motion from the wrath of the God of love to the mercy of the God of love, is ruled out of court by strong simplicity. That is to say, the free God of the Bible is ruled out, which is further to say: if instead we had begun with the who of God as made known in His historical choices and let that biblical question and answer govern our theological determination of God's oneness in being, we surely would still be left with aporias—we surely would still cry of our dereliction (Rom. 8:22).

But these would be the cries of the just, who live by hope for what is not yet seen: the glorious liberty of the children of God, the coming redemption of our bodies. It would not be a cry of incomprehension at God's ways that anesthetizes the pain of hope by neutralizing the genuine contradiction between the doing of God's will in heaven and what cruelty is yet done on the earth (Rom. 7:24) and, so anesthetized, misses the astonishing divine self-surpassing for us that is the resurrection of the Crucified One (Rom. 7:25). What Paul celebrates as God's inscrutable way is the triumph of His costly mercy for all, not the conundrum of ascribing freedom to the necessary being. Ascribing freedom to the necessary being is the conceptual pastiche that comes from hybridizing two thoughts of God's oneness with divergent trajectories, as I have abundantly shown in the preceding pages.

To rule out the free God of the Bible is, methodologically, to permit some other *Fragestellung* than the Bible's canonical narrative ("myth," if you prefer) to become the matrix of theological reasoning. That is the good reason that until now, by way of conclusion of this inquiry, I have not taken up Dolezal's countercase, even though I laud it as the best alternative to my own position. We have to do here methodologically with the power of a question to frame an investigation, to set the agenda for inquiry, and to that extent to steer the outcome. I can, hypothetically, ask how the Three of the gospel narrative are the one true God. In this case, epistemic primacy[9] is accorded to Jesus, His Father, and their Spirit, taken as the Father's sending of the Son in the Spirit for us and our salvation—understood, as we today must understand, historically and critically, as rooted in the concrete humanity of Jesus and His way to and through Golgotha. This epistemic primacy frames the question about God's unity, so that the eschatological answer of 1 Corinthians 15:15, in tandem with the eschatological reading of Zechariah 14:9, tells of God who is one in God and for God as the Beloved Community and as such also truthfully for us in time as the coming of the Beloved Community. The Triune God is the eternal communion of love that is freely self-determined to be the same one for us also by our final incorporation into its own eternal life.

Or, hypothetically, I can ask how the one true God can also be understood as the Three of the gospel narrative. Here the cosmological determination of protological simplicity and metaphysical absoluteness (with its optical illusion that it has achieved insight into God's absoluteness rather than a superlative in relation to us imperfect beings) frames the question about God's threeness, so that the anthropomorphism of the biblical narrative in speaking of the Father of the Son in the Spirit is drastically qualified as an accommodation, a figure of speech, a religious representation to finite minds of what in itself is and must be an incomprehensible tautology: God Is He Who Is.

Certainly, as we have seen (and as Dolezal exhibits with his appeal to the Westminster Confession), the Christian tradition, empirically speaking, is of a divided mind at the juncture between these two ways. But I argue that we face here a hermeneutical crux today. I have shown in the preceding that the two ways of inquiry manifest, and must manifest, different trajectories. Moreover, it is only when we permit the complex answer of strong trinitarian

---

9. For the notion of epistemic primacy, see Bruce D. Marshall, *Trinity and Truth* (Cambridge: Cambridge University Press, 2000).

personalism to the question about divine unity to develop on its own terms, according to its own entelechy, that we see clearly the error of protological simplicity as a fundamental alternative—and, as such, the danger that it poses to the Christian doctrine of God as the One who comes from God to us and for us so that we might live now and ever more in God. In any case, the argumentative way of this book has been hermeneutical rather than propositional, pragmatic rather than theoretical. If, argumentatively, on the other hand, I had directly engaged in the propositional and theoretical manner in which Dolezal advocates strong simplicity and prosecutes his case for simplicity as a metaphysical insight, I would have surrendered in advance to ground rules that would have forced me upon the horns of the same dilemma on which, in the end, Dolezal willingly impales himself.

The Rule Theory of Doctrine

The rule theory of Christian doctrine is above all credited in recent times to George Lindbeck's seminal critique of propositionalism in theology, *The Nature of Doctrine*.[10] Dolezal's book is a textbook case, hermeneutically, for propositionalism in that the diverse testimonies of Scripture are ahistorically and uncritically torn from their context in God's history with His people, principlized (i.e., turned into free-floating abstractions) and as such harmonized[11] according to an agenda other than the revelation: "God consigned all to sin in order to have mercy on all." Lindbeck's hermeneutical critique of propositionalism, however, does not amount to noncognitivism in theology; rather, it specifies the way in which cognitive claims regarding God are to be made—that is, in first-order, directly Spirited discourse ("Be of good cheer, your sins are forgiven!" For "Jesus is Lord." And Jesus is Lord because "God has highly exalted Him" who undertook your lot and bore your burden. And God exalted Jesus because God freely chose to surpass the wrath of His love by the mercy of His love).

Lindbeck sometimes called the propositionalist method "cognitivist," and this, I believe, confused the matter. As he himself put it, "There is nothing in the cultural-linguistic approach that requires the rejection (or the acceptance) of epistemological realism and the correspondence theory of truth, which, according to most of the theological tradition, is implicit in the conviction of believers that when they rightly use a sentence such as 'Christ is Lord' they

10. George A. Lindbeck, *The Nature of Doctrine: Religion and Theology in a Postliberal Age* (Philadelphia: Westminster, 1984).
11. For a fuller critique of "scholasticism" as a hermeneutic, see Paul R. Hinlicky, *Beloved Community: Critical Dogmatics after Christendom* (Grand Rapids: Eerdmans, 2015), esp. 46–48.

are uttering a true first-order proposition."[12] Rather, "grammar"—that is, "second-order" theological discourse—sorts out the right usage of possible first-order cognitive claims in theology. In this case, as I would put it in arguing for a rule version, simplicity "says nothing true or false about God and his relation to creatures"[13] but only speaks about any such assertions. That would be the "weak" simplicity that simply forbids dualism in theology. So assert, then, the forgiveness of sins on account of Christ, God's Son come in the flesh for us, that God's singularity in this act is honored, the holiness of the event of Christ made to be sin for us is respected, and the wonder of the God of love surpassing wrath to achieve mercy is adored by the forgiven. The rule of simplicity thus makes an apophatic qualification of the epistemically primary kataphatic word of God's deliverance. This, precisely, is the pattern exhibited in the first table of the Decalogue, as I will now exhibit by way of conclusion.

But first, one more hermeneutical point must be made. I have noted in passing, beginning with Jüngel's account of Jesus as the vestige of the Trinity in chapter 4, that our understanding of the gospel narrative is historical and critical today. It is surely the case that the historical-critical understanding of the Bible subverts theology taken as contextless abstraction of principles from Scripture that harmonizes them into a scheme driven by philosophical ambitions to know the protological *archē* and to organize the world into a cosmic system on that basis—even, if not especially, when we call this product of our own manufacture the "biblical worldview." This kind of theology is, of course, the very habitat of propositionalism. All to the good, then, that historical criticism subverts such theology, especially when it claims the authority of Scripture for the conceptual idolatry that it erects. But the rule version of weak simplicity can claim biblical warrant when it is clear that the Word of God in the Bible is the kerygma, or proclamation, the "good news" of the coming of God (Isa. 40:9–11) to us and for us, addressed through Israel (Mark 1:15) to all nations (Mark 13:10). In this understanding of theology as "critical dogmatics,"[14] the theologically disciplined appropriation of historical criticism proves its mettle in warranting the rule version of weak simplicity, as I will now show.

The Decalogue's First Table as the Rule of Weak Simplicity

In his commentary on the Decalogue (Exod. 20:1–17), Brevard Childs put the hermeneutical point that I just made thusly: "If one assumes, as I do, that a

12. Lindbeck, *Nature of Doctrine*, 68–69.
13. See ibid., 69.
14. See further Hinlicky, *Beloved Community*, 3–55.

major purpose of biblical exegesis is the interpretation of the final form of the text, the study of the earlier dimensions of historical development should serve to bring the final stage of redaction into sharper focus."[15] Giving authority to Scripture in Christian theology by exegetically establishing the final form of the text is not an arbitrarily imposed dogmatic framework on heterogeneous literature, though it is indeed the founding act of Jewish, and then of Christian, orthodoxy. For Christian theology, it is the first and ever-foundational dogmatic decision against dualism in theology and docetism in Christology.[16] Historical criticism serves to unveil this trajectory against dualism and for unity in the doctrine of God within the scriptural literature itself and thus clarifies the sense of the final—that is, canonical—form of the text as telling one story from Genesis to Revelation of the one God resolved to redeem and fulfill the creation by the missions of His Son and Spirit. Historical criticism thus provides, in an appropriately deliteralized way, the insight of precritical *prisca theologia* that Scripture exists as the precipitate of the ancient promise of creation as the coming of the Beloved Community.[17] Scripture from the

15. Brevard S. Childs, *The Book of Exodus: A Critical, Theological Commentary* (Philadelphia: Westminster, 1974), 393. Frank Crüsemann writes,

> What happens theologically in this step-wise association of the Mount of God and divine law must be understood against the background of ancient Near Eastern culture. Law that is not custom or tradition comes from the king. The divine dignity of the state underlies its law, and the same is true of its cult. Sinai is, however, a utopian place. It is temporally and physically outside state authority. The association of divine law with this place is completed by steps, which the catastrophe of Israel both enabled and compelled. Sinai became the fulcrum of a legal system not connected with the power of a state and therefore not a mere expression of its tradition and custom. . . . A place was created for an alternative to royal law and cult. . . . Torah itself became the important form of rescue as cult and law were anchored in this place from which God had already been rescuing. (*The Torah: Theology and Social History of Old Testament Law*, trans. Allan W. Mahnke [Minneapolis: Fortress, 1996], 56–57)

The frank acknowledgment that by this "fictional place in an invented past" Israel escaped "every earthly power" is on one level true and on another false, since "Torah is the other side of the exodus" (ibid.). What is primary is Israel's memory of the redeeming God, in terms of which the imponderables of origin and eschaton were parsed.

16. Paul R. Hinlicky, *Divine Complexity: The Rise of Creedal Christianity* (Minneapolis: Fortress, 2009), 69–108.

17. Oswald Bayer, *A Contemporary in Dissent: Johann Georg Hamann as a Radical Enlightener*, trans. Roy A. Harrisville and Mark C. Mattes (Grand Rapids: Eerdmans, 2012) (originally published as *Zeitgenosse in Widerspruch: Johann Georg Hamann als radikaler Aufklärer* [Munich: Piper, 1988]). As I wrote in a review of this book (*Lutheran Quarterly* 27, no. 1 [2013]: 94–96),

> Hamann's two key moves are the theological critique of epistemology and the Trinitarian revision of metaphysics. The theological self is *matter* addressed by God *through matter*: "the transient and voided human being who is nonetheless immortal because God has addressed him and thus will have to do with him in eternity, whether in anger or in grace . . ." (33). Thus in the very place of Kantian transcendentalism comes instead

beginning and all the way down is the promise of the new creation, handed on through generations and finding traction in every new circumstance, "written . . . that we might have hope" (Rom. 15:4). Scripture is the tradition of the gospel in its normatively prophetic and apostolic modalities. It tells of the Lord, who faithfully works renewal from historical disasters in the pattern of the exodus by the remembrance of His Word in the Spirit's community, as Jewish philosopher Peter Ochs urges in his endeavor to reclaim for the present this way of scriptural reasoning: from the Babylonian exile, from the destruction of the temple and loss of the land, and now from the Shoah,[18] the promise encoded in the holy Scriptures works the renewal of life on the way to the end of days. That is how the one Bible tells the one God.

The expository commands, then, follow from the indicative statement[19] of the Decalogue's preface, "I am the LORD your God, who brought you up . . .": have no other gods, make no images for yourselves, and do not abuse the divinely given Name, but rather attend to it on the Sabbath. "Yahweh has identified himself as the redeemer God. The formula identifies the authority and right of God to make known his will because he has already graciously acted on Israel's behalf."[20] All these commandments, accordingly, qualify the God who identifies Himself with Israel by way of negative prohibitions that would prevent the lethal misunderstanding of free election (Amos 3:2) that reduces God to Israel, whether in pride or despair. They work to preserve the freedom of God in election (as did also John the Baptist in the fullness of time [Luke 3:8]) and to warn against reduction (also the reduction of abstraction)

the auditory event of being addressed by God. Kant would object to this: How could one ever tell that some finite and sensuous word is the word of the Infinite? Kant is thus thinking that the issue is one of epistemological justification for an outrageous, "enthusiastic" claim to know the Infinite in the finite. For Hamann, however, the biblical text on the *imago Dei*, Genesis 1:26–28, is the "historical a priori." It decodes all human experience, most basically the child's experience of being addressed by elders and parents and hence summoned to adult dignity and responsibility. God thus speaks to the creature through the creature continuing, enjoying, preserving, and expanding the work of creation, eminently and decisively in the new man Jesus Christ, in whom creation is redeemed. The epistemic warrant of this theological interpretation of nature and history is biblical narrative, which displays the structure of Trinitarian advent: "the condescension of the triune God who has interlaced his eternity with time, not only with his incarnation and death on the cross but as the Creator who addresses the creature through the creature, and as the Spirit who kills and makes alive through modest, particular, temporal events, as narrated by the Bible" (196). Creator and creation, eternity and time are not separated but united in Christ, and thus Christ is the Bible's key to interpreting nature and history.

18. Peter Ochs, *Another Reformation: Postliberal Christianity and the Jews* (Grand Rapids: Baker Academic, 2011).

19. Childs, *Book of Exodus*, 401–2.

20. Ibid., 401.

of the Name of this "One," who delivered from bondage and thus made Israel His people, into something other than the One who comes as redeemer of His freely chosen creature to all nations of the earth.

Historical-critical study makes abundantly clear what should be clear already from close reading of the final canonical form: the commandments do not assert the monotheism of the ontologically One but rather command henotheism in a conflicted and contested world: the "literal meaning [of the Hebrew of the first commandment] 'before my face'" provides "the original setting which prohibited setting up idols in the presence of Yahweh."[21] Thus, "the claim for Yahweh's exclusiveness in the sense that Yahweh alone has existence is not contained in the first commandment,"[22] though, Childs notes, by the time of Second Isaiah (Isa. 45:6, 14, 21), this first commandment expands its claim to universality in this direction. But this expansion, due to the encounter with Babylon in the exile, can be misleading. "Israel's adherence to one God alone is reflected in the earliest level of tradition. Israel did not gradually progress to a belief in one God, but this confession was constitutive to the covenantal tradition from the outset."[23] That may be seen in the following commandments.

The prohibition of graven images—that is, setting up idols beside Yahweh, who reigns invisibly on the throne which is the ark of the covenant—interprets the first commandment as an expression of Yahweh's zealous—indeed jealous, because holy—love for Israel.[24] Originally an independent command that has been redacted as the second commandment now expositing the first, the prohibition of images "provides a good example of how the recognition of the historical dimension leading up to the development of the final form of the text can bring the interpretation of the latter into sharper focus."[25] It makes the first commandment "more inclusive" by spanning the known universe for possible analogues of God in order to forbid them. It intimates, without saying exactly why, that such "worship of images is understood as encroaching on a prerogative of God. . . . God's right as Yahweh is somehow at stake."[26] Childs discusses several possibilities in this connection but dismisses every attempt to align the second commandment with Platonic iconoclasm: "Much of the traditional contrast between crude primitive materialism and spiritual religion seems misplaced."[27] The substitution of a concept for an image in Platonic

21. Ibid., 402–3.
22. Ibid., 403.
23. Ibid.
24. Ibid., 405.
25. Ibid., 406.
26. Ibid., 407.
27. Ibid., 408.

iconoclasm does not fulfill the second commandment but rather violates it in a sophisticated way. Instead, "because the freedom of God to relate himself to his world was encroached upon by the image, it was forbidden."[28] In divine freedom, God has decided. God is revealed in His self-determination to be and ever become Israel's God. "The prohibition of images is grounded in the self-introductory formula, 'I am Yahweh,' which summarizes God's own testimony to himself" in acquiring the extrinsic property, Israel, as His freely chosen covenant partner. "The contrast to this true witness, the substitution of an image—regardless of whether spiritual or crass—is judged to be a false witness . . . a rival human witness, and therefore false."[29] The substitution of an intellectual concept, a vicious abstraction, then, is no less idolatrous than bowing down to material formed by human hands, for the idea is but the idol made by the mind.

The original *Sitz im Leben* of the third commandment prohibiting taking the Lord's name in vain is the oath, where lying under oath in the name of Yahweh treats Yahweh as unreal, a vanity. "It is a 'lie' in Old Testament thought, not because of the intention to deceive, but because it is objectively without any reality, and therefore false."[30] The prohibition thus "attempt[s] to protect the divine name, which of course was identified with God's being itself, from abuse within and without the cult."[31] Childs makes no further comment here on his passing remark that the name of God was "of course" identified with the being of God (just as the taking of the name in vain treated the being of God as a vanity), but the prototrinitarianism is worth taking note of here. God *is* God's name, also on human lips, whether it is there sanctified or profaned. The fourth commandment, on keeping the Sabbath, accordingly commands the sanctification of God's name on human lips by recalling God's sanctifying election of Israel. The "earliest tradition did not carry a particular motivation with it. Rather, the command to observe, or not to desecrate, the Sabbath was the bare datum of the tradition" that then was provided several different motives: to remember God's gift of creation, as in the Exodus recension, or to remember the exodus, as in the Deuteronomic recension. In either case, Israel sanctifies the Sabbath by remembering the name of the God of creation and exodus, completing the circle of the first table back to the preface telling of the God who creates Israel in the act of free election.[32]

28. Ibid.
29. Ibid., 409.
30. Ibid., 411.
31. Ibid., 412.
32. Ibid., 415–17.

The second table of duties, toward fellows, flows from this declaration of "Yahweh our God, Yahweh alone," just as the command to love the neighbor as oneself flows from the command to love this liberating God before all others—even if that makes Yahweh an ontotheological "being alongside other beings"! Just this *ordo caritatis*, however, is the sense of the Shema, which Jesus exposited as the double love commandment, which Augustine (in a better frame of mind than in books 5–7 of *De Trinitate*) isolated as the chief content of Christian teaching, the Beloved Community (*civitas Dei*) that comes by the folly of preaching the cross as wisdom hidden for ages but now being made known as the power to save. So Luther exposited the Shema:

> Notice that [Moses] explains the First Commandment in a positive way, namely, that the Lord is one. For the name used here is the Tetragrammaton, which is applicable solely to God. But he treats this unity of God in the Spirit; that is, he makes the point not only that God is one, but also that He should be regarded as one by us. Merely to say that He is one God conveys no meaning to us. However, that He is regarded as one God and as our God (as he says here) is salvation and life and the fullness of all the Commandments. Thus in Genesis 28:21, Jacob says: "The Lord shall be God to me." In what way shall the Lord be God to him? As though He had not been that before? It is only that through a particular rite and worship he determined to have none but the Lord as God. Thus God becomes God and changes in accordance with the change in our feelings toward Him. . . . No one can have one God unless he clings to Him alone and trusts in Him alone; otherwise he will be snatched off into a variety of works and various gods. . . . For nature cannot but commit idolatry. When, therefore, he says: "The Lord your God is one Lord," he takes away all confidence in yourself. When he says, "You shall love the Lord," he arouses joyous and free service to God. For when I love God truly, I want everything God wants, nor is anything sweeter than to hear and do what God wants, as also human love does with its beloved. Thus through oneness with God in faith we received everything freely from God, through love, we do everything freely toward God.[33]

The rule of weak simplicity may be formulated in a variety of ways, as witnessed in the preceding pages. At heart it commands this: so speak of God that God becomes the one God (that God the Holy Trinity is) for you,

33. Martin Luther, *Luther's Works: The American Edition*, ed. Jaroslav Pelikan and Helmut T. Lehmann (St. Louis: Concordia; Philadelphia: Fortress, 1955–86), 9:67–68. Luther's statement, "Thus God becomes God and changes in accordance with the change in our feelings toward Him," exposits Paul's critique of the strong party in Corinth, those who know the One God falsely. To know the One God truly, "in the Spirit," is to know God as our One and Only, in whom and under whom all other creatures are to be loved as others also to be set free for the glorious liberty of the children of God.

as indeed the One of all the so-called gods in heaven and on earth who freely comes to set free the captive from whatever captivity keeps one from loving this liberating God above all and all other creatures as those also to be set free. It is the rule of faith that hopes for that day when all of us are thus changed by the Spirit (1 Cor. 15:51) by unification with the Son—that is to say, changed by God to love God in God with all others beloved of God, so that God will become *panta en pasin*. On that day, "The LORD will become king over all the earth; on that day the LORD will be one and his name one" (Zech. 14:9).

Glossary of Foreign Words and Phrases

actus (Lat.): act

actus purus (Lat.): pure act

ad aliquid (Lat.): in relation to another

ad extra (Lat.): in relation to what is outside

ad infernos (Lat.): (descent) into hell

ad intra (Lat.): in relation to what is within

ad se (Lat.): to oneself

agere sequitur esse (Lat.): doing follows being

aliud (Lat.): another

Alleinwirksamkeit Gottes (Ger.): the sole causality of God

Alleswirksamkeit Gottes (Ger.): God active in all things

anabasis (Gk.): ascent

analogia entis (Lat.): analogy of being

analogia fidei (Lat.): analogy of faith

anankē (Gk.): necessity

anhypostasis (Gk.): without a hypostasis of its own

apatheia (Gk.): passionlessness

apeiron (Gk.): infinite

apophasis (Gk.): negative knowledge

archē (Gk.): origin, cause (= *principium* [Lat.])

a se (Lat.): from oneself

assumptio carnis (Lat.): assumption of flesh

Aufhebung (Ger.): fulfilled, canceled, and overcome

Auseinandersetzung (Ger.): comparison and contrast

bona naturalia manent (Lat.): natural goods remain

capax Dei per gratiam (Lat.): by grace capable of God

causa sui (Lat.): cause of itself

Christo remoto (Lat.): by way of removing Christ from consideration

Christus crucifixus (Lat.): Christ crucified

Christus pro nobis (Lat.): Christ for us

civitas Dei (Lat.): city of God

coincidentia oppositorum (Lat.): coincidence of opposites

commercium admirabile (Lat.): wonderful exchange

communicatio idiomatum (Lat.): communication of attributes

conformitas Christi (Lat.): conformation to Christ

consensus fidelium (Lat.): consensus of the faithful

contra mundum (Lat.): against the world

creatio continua (Lat.): continuous creation

creatio ex nihilo (Lat.): creation out of nothing

creatio ex vetere (Lat.): creation out of the old

cum grano salis (Lat.): with a grain of salt

Dasein (Ger.): being there, existence

de Deo uno (Lat.): concerning the one God

de dicto (Lat.): concerning words

de re (Lat.): concerning reality

der zeitliche Ursprung (Ger.): the temporal origin

der zeitlose Grund (Ger.): the timeless ground

Destruktion (Ger.): destruction

Deus absconditus (Lat.): God hidden

Deus actuosissimus (Lat.): God most actual

deus exlex (Lat.): arbitrary deity

deus ex machina (Lat.): god out of a machine

Deus incarnatus (Lat.): God incarnate

enhypostasis (Gk.): hypostasized in

eo ipso (Lat.): by itself

epaphax (Gk.): once for all

esse (Lat.): to be, or being

esse Deum dare (Lat.): to be God is to give

esse ipsum subsistens (Lat.): being itself subsisting

essentia (Lat.): essence

essentia nuda (Lat.): nude essence

est (Lat.): he, she, or it is

ex necessitate naturae (Lat.): by necessity of nature

ex nihilo nihil fit (Lat.): out of nothing, nothing comes

extra Calvinisticum (Lat.): Calvin's teaching that the divine Son exceeds the man Jesus

fides caritate formata (Lat.): faith formed by love

fides Christo formata (Lat.): faith formed by Christ

fides quaerens intellectum (Lat.): faith seeking understanding

figura (Lat.): figure

filioque (Lat.): and the Son

finis (Lat.): end (= *telos* [Gk.])

finiti ad infinitum non est proportio (Lat.): there is no proportion of the finite to the infinite

finitum non capax infiniti (Lat.): the finite is not capable of the infinite

Fragestellung (Ger.): framing of the question

fröhliche Wechsel (Ger.): joyful exchange

gratia non destruit, sed supponit et perfecit naturam (Lat.): grace does not destroy but supports and perfects nature

homoousios (Gk.): of the same being

Hunc audite! (Lat.): Listen to Him!

hypostasis (Gk.): way of being (= *persona* [Lat.])

imago Dei (Lat.): image of God

in divinis (Lat.): in divine things

in fide ipsa Christus adest (Lat.): Christ is present in faith itself

in medias res (Lat.): in the midst of things

ipsum esse (Lat.) = *esse ipsum*, being itself

kai ho logos sarx egeneto (Gk.): and the Word became flesh

katabasis (Gk.): descent

kataphasis (Gk.): positive knowledge

kat' epinoian (Gk.): according to thought

lex talionis (Lat.): law of retribution

libido dominandi (Lat.): lust for domination

logos (Gk.): word or reason

Logos asarkos (Gk.): the Logos without flesh

Logos ensarkos (Gk.): the Logos enfleshed

metaphora rerum/verborum (Lat.): change of things/words

mia ousia treis hypostaseis (Gk.): one being, three persons

Nachdenken (Ger.): to consider, reflect; literally, to think after

natura (Lat.): nature

naturaliter (Lat.): naturally

naturaliter anima est gratiae capax (Lat.): the soul is naturally capable of grace

natura naturans (Lat.): nature naturing

natura naturata (Lat.): nature natured

non aliud (Lat.): not-other

non in genere (Lat.): not in a genus/class

non posse peccare (Lat.): not able to sin

non solum est verborum, sed et rerum metaphora (Lat.): a change not only of words but of things

novum (Lat.): novelty

oikonomia (Gk.): plan, management, economy (of God)

opera Dei ad extra (Lat.): the external works of God

opera Dei ad extra indivisa sunt (Lat.): the external works of God are indivisible

operatio (Lat.): operation

ordo caritatis (Lat.): the order of love

origio (Lat.): origin

ousia (Gk.): being

panta en pasin (Gk.): all in all

pars pro toto (Lat.): part for the whole

per gratiam (Lat.): by grace

perpetuum mobile (Lat.): perpetual motion

persona (Lat.): person (= *hypostasis* [Gk.])

philosophia perennis (Lat.): the perennial philosophy

physis (Gk.): nature

principium (Lat.): beginning, cause (= *archē* [Gk.])

prisca theologia (Lat.): ancient theology

prosōpon (Gk.): face, appearance (= *persona* [Lat.])

Punkt (Ger.): period

Realdialektik (Ger.): a movement of yes and no in reality

redivivus (Lat.): alive again

res non generans neque genita nec procedens (Lat.): a thing not generating
    nor generated nor proceeding

satis est (Lat.): it suffices

scientia sacra (Lat.): sacred gnosis

securitas (Lat.): security

sic et non (Lat.): yes and no, dialectic

sicut Deus eritis (Lat.): you shall be God

significat (Lat.): he, she, or it signifies

simplicitas (Lat.): simplicity

simpliciter (Lat.): simply

Sitz im Leben (Ger.): setting in life

soli Deo gloria (Lat.): glory to God only

sophrosynē (Gk.): prudence

sub Pontio Pilato (Lat.): under Pontius Pilate

subsistere (Lat.): to subsist

substantia (Lat.): substance

sui generis (Lat.): in a genus/class by itself

superbia (Lat.): pride

telos (Gk.): end (= *finis* [Lat.])

terminus ad quem (Lat.): point to which

terminus a quo (Lat.): point from which

tertium non datur (Lat.): there is no third (way)

theosis (Gk.): deification

translatio rerum/verborum (Lat.): change of things/words

tria quaedam (Lat.): three certain things

ubi et quando Deo visum est (Lat.): where and when it pleases God

ubivolipraesens (Lat.): present where He (Christ) wills
Veni, Creator Spiritus (Lat.): Come, Creator Spirit
verbum externum (Lat.): external word
via eminentiae (Lat.): way of eminence
via negativa (Lat.): way of negation
vinculum caritatis (Lat.): chain of love

Works Cited

Adkins, Brent, and Paul R. Hinlicky. *Rethinking Philosophy and Theology with Deleuze: A New Cartography*. London: Bloomsbury Academic, 2013.

Alfsvåg, Knut. *What No Mind Has Conceived: On the Significance of Christological Apophaticism*. Leuven: Peeters, 2010.

Allen, R. Michael. *The Christ's Faith: A Dogmatic Account*. London: T&T Clark, 2009.

Aquinas, Thomas. *Summa contra Gentiles*. Translated by Vernon J. Bourke. 5 vols. Notre Dame, IN: University of Notre Dame Press, 1975.

———. *Summa Theologiae: A Concise Translation*. Edited by Timothy McDermott. Allen, TX: Christian Classics, 1991.

Augustine. *On Christian Teaching*. Translated by R. P. H. Green. Oxford: Oxford University Press, 1999.

———. *On the Trinity*. Translated by Edmund Hill. New York: New City Press, 1991.

Ayres, Lewis. *Nicaea and Its Legacy: An Approach to Fourth-Century Trinitarian Theology*. Oxford: Oxford University Press, 2006.

Barth, Karl. *Church Dogmatics*. Translated by G. W. Bromiley. Edited by G. W. Bromiley and T. F. Torrance. 4 vols. Edinburgh: T&T Clark, 1975.

Bayer, Oswald. *A Contemporary in Dissent: Johann Georg Hamann as a Radical Enlightener*. Translated by Roy A. Harrisville and Mark C. Mattes. Grand Rapids: Eerdmans, 2012. Originally published as *Zeitgenosse in Widerspruch: Johann Georg Hamann als radikaler Aufklärer*. Munich: Piper, 1988.

———. *Martin Luther's Theology: A Contemporary Interpretation*. Translated by Thomas H. Trapp. Grand Rapids: Eerdmans, 2007.

Bayer, Oswald, and Benjamin Gleede, eds. *Creator Est Creatura: Luthers Christologie als Lehre von der Idiomenkommunikation*. Berlin: de Gruyter, 2007.

Bettenson, Henry, ed. *Documents of the Christian Church*. London: Oxford University Press, 1947.

Betz, John R. Introduction to *Analogia Entis: Metaphysics; Original Structure and Universal Rhythm*, by Erich Przywara, 1–115. Translated by John R. Betz and David Bentley Hart. Grand Rapids: Eerdmans, 2014.

Bielfeldt, Dennis, Mickey L. Mattox, and Paul R. Hinlicky. *The Substance of the Faith: Luther's Doctrinal Theology for Today*. Minneapolis: Fortress, 2008.

Bond, H. Lawrence. "Nicolas of Cusa and the Reconstruction of Theology: The Centrality of Christology in the Coincidence of Opposites." In *Contemporary Reflections on the Medieval Christian Tradition: Essays in Honor of Ray C. Petry*, edited by George H. Shriver, 81–94. Durham, NC: Duke University Press, 1974.

Brueggemann, Walter. *Theology of the Old Testament: Testimony, Dispute, Advocacy*. Minneapolis: Fortress, 1997.

Burrell, David B. "Analogy, Creation, and Theological Language." In *The Theology of Thomas Aquinas*, edited by Rik Van Nieuwenhove and Joseph Wawrykow, 77–98. Notre Dame, IN: University of Notre Dame Press, 2005.

———. "Creator/Creatures Relation: 'The Distinction' vs. 'Onto-theology.'" *Faith and Philosophy* 25, no. 2 (April 2008): 177–89.

———. *Freedom and Creation in Three Traditions*. Notre Dame, IN: University of Notre Dame Press, 1993.

Childs, Brevard S. *The Book of Exodus: A Critical, Theological Commentary*. Philadelphia: Westminster, 1974.

Cicero. *The Nature of the Gods*. Translated by Horace C. P. McGregor. Harmondsworth, UK: Penguin, 1972.

Conzelmann, Hans. *1 Corinthians: A Commentary on the First Epistle to the Corinthians*. Translated by James W. Leitch. Hermeneia. Philadelphia: Fortress, 1975.

Cooper, Jordan. *Christification: A Lutheran Approach to Theosis*. Eugene, OR: Wipf & Stock, 2014.

Cross, Richard. *Duns Scotus on God*. Burlington, VT: Ashgate, 2005.

———. "Idolatry and Religious Language." *Faith and Philosophy* 25, no. 2 (April 2008): 190–96.

Crowe, Benjamin D. *Heidegger's Religious Origins: Destruction and Authenticity*. Bloomington: Indiana University Press, 2006.

Crüsemann, Frank. *The Torah: Theology and Social History of Old Testament Law*. Translated by Allan W. Mahnke. Minneapolis: Fortress, 1996.

DeJonge, Michael P. *Bonhoeffer's Theological Formation: Berlin, Barth, and Protestant Theology*. Oxford: Oxford University Press, 2012.

Dodd, C. H. *The Interpretation of the Fourth Gospel*. Cambridge: Cambridge University Press, 1995.

Dolezal, James E. *God without Parts: Divine Simplicity and the Metaphysics of God's Absoluteness*. Eugene, OR: Pickwick, 2011.

Drozdek, Adam. *Greek Philosophers as Theologians: The Divine* Arche. Burlington, VT: Ashgate, 2007.

Duby, Steven J. "Divine Simplicity, Divine Freedom, and the Contingency of Creation: Dogmatic Responses to Some Analytic Questions." *Journal of Reformed Theology* 6 (2012): 115–42.

Frend, W. H. C. *The Rise of Christianity*. Philadelphia: Fortress, 1984.

Gäbler, Ulrich. *Huldrych Zwingli: His Life and Work*. Translated by Ruth C. L. Gritsch. Philadelphia: Fortress, 1986.

Greene, John C. *The Death of Adam: Evolution and Its Impact on Western Thought*. Ames: Iowa State University Press, 1996.

Grillmeier, Aloys. *Christ in Christian Tradition*. Vol. 1, *From the Apostolic Age to Chalcedon (451)*. Translated by John Bowden. 2nd rev. ed. Atlanta: John Knox, 1975.

Gunton, Colin E. *Act and Being: Towards a Theology of the Divine Attributes*. Grand Rapids: Eerdmans, 2003.

———. "Augustine, the Trinity and the Theological Crisis of the West." *Scottish Journal of Theology* 43, no. 1 (February 1990): 33–58.

Harnack, Adolph von. *History of Dogma*. Translated by Neil Buchanan. 7 vols. New York: Dover, 1961.

Haugh, Richard S. *Photius and the Carolingians: The Trinitarian Controversy*. Belmont, MA: Nordland, 1975.

Hegel, G. W. F. *Lectures on the Philosophy of Religion: The Lectures of 1827*. Edited by Peter C. Hodgson. Translated by R. F. Brown et al. One-volume ed. Berkeley: University of California Press, 1988.

Hinlicky, Paul R. "Anthropology." In *Dictionary of Luther and the Lutheran Traditions*. Grand Rapids: Baker Academic, forthcoming.

———. *Before Auschwitz: What Christian Theology Must Learn from the Rise of Nazism*. Eugene, OR: Cascade, 2013.

———. *Beloved Community: Critical Dogmatics after Christendom*. Grand Rapids: Eerdmans, 2015.

―――. *Divine Complexity: The Rise of Creedal Christianity*. Minneapolis: Fortress, 2009.

―――. "Leibniz and the Theology of the Beloved Community." *Pro Ecclesia* 21, no. 1 (2012): 25–50.

―――. *Luther and the Beloved Community: A Path for Christian Theology after Christendom*. Grand Rapids: Eerdmans, 2010.

―――. "Luther's Anti-Docetism in the Disputatio de divinitate et humanitate Christi (1540)." In Bayer and Gleede, *Creator Est Creatura*, 139–81.

―――. "Metaphorical Truth and the Language of Christian Theology." In *Indicative of Grace—Imperative of Freedom: Essays in Honour of Eberhard Jüngel in His 80th Year*, edited by R. David Nelson, 89–100. London: Bloomsbury, 2014.

―――. *Paths Not Taken: Fates of Theology from Luther through Leibniz*. Grand Rapids: Eerdmans, 2009.

―――. Review of *A Contemporary in Dissent: Johann Georg Hamann as a Radical Enlightener*, by Oswald Bayer. *Lutheran Quarterly* 27, no. 1 (2013): 94–96.

―――. "Verbum Externum: Dietrich Bonhoeffer's Bethel Confession." In *God Speaks to Us: Dietrich Bonhoeffer's Biblical Hermeneutics*, edited by Ralf K. Wüstenberg and Jens Zimmermann, 189–215. International Bonhoeffer Interpretations 5. Frankfurt: Peter Lang, 2013.

Hinlicky Wilson, Sarah. *Woman, Women, and the Priesthood in the Trinitarian Theology of Elisabeth Behr-Sigel*. London: Bloomsbury, 2013.

Hopko, Thomas. "The Trinity in the Cappadocians." In *Christian Spirituality: Origins to the Twelfth Century*, edited by Bernard McGinn, John Meyendorff, and Jean Leclerq, 263–70. World Spirituality 16. New York: Crossroad, 1989.

Horan, Daniel P. *Postmodernity and Univocity: A Critical Account of Radical Orthodoxy and John Duns Scotus*. Minneapolis: Fortress, 2014.

Jenson, Robert W. *America's Theologian: A Recommendation of Jonathan Edwards*. New York: Oxford University Press, 1986.

―――. "How the World Lost Its Story." *First Things* 36 (1993): 19–24. Online: http://www.firstthings.com/article/2010/03/how-the-world-lost-its-story.

―――. *Systematic Theology*. 2 vols. Oxford: Oxford University Press, 1997.

―――. *The Triune Identity: God according to the Gospel*. Philadelphia: Fortress, 1982.

―――. *Unbaptized God: The Basic Flaw in Ecumenical Theology*. Minneapolis: Fortress, 1992.

Johnson, Keith L. *Karl Barth and the* Analogia Entis. London: T&T Clark, 2011.

Jüngel, Eberhard. *God as the Mystery of the World: On the Foundation of the Theology of the Crucified One in the Dispute between Theism and Atheism.* Translated by Darrell L. Guder. Grand Rapids: Eerdmans, 1983.

———. *Theological Essays I.* Translated by J. B. Webster. Edinburgh: T&T Clark, 1989.

Kärkkäinen, Pekka, ed. *Trinitarian Theology in the Medieval West.* Schriften der Luther-Agricola-Gesellschaft 61. Helsinki: Luther-Agricola-Society, 2007.

Kaufman, Dan. "Divine Simplicity and the Eternal Truths in Descartes." *British Journal for the History of Philosophy* 11, no. 4 (2003): 553–79.

Kermode, Frank. *The Genesis of Secrecy: On the Interpretation of Narrative.* Cambridge, MA: Harvard University Press, 1979.

Kerr, Fergus. *After Aquinas: Versions of Thomism.* Malden, MA: Blackwell, 2002.

Kusukawa, Sachiko. *The Transformation of Natural Philosophy: The Case of Philip Melanchthon.* Ideas in Context. Cambridge: Cambridge University Press, 1995.

Lee, Philip J. *Against the Protestant Gnostics.* New York: Oxford University Press, 1987.

Lietzmann, Hans. *A History of the Early Church.* Translated by Bertram Lee Woolf. 4 vols. New York: World Publishing, 1961.

Lindbeck, George A. *The Nature of Doctrine: Religion and Theology in a Post-liberal Age.* Philadelphia: Westminster, 1984.

Lossky, Vladimir. *In the Image and Likeness of God.* Edited by John H. Erickson and Thomas E. Bird. Crestwood, NY: St. Vladimir's Seminary Press, 1985.

Lovejoy, Arthur O. *The Great Chain of Being: A Study of the History of an Idea.* Cambridge, MA: Harvard University Press, 1964.

Luther, Martin. *The Bondage of the Will.* Translated by J. I. Packer and O. R. Johnston. Old Tappan, NJ: Revell, 1957.

———. *D. Martin Luthers Werke: Kritische Gesamtausgabe.* 50 vols. Weimar: Hermann Böhlau, 1883–2007.

———. *Luther: Lectures on Romans.* Edited and translated by Wilhelm Pauck. Library of Christian Classics. Philadelphia: Westminster, 1961.

———. *Luther's Works: The American Edition.* Edited by Jaroslav Pelikan and Helmut T. Lehmann. 55 vols. St. Louis: Concordia; Philadelphia: Fortress, 1955–86.

Marenbon, John. *Medieval Philosophy: An Historical and Philosophical Introduction.* London: Routledge, 2007.

Marshall, Bruce D. "Faith and Reason Reconsidered: Aquinas and Luther on Deciding What Is True." *The Thomist* 63 (1999): 1–48.

———. "Justification as Declaration and Deification." *International Journal of Systematic Theology* 4, no. 1 (March 2002): 3–28.

———. *Trinity and Truth*. Cambridge: Cambridge University Press, 2000.

McClymond, Michael J., and Gerald R. McDermott. *The Theology of Jonathan Edwards*. New York: Oxford University Press, 2012.

McCormack, Bruce L. *Karl Barth's Critically Realistic Dialectical Theology: Its Genesis and Development, 1909–1936*. Oxford: Clarendon; New York: Oxford University Press, 1995.

———. *Orthodox and Modern: Studies in the Theology of Karl Barth*. Grand Rapids: Baker Academic, 2008.

McDermott, Gerald R. *God's Rivals: Why Has God Allowed Different Religions? Insights from the Bible and the Early Church*. Downers Grove, IL: IVP Academic, 2007.

———, ed. *The Oxford Handbook of Evangelical Theology*. New York: Oxford University Press, 2010.

McDermott, Gerald R., and Harold Netland. *A Trinitarian Theology of Religions: An Evangelical Proposal*. Oxford: Oxford University Press, 2014.

McGiffert, Arthur Cushman. *A History of Christian Thought*. Vol. 1, *Early and Eastern, from Jesus to John of Damascus*. New York: Scribner, 1954.

McGrath, Alister E. *A Fine-Tuned Universe: The Quest for God in Science and Theology*. Louisville: Westminster John Knox, 2009.

Melanchthon, Philip. *On Christian Doctrine: Loci Communes, 1555*. Translated and edited by Clyde L. Manschreck. Grand Rapids: Baker, 1982.

Meyendorff, John. *Byzantine Theology: Historical Trends and Doctrinal Themes*. New York: Fordham University Press, 1979.

———. *Christ in Eastern Christian Thought*. Crestwood, NY: St. Vladimir's Seminary Press, 1987.

Miles, Margaret R. *Plotinus on Body and Beauty: Society, Philosophy, and Religion in Third-Century Rome*. Oxford: Blackwell, 1999.

Muller, Richard A. *Dictionary of Latin and Greek Theological Terms Drawn Principally from Protestant Scholastic Theology*. Grand Rapids: Baker, 1985.

———. *Post-Reformation Reformed Dogmatics: The Rise and Development of Reformed Orthodoxy, ca. 1520 to ca. 1725*. 4 vols. 2nd ed. Grand Rapids: Baker Academic, 2003.

Mullins, R. T. "Simply Impossible: A Case against Divine Simplicity." *Journal of Reformed Theology* 7 (2013): 181–203.

Murphy, George L. *The Cosmos in the Light of the Cross*. Harrisburg, PA: Trinity Press International, 2003.

Nasr, Seyyed Hossein. *Knowledge and the Sacred*. Albany: State University of New York Press, 1989.

Nygren, Anders. *Agape and Eros*. Translated by Philip S. Watson. New York: Harper & Row, 1969.

Ochs, Peter. *Another Reformation: Postliberal Christianity and the Jews*. Grand Rapids: Baker Academic, 2011.

Ortlund, Gavin. "Divine Simplicity in Historical Perspective: Resourcing a Contemporary Discussion." *Modern Theology* 16, no. 4 (October 2014): 436–52.

Pannenberg, Wolfhart. *Basic Questions in Theology: Collected Essays*. Translated by George H. Kehm. 2 vols. Philadelphia: Fortress, 1972.

Pelikan, Jaroslav. *The Christian Tradition: A History of the Development of Doctrine*. Vol. 1, *The Emergence of the Catholic Tradition (100–600)*. Chicago: University of Chicago Press, 1971.

Polkinghorne, John. *The Faith of a Physicist: Reflections of a Bottom-Up Thinker*. Princeton: Princeton University Press, 1994.

Preus, Robert D. *The Theology of Post-Reformation Lutheranism*. 2 vols. St. Louis: Concordia, 1972.

Przywara, Erich. *Analogia Entis: Metaphysics; Original Structure and Universal Rhythm*. Translated by John R. Betz and David Bentley Hart. Ressourcement: Retrieval and Renewal in Catholic Thought. Grand Rapids: Eerdmans, 2014.

Rad, Gerhard von. *Old Testament Theology*. Translated by D. M. G. Stalker. 2 vols. New York: Harper & Row, 1962.

Rinehart, Larry. "Confessions of a Lutheran Perennialist." *Lutheran Forum* 45, no. 3 (2011): 58–61.

———. *Esse & Evangel: Metaphysical Order in Evangelical Doctrine*. North Charleston, SC: CreateSpace, 2015.

Roberts, Alexander, and James Donaldson, eds. *The Ante-Nicene Fathers*. Vol. 2, *Fathers of the Second Century: Hermas, Tatian, Athenagoras, Theophilus, and Clement of Alexandria*. Reprint, Peabody, MA: Hendrickson, 2004.

Rorem, Paul. "Martin Luther's Christocentric Critique of Pseudo-Dionysian Spirituality." *Lutheran Quarterly* 11, no. 3 (August 1997): 291–307.

———. "The Uplifting Spirituality of Pseudo-Dionysius." In *Christian Spirituality: Origins to the Twelfth Century*, edited by Bernard McGinn, John Meyendorff, and Jean Leclerq, 132–51. World Spirituality 16. New York: Crossroad, 1989.

Royce, Josiah. *The Problem of Christianity*. Washington, DC: Catholic University of America Press, 2001.

Schmitt, Yann. "The Deadlock of Absolute Divine Simplicity." *International Journal of the Philosophy of Religion* 74 (2013): 117–30.

Soskice, Janet Martin. *Metaphor and Religious Language*. Oxford: Clarendon, 1987.

Soulen, R. Kendall. *The Divine Name(s) and the Holy Trinity*. Vol. 1, *Distinguishing the Voices*. Louisville: Westminster John Knox, 2011.

Spinoza, Baruch. *The Ethics; Treatise on the Emendation of the Intellect; Selected Letters*. Translated by Samuel Shirley. Edited by Seymour Feldman. 2nd ed. Indianapolis: Hackett, 1992.

Stead, Christopher. *Divine Substance*. Oxford: Clarendon, 1977.

Theissen, Gerd. *Biblical Faith: An Evolutionary Approach*. Philadelphia: Fortress, 1985.

Tillich, Paul. *Systematic Theology*. 3 vols. Chicago: University of Chicago Press, 1967.

Torrance, T. F. *The Trinitarian Faith: The Evangelical Theology of the Ancient Catholic Church*. Edinburgh: T&T Clark, 1993.

Vind, Anna. "'Christus factus est peccatum metaphorice': Über die theologische Verwendung rhetorischer Figuren bei Luther unter Einbeziehung Quintilians." In Bayer and Gleede, *Creator Est Creatura*, 95–124.

Westhelle, Vítor. *After Heresy: Colonial Practices and Post-Colonial Theologies*. Eugene, OR: Cascade, 2010.

Williams, Rowan. *On Christian Theology*. Challenges in Contemporary Theology. Oxford: Blackwell, 2000.

Wisse, Maarten. *Trinitarian Theology beyond Participation: Augustine's "De Trinitate" and Contemporary Theology*. London and New York: T&T Clark, 2013.

Zizioulas, John D. *Being as Communion: Studies in Personhood and the Church*. Crestwood, NY: St. Vladimir's Seminary Press, 1993.

Index